Images of
Conflict

Images of
Conflict

Albert F. Eldridge

New York   St. Martin's Press

For the students of Duke University,
who patiently listened
so that we all might learn

Library of Congress Catalog Card Number: 77–85994
Copyright © 1979 by St. Martin's Press, Inc.
All Rights Reserved.
Manufactured in the United States of America.
32109
fedcba
For information, write St. Martin's Press, Inc.,
175 Fifth Avenue, New York, N. Y. 10010

cover design: Melissa Tardiff

cloth ISBN: 0–312–40923–0
paper ISBN: 0–312–40924–9

Preface

Each of the social sciences treats conflict as an important theoretical issue. Anthropologists study ethnocentrism and cultural bias; political scientists study war and revolution; sociologists analyze riots and crowd behavior; and psychologists examine violence and aggression. These fields have all added greatly to our understanding of social conflict. In fact, most of the literature on conflict has a particular disciplinary focus. It becomes increasingly apparent, however, that we cannot fully understand human conflict until we have integrated these contributions.

This text uses an interdisciplinary perspective, drawing especially upon political science, psychology, and sociology. I believe that the juncture of these fields provides a logical starting point for an integrated analysis of human conflict. Indeed, on one level this text is a study of the interrelationships among the various behavioral sciences as they illuminate human conflict. For this reason, conflict will not be analyzed at a single level, such as the individual, the group, or the culture. Instead, I will try to show how each level of analysis is relevant to social conflict and its resolution.

The text explores various dimensions of conflict by proceeding from some of the basic elements of conflict to a more sophisticated and detailed analysis of the relationships that exist among them. Chapter 1 focuses on the various definitions, approaches, and models which shape and in turn reflect our dispositions toward conflict. Chapter 2 elaborates on the basic processes of perception and discusses how perception enables us to match objective and subjective realities. In chapter 3 we examine the conditions of stress, anxiety, tension, and conformity which seem particularly to encourage perceptions of conflict and often initiate violent behavior. Chapters 4, 5, and 6 describe and analyze patterns of change in perception in various contexts—in groups, nations, and international systems—that have experienced violence.

Chapter 7, which deals with bargaining theory, stresses the perceptions, choices, and decisions entailed in the resolution of conflict. The various strategies involved in using threats and promises are explored. Next, drawing upon the example of the Strategic Arms Limitation Talks (SALT) of 1969–1972, chapter 8 analyzes negotiations from the perspective of one key negotiator—Henry Kissinger. We will look at his methods of negotiating, the processes of communication during the "back-channel" negotiations, the situational conditions during the SALT talks, and the interrelationships among all of these factors. Chapter 9, the concluding chapter, has two purposes. First, it attempts to synthesize theory and findings with policy observations. Second, it deals with the ways in which this synthesis can be applied, on both the personal and societal levels, to reduce the potential for conflict in the world today.

In writing *Images of Conflict* I have been indebted to a number of people whose advice and admonitions have strengthened the book considerably. I am particularly grateful to the students who have taken my course on conflict resolution. Their questions have impelled me to examine my own attitudes, values, and perceptions more closely than I might otherwise have done. I also have drawn upon the work of hundreds of my academic colleagues, whose individual contributions I have done my best to acknowledge. I, of course, retain full responsibility for errors of commission or omission in the presentation and analysis of their work.

Many individuals have helped to prepare the manuscript for publication. Louise Walker, Doris Ralston, and Patsy McFarland worked with patience and professionalism in transforming my various drafts into readable copy. John Borawski, Wendy Aims, and Vivianne Lake spent long hours providing sources, checking various drafts for error, and volunteering valuable insights. Last, but certainly not least, I wish to thank Bert Lummus of St. Martin's Press. His patience and encouragement throughout the publication process made this book possible.

A. F. E.

Contents

1 | SOCIAL CONFLICT, PERCEPTION, AND COMMUNICATION: AN ORGANIZING FRAMEWORK

Social conflict is a complex subject that presents many problems. Before exploring some of the basic concepts, approaches, and theories, let us examine three of these basic problems.

The Problem of Meaning

Before we can investigate conflict, we must define it. Unfortunately the definitions of conflict constitute an embarrassment of riches. Not only are there too many definitions; many of the meanings overlap, and when they do not overlap, their distinctions are confusing. For example, some see conflict as "a form of social behavior in which one individual injures another person." Others maintain that injury is unnecessary; conflict occurs when "two or more individuals feel hostile or threatening towards each other." On the other hand, some scholars contend that conflict can be present even without overt hostility. Many of them accept the notion that conflict implies opposition but disagree that it must always be conscious. We can talk about unconscious conflict. Think of students competing for grades. In most cases, they are unconscious of the inherent conflict in their competition. Does this mean that conflict is competition? Again disagreement. Some say conflict is competition only when competition implies the use of violence. Does this mean that conflict is a form of violence? What about aggression, hostility, anger, and related concepts? Are they synonymous with conflict? Are they dimensions of conflict, or are they actually quite different?

There is probably no single precise, inclusive, or manageable definition that adequately captures the diversity and complexity of conflict. If definitions are by nature arbitrary, then perhaps any defini-

1

tion that creates a foundation for shared knowledge is adequate for our purposes.

In this spirit, the definition of conflict I will use is intended to be neither restrictive nor exhaustive, but only to provide a working basis for discussion. This definition is a social-psychological one: *conflict* is a situation in which one actor (either an individual, a group, or a nation) is engaged in opposition (violent or nonviolent) to another actor(s) who is pursuing what are, or appear to be, incompatible goals. Let us look at this definition in detail.

First, the definition rules out the intrapersonal. Social conflict involves transactions between actors; it is a form of social behavior. A student struggling with a term paper, a farmer struggling with the natural environment, or a person struggling with emotion is not engaged in social conflict according to our definition. This limitation simplifies our study while helping us to recognize that some intrapersonal conflicts may illuminate conflicts between individuals.[1]

Second, the definition focuses on motive behavior. Human action is motivated, or goal-directed. It is for this reason that we think of conflict as beginning with the arousal of wants. In the ensuing conflict, each phase follows the other in a consistent manner, leading to the achievement of the goal. Consequently, conflict behavior can be characterized as an instrumental act.[2] This behavior may be intentional or unintentional, conscious or unconscious.

Third, the definition assumes that conflict behavior is an integrated act. That is, it reflects the influence of both the actor's wants and goals upon his or her emotions, thoughts, perceptions, and memories. We are not asserting that conflict begins solely in the mind.[3] What we are contending is that cognitions, beliefs, values, and perceptions work together with situational factors to influence action. Our task is to illuminate the nature and influence of these enduring mental and varying situational factors.[4]

Fourth, we should consider the implications of the phrase "engaged in opposition." The concept of "opposition" is rather ambiguous. It implies that individuals are attempting to prevent others from achieving their goals, and that this thwarting is the essence of conflict. This opposition can take many forms. It may be violent, using destructive action, or nonviolent, employing confrontation. It may or may not be verbal. Later on, we will examine the various circumstances that call forth one type of adaptive behavior rather than another.

Finally, the definition assumes that conflict is a continuous process; it does not simply begin and end. Each participant acts with reference to the other. The actions of one actor call forth a response from the opposing actor, in a pattern of action and reaction that may create renewed cycles of conflict.[5]

The Problem of Approach

Since no single theory of conflict exists, students have tried to gain insights using the perspective of various social sciences. Within these disciplines, standard approaches have developed. Although a full discussion is impossible here, a brief enumeration of these approaches would be useful.[6] For convenience, we have divided the social sciences into three sets, depending upon whether they utilize a micro, macro, or combined approach in studying conflict. While no academic discipline is solely micro or macro in orientation, generally speaking psychology focuses on individual behavior; sociology and anthropology deal with larger collectives of actors; and economics and political science utilize both perspectives.

CONFLICT IN THE MIND

Psychologists have conceptualized conflict generally within the framework of human aggression. Their central question is: Does aggression originate in the mind? They have formulated three possible answers to this question: (1) physiological—aggression results from a malfunctioning of the brain or from instinctual drives; (2) motivational—people are aggressive because of goal-directed behavior; and (3) learning—aggression may result from some past experience when one was either rewarded or punished for aggressive behavior. Related psychological research also has analyzed such related concepts as hostility, anger, and hatred.[7]

One of the most controversial explanations of aggression is the frustration-aggression thesis. In 1939 a group of researchers at Yale University published a study entitled "Frustration and Aggression," which suggested that aggression was always a consequence of frustration. Later research, however, was to show that not every frustrating situation produces overt aggression.[8] It could be inhibited by punishment or dire circumstances, for example. Later on, we will analyze this thesis in greater detail.

CONFLICT AND SOCIAL INSTITUTIONS

Sociologists tend to regard conflict as a normal dimension of group existence, serving positive social functions. Conflict may promote integration of a group or nation; it helps establish identity and reinforces group solidarity. While serving these functions, conflict may generate *inter*group hostilities, expressed in classic form as "in-groups" versus "outgroups." You are probably familiar with this kind of social conflict by other names: "haves versus have-nots" or "ins versus outs." Some research in sociology has attempted to identify those structures and collective behaviors that generate conflict. Among them are social stratification systems (economic, political, and educational status, etc.), culture (beliefs, customs, values, norms), milling behavior (rumor transmission, crowd actions), competition (in role behavior, sex, and age groups), and conformity. If the psychologist tries to understand conflict by studying the individual mind, the sociologist analyzes social institutions and processes.

CONFLICT AND CULTURE

Like the sociologist, the anthropologist sees conflict as a product of the social environment. Of particular interest are those norms and values that are conducive to conflict. Probably the most controversial findings deal with the notion of *national character*. The cultural approach assumes that all members of a given culture share the same cultural characteristics, including attitudes toward strength and weakness; definitions of "compromise" and "surrender"; bases of self-identification (e.g., family, peer, or nation); orientation to social structures (e.g., active or passive relationships with government, etc.); and beliefs and values (e.g., the Russian preoccupation with strength or the American infatuation with pragmatism). Anthropology has also made some significant contributions to the study of cross-cultural communications. Language, for example, expresses both the mental images we wish to transmit to others and our connotations of these images. For example, during the Vietnam War negotiations, it was important to know how the Americans and the Vietnamese defined the term "compromise," and also whether compromise was evaluated as good or bad. Linguistic analysis by anthropologists can contribute to such an understanding. Both communications and linguistics will be discussed further later on.

THE CONFLICT OF SCARCITY

In economics, conflict analysis is the study of the distribution patterns between actors when some item is scarce and valued.[9] Some of the most controversial explanations of imperialism and war can be traced to studies of economic factors, including Karl Marx's theory of the inevitability of violence among capitalist nations, known as dialectical materialism. Economics is the parent discipline of many specialized fields that focus on particular dimensions of economic behavior. Among these are decision-making analysis and game theory. A later discussion of the methods of conflict resolution will draw heavily upon these subfields of analysis, particularly in the areas of nuclear deterrence and conflict negotiations.

THE POLITICS OF CONFLICT

Political scientists have analyzed conflict on both the micro and macro levels. Most studies of political conflict center on the interrelationships among power, influence, and authority in social behavior. Political scientists have looked at the authoritative allocation of values in societies. They have analyzed the decision-making power of various social institutions, examined the coercive potential of nations, and studied the political influence of individuals, groups, and nations. The settings of political conflict may be interpersonal (e.g., among decision makers in a legislature or bureaucracy), societal (e.g., among various governmental structures), or systemic (e.g., among multinational alliances struggling for global power). By studying various actors, settings, and types of interactions, political scientists have been able to evaluate the amount, causes, and "success" of political conflict.

A MULTIDISCIPLINARY APPROACH

Where do these bodies of specialized knowledge leave us? Each of these disciplines provides many valuable pieces of information, but none of them deals with human conflict in a comprehensive manner. This text views people as the product of their psychological environment and the social structures and processes of which they are a part. For this reason, the causes of conflict will not be traced back to the findings in any one discipline or level of analysis. Rather, this text will try to convey an understanding of how various approaches, factors, and causes in the social sciences discussed above are interrelated, and how these interrelationships can provide us with a more powerful tool of analysis.

The Problem of Organization

Many laymen believe that learning about conflict is a mechanical process of gathering information. Once a "critical mass" has been accumulated, understanding will follow. However, as the above section implies, this approach is inadequate. To be meaningful, information must be organized. This is an intellectual process of relating information to a set of concepts, variables, hypotheses, and theories. One organizational scheme already mentioned is the psychological-versus-motivational framework for studying aggression. At this point, let us survey several other organizing frameworks that are useful in bringing together the dimensions of conflict into a comprehensible whole.

Before beginning, let us emphasize that the order imposed by these frameworks is largely arbitrary. Each is based on the distinctions, definitions, objectives, and even values of the social scientist. For this reason, it is crucial to identify and, where possible, justify the pathways we select.

Added to the cornucopia of definitions and approaches in the study of conflict is an overabundance of organizing frameworks. We can eliminate a number of them immediately by referring to our definition of conflict—a situation in which one identifiable actor is in opposition to another identifiable actor. This definition forms a conceptual framework. That is, it establishes the boundaries of our discussion by excluding intrapersonal conflict, nonmotive behavior, and unintegrated activities. This framework also identifies many relevant variables and suggests possible interrelationships among them.

The Nature of Perception

Our definition of conflict states that actors engage in conflict because they see a situation as blocking their goals. This notion of "seeing" or defining situations suggests the importance of the term "perception."

Perception is the process by which we receive and extract information about our environment. It is sometimes referred to as "the pictures in our minds" because it reflects our mental observations about our world. Each person's perceptions are unique. They are the products of our physical makeup and social setting, our wants and needs, and our personal experiences. However, although no two people have precisely the same image of their environment, there are perceptual features we all share.

Since perception involves receiving and extracting information, many scholars believe it deals primarily with knowledge—called, in psychology, the *cognitive process*. This process has two other aspects: learning and thinking. If we think of perception as the process of receiving and extracting information, then learning can be viewed as the acquisition of that information through experience. Once acquired, this information is stored for future reference. Learning therefore facilitates perception because the stored information can act as a model or guide for future perceptions. For example, if I have previously learned that a certain social situation makes me uncomfortable, I am more likely to recognize this situation as it develops. That is, I am more receptive to certain cues in this situation and become more selective in my mental reaction to them. If I must then decide how to extricate myself from the situation, I will engage in thinking. Thinking is the cognitive process of problem solving. The more complex the problem, the more information needed to solve it, and the greater one's reliance on thinking.

Most psychologists agree that perception, learning, and thinking are so closely interrelated as to be practically inseparable.[10] When we talk about extracting information, perception is viewed as the most inclusive concept. In this process, learning and thinking play an important though secondary role.

The Perceptual Process

In organizing our discussion of conflict, the perceptual process is crucial. Perception consists of three basic stages: stimulus input, intervening mental activity, and response. We will briefly discuss each of these stages now, and examine them in more detail later on in this chapter.

THE THREE STAGES

The perceptual process begins with a particular set of events, persons, or conditions in the individual's environment. Our senses are constantly bombarded by stimuli to which we do not react. The human eye, for example, can only see colors of specific wavelengths. What happens when some word, action, or object is picked up by our senses (the first stage of the perceptual process) and passed on to the brain? This takes us to the second stage.

When stimuli are transmitted to the brain during the second stage, either of two related mental processes may occur. The mind can simply receive the stimuli, extract the information, and respond to it immediately. When this occurs, we have *reception* and *relay*. Usually, however, the mind will do more. The stimuli, for example, may be so filled with information that the mind must organize it into a pattern. Once it is organized, the mind may select certain pieces of this information and pass it on for response. This process of organization and modification, known as *selection*, allows us to extract more varied information from the stimulus. As such, selection is crucial for problem solving or thinking—particularly in social situations, as we shall soon see.

The final step in the perceptual process is the response. This usually consists of speaking or some other overt act; occasionally it involves simply continued reception and selection, eventually leading to action. We realize that perception has taken place when the person lets us know that he or she has received, processed, and now is acting on the stimulus input. When this occurs, we have witnessed *adaptive behavior*.

Let us consider two examples. Suppose someone throws a rock at you, and you jump out of the way. What has happened? The rock hurtling through the air is a visual stimulus. This stimulus is received by the eye and transmitted to the brain. The brain receives this information, processes it (e.g., creates an image of harm), relays this image to the response center, and causes you to jump out of the way. The stimulus for action is responded to immediately and automatically. In social interaction, however, the perceptual process is usually more complicated. Suppose you are walking along a dimly lit street in a large city when suddenly a stranger steps out of the shadows and orders you to stop. Several stimuli are involved: the dark street, the other person, his statement, and the urban setting. While the verbal statement "Stop" may be the primary stimulus the senses are receptive to the situationed stimuli as well. These stimuli are all transmitted to the brain—where, either through learning or thinking, the information is organized and integrated into patterns. These patterns may be further reorganized according to the impact of your particular beliefs (e.g., the setting is potentially dangerous), motivations (e.g., you do not want to be harmed), and attitudes (e.g., you are predisposed to dislike and fear this situation). Sufficient information may be extracted at this point for you to perceive this situation as threatening. You may either respond with action or extract further information as the event unfolds. The original perception of threat may be confirmed or proven erroneous. In this example, the time elapsed between stimulus and response is probably very brief. In many less dramatic situations, there may be lengthy deliberation as the information is extracted and modified before being translated into adaptive behavior.

AN INTERACTION MODEL

The following three-step model is useful in examining simple as well as complex perceptions. It permits us to analyze a variety of conditions, events, and interactions that comprise conflict.

Our lives are based upon our interactions, including conflicts, with other people. As you will recall, we have defined conflict in terms of interactive behaviors: the opposition between one or more actors. A perceptual-behavioral interaction sequence between two actors is presented in Figure 1.1. Here, two actors (individuals, groups, or nations) are generating stimuli, extracting information through the perceptual processes, and then responding. Their responses are sent into the environment and serve as additional stimuli for the ongoing interactions that link them. Both actors perceive the factors in the relationship between them (in some cases similarly and in others quite differently). Each is formulating images of these factors and the other; each, consequently, is engaging in adaptive behavior. Conflict is one type of adaptive behavior.

Figure 1.1 THE PROCESS OF PERCEPTION

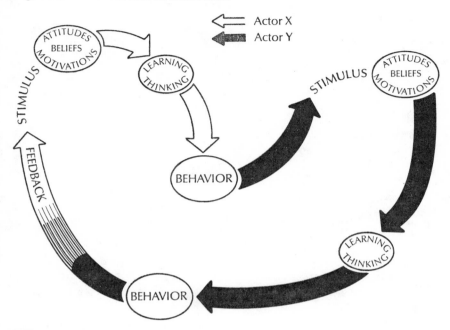

SOURCE: Modified from Ronald H. Forgus, *Perception: The Basic Process in Cognitive Development* (New York: McGraw-Hill, 1966), p. 4.

Let us now consider the principles underlying the perceptual process, particularly when the response is conflict. Since the communication process is particularly useful in a detailed discussion of perceptions, we will reexamine social interaction and perception from this perspective.

The Nature of Communication

Any communication process, regardless of its form, is an attempt to share information. This process consists of at least three elements—a *source,* a *message,* and a *destination.* This is a linear, one-way model. Some communications theorists, however, such as Harold Lasswell, include the *channel* in which the information is transmitted and the *effect* of the information on the source and the destination. The notion of *effect* modifies this view of communication as a linear process. If communication has an effect, sometimes referred to as *feedback,* the process is seen as curvilinear or continuous. Figure 1.2 illustrates an information source; a message that is being transmitted through a channel; the transformation of that message into a signal,

Figure 1.2 A HUMAN COMMUNICATION SYSTEM

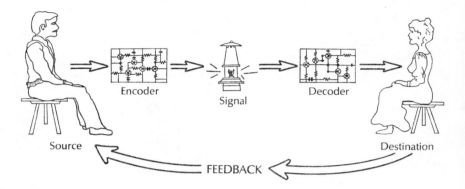

which is sent to a destination; a response to the message; and in responding, the transmission of a return signal to the original source. Feedback is important in communication. A sender uses it to check the success of the message by observing the reactions of the receiver.

The Communication Process

In our attempts to share information, what role is played by perception, learning, and thinking? In other words, what is the relationship between information transmission and information extraction? Information theory, the study of the communication process, posits that communication is a continuous, dynamic, interactive process. Let us examine what occurs when a sender attempts to share information with a receiver. First, the information must be put into a transmittable form. When thoughts are translated into a spoken, written, or visual form, we say that they are *encoded*. This encoded message is then transmitted as a signal that becomes a stimulus, perceived or not by the receiver. Communication theorist Wilbur Schramm suggests this is a critical point. If the message is not encoded fully, accurately, or effectively, it may not be received. Another problem is that sufficient transmission channels may not exist. Or, where they do exist, they may contain so much "noise" as to interfere with reception of the message (1965: 4).

Let us assume, however, that the signal is received and that the receiver is paying attention. This signal must then be *decoded;* that is, the information contained in the signal must be extracted. Here is where learning and thinking take over. Once the information has been extracted and interpreted, the receiver begins to encode his

Figure 1.3   THE RAYMOND ROSS MODEL OF HUMAN COMMUNICATION

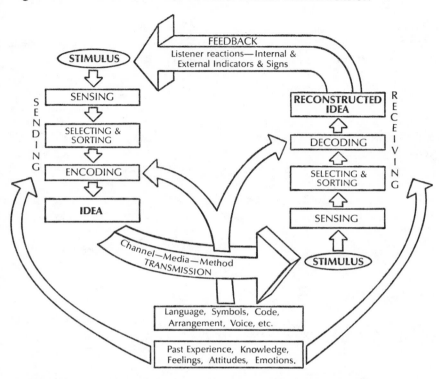

SOURCE: Modified from Raymond S. Ross, *Speech Communication: Fundamentals and Practice*, 4th ed., © 1977, p. 15. Adapted by permission of Prentice-Hall, Inc., Englewood Cliffs, N.J.

own message as he prepares to respond. It is not certain whether this encoding process will result in some overt communication. It depends on the situation, including the social climate of the actors, the rules of their culture, and other elements. But whatever the results, feedback occurs: Signals are returned to the original sender, and the process continues through countless cycles. In this sense, then, communication neither begins nor ends. It is a continuous and dynamic process. Figure 1.3 summarizes the various elements of communication and perception and depicts the basic analytical framework we will use to study conflict.

At this point, a word of caution is needed. First, no conceptual framework can identify all the variables that may affect communication or perception. Even if such a framework were possible, so many elements would have to be incorporated that it would become unmanageable. The variables and relationships found in Figures 1.1, 1.2, and 1.3 are the basic elements of our inquiry. As we explore these elements in the following chapters, they will be modified.

A second point to remember is that these processes are dynamic. Perception and communication are highly complex interacting systems. A variation in one part of one system may affect any other part of both systems.

We study perception and communication processes to try to understand their role in conflict. It was once thought that perception was an identical copy of the external stimulus; if one could identify the stimulus being communicated, one would know the exact perception evoked (Forgus, 1966: 12). We now know that there is no simple, predictable relationship among communication, perception, and conflict. Today, most theorists know that stimulus and perception may hardly correspond. When deviation does occur, it can be attributed to two groups of factors. The first deals with the relationship among the elements of communication. The second focuses on the factors and relationships in perception. This latter set of factors also accounts for individual differences in perception caused by psychological variables such as beliefs, attitudes, and values. In the next two chapters, we shall examine these variables, which are believed to be conducive to conflict. Before beginning, however, let us summarize our three organizing concepts and frameworks.

Summary

Social conflict is a situation in which individuals, groups, or nations are engaged in conscious opposition to one another in the pursuit of incompatible goals. This definition has four distinguishing characteristics. (1) Social conflict takes the form of motive and adaptive behavior. (2) Such behavior occurs in response to the combined influence of psychological and situational forces. (3) These forces emerge from the interactions of individuals, groups, or nations with their social environment. (4) Such interactions are continuous and dynamic as each actor receives, extracts, and responds to information from the environment.

Several perspectives can be employed to analyze social conflict. Each of the social sciences has its own approach. Psychologists analyze individual mental predispositions; sociologists examine society's structures and processes; anthropologists focus on the norms and values of culture; political scientists analyze the effect of power, influence, and authority. Whatever the perspective, each discipline tries to understand the causes of changes in human behavior. Our task is to integrate the diverse contributions into a comprehensible whole. One organizational framework rests on the assumption that behavior is a response not to "objective" facts but to one's perception of the situation. In economist Kenneth Boulding's words, we assume that "it is what we think the world is like, not what it is really like, that determines our behavior" (1962: 423). The way we extract information from, or perceive, our environment provides the basis for our actions.

We have noted that conflict behavior is an integrated response. This response is based on the information we extract about our environment and our own interests, as well as the interests of others. In some cases, a great deal of information will be extracted; in other cases, very little. In some situations, this information provides a fairly complete and accurate picture of the environment; in other situations, these images will be incomplete and even wrong. In all cases, however, there is an interaction among perception, learning, thinking, and responding. The beliefs, values, and experiences of every individual will result in unique thoughts and behavior.

Perception also requires information to be transmitted, usually through social interaction. Social interaction is influenced by a number of factors, and these, in turn, affect the quantity and quality of the information extracted. An organizing framework is needed to identify these interaction variables. This framework should suggest important relationships among the variables and between the entire set of variables and the perception process. Information theory is such a framework. It posits the continuous, dynamic, and interactive process by which information is encoded at a source, transmitted through a channel to a receiver, decoded by that receiver, and acted upon. The model of these processes (presented in Figure 1.3) identifies not only sender, receiver, and message variables but also such environmental variables as climate, situation, and culture. By including these environmental factors, we can examine the conditions that are believed to affect perceptions and conflict responses. While focusing on the effects of communication on the behavior of senders and receivers, we must be concerned with other factors. The influence of different channels on message transmission, the ways in which messages are filtered and distorted by perceptions, and the ways various contexts affect perceptions and response are additional determinants in perception.

Social conflict results from relationships between people, and these relationships depend upon communication and perception. In the next chapter, we will examine the underlying principles.

Notes*

1. The study of intrapersonal conflict is a diverse and complex field. Originating in psychology, it has been divided into a number of subfields, such as physiological psychology. Intrapersonal conflict has traditionally focused on "aggressiveness"—manifested in either feelings and/or behavior. Two schools have emerged—the "in-

*Complete citations for the works mentioned here will be found in the Bibliography, page 15.

stinctivists" (e.g., Sigmund Freud, Konrad Lorenz, and Robert Ardrey) and the "environmentalists" (e.g., Ashley Montagu). Both approaches have been criticized by Leonard Berkowitz, who claims that "aggressiveness" results from a complex interaction between nature (instinct) and nurture (environment). Berkowitz's thesis is presented and examined in Terry Maple and Douglas W. Matheson, eds., *Aggression, Hostility and Violence: Nature or Nurture.*

2. For a detailed examination of the instrumentalities of conflict, see Lewis Coser's *The Functions of Social Conflict* and his *Continuities in the Study of Social Conflict.*

3. The notion that wars begin in the mind has been popular for some time (e.g., see Otto Klineberg's *The Human Dimension in International Relations*). Increasingly such personal (micro) orientations have given way to orientations which stress the interaction between personal and environmental (macro) variables. Decision-making analysis of conflict embodies both notions. One of the central concepts in decision-making analysis is, of course, "perception." A good collection of readings based on micro, macro, and micro-macro approaches is Dean G. Pruitt and Richard C. Snyder, eds., *Theory and Research on the Causes of War.*

4. Attitudes, values, and beliefs are, of course, subject to change. In chapters 7 and 8, we will examine how individuals, groups and nations change their own and each others' mental images.

5. Conflict cycles may terminate when one or more actors realize or think that objectives have been realized.

6. A number of texts examine various approaches to the study of conflict. One early interdisciplinary collection of readings is Elton B. McNeil's *The Nature of Human Conflict.* A more recent work is Klaus R. Scherer et al., *Human Aggression and Conflict: Interdisciplinary Perspectives* (Englewood Cliffs, N.J.: Prentice-Hall, 1975).

7. One scholar who has done considerable work on emotional states (e.g., rage or anger) is Leonard Berkowitz. Some of his more interesting findings are reported in: "The Case for Bottling Up Rage," "Aggressive Humor as a Stimulus to Aggressive Behavior," and "Impulsive Aggression: Reactivity to Aggressiveness under Emotional Arousal."

8. The Dollard-Dobb hypothesis has been modified since the 1940s. For a discussion of these modifications, consult Leonard Berkowitz, *Aggression: A Social Psychological Analysis.* Another excellent survey of modifications of the frustration-aggression theory is Elton B. McNeil's "Psychology and Aggression."

9. A prolific scholar in the field of economics and conflict is Kenneth E. Boulding. One of Boulding's most widely read works is *Conflict and Defense: A General Theory.*

10. See Ronald Forgus, *Perception: The Basic Process in Cognitive Development,* pp. 1–10.

Bibliography

BERKOWITZ, LEONARD, and ANTHONY LEPAGE. "Weapons as Aggression Eliciting Stimuli." In Maple, Terry and Douglas W. Matheson, (eds.). *Aggression, Hostility and Violence: Nature or Nurture.* New York: Holt, 1973, pp. 141–151.

————. "Aggressive Humor as a Stimulus to Aggressive Behavior." *Journal of Personality and Social Psychology,* 16 (1970), 710–717.

————. "The Case for Bottling Up Rage." *Psychology Today,* (1973), 24–31.

————. "Impulsive Aggression: Relativity to Aggressiveness Under Emotional Arousal." in *Journal of Personality,* 35 (1967), 415–424.

————. *"Aggression: A Social Psychological Analysis.* New York: McGraw-Hill, 1962.

BOULDING, KENNETH E. *Conflict and Defense: A General Theory.* New York: Harper, 1962.

COSER, LEWIS. *Continuities in the Study of Social Conflict.* New York: Free Press, 1967.

————. *The Functions of Social Conflict.* New York: Free Press, 1956.

FORGUS, RONALD. *Perception: The Basic Process in Cognitive Development.* New York: McGraw-Hill, 1966.

KLEINBERG, OTTO. *The Human Dimension in International Relations.* New York: Holt, 1964.

MCNEIL, ELTON B. (ed.). "Psychology and Aggression." *Journal of Conflict Resolution,* 3 (1959), 193–293.

PRUITT, DEAN G., and RICHARD SNYDER (eds.). *Theory and Research on the Causes of War.* Englewood Cliffs, N.J.: Prentice-Hall, 1975.

SCHRAMM, WILBUR (ed.). *The Process and Effects of Mass Communication.* Urbana, Ill.: University of Illinois Press, 1965.

2 | SOME PSYCHOLOGICAL DIMENSIONS OF PERCEPTION

In the previous chapter, we stated that people act on their ideas. By receiving, interpreting, and reacting to information from the physical and social environment, they attempt to find meaning in the world. As a first step in defining the world, they must gather information. We have discussed the concept of "communication"—the process by which we gather and perceive environmental information. However, since perceptions are biased, each person has a unique image of the world. That is, certain psychological and environmental factors influence the gathering, extraction, and evaluation of information. In this chapter, we will see how this happens.

Selective Organization of Images

Our beliefs about persons and objects are selective. Among all the characteristics of everything in our environment, only certain ones catch our attention and enter our image of the world. A brief experiment will illustrate this point. Put down this book and look around the room. Try to describe it in your mind. Did you think about the furnishings? Did your image include colors, textures, and dimensions? If not, your image was partial. What determines this selectivity? A number of factors, some pertaining to the phenomena being viewed and others unique to the person doing the viewing. The first category includes the frequency, intensity, and number of stimuli. In the second category are attention span, personal disposition (such as sensitivity to certain persons and objects), and emotions (such as fear or anger).[1]

Not only are our beliefs selectively organized, they are also grouped into enduring systems of ideas. How does this grouping come about? One of the most widely accepted explanations is that our past experiences are responsible; that is, we learn belief systems.[2] Thus, for example, a soldier might view a combat scene and perceive the firepower of the combatants' weapons. All combat events involving firepower will be organized into a common cognitive system—"tactical combat." Other people may view the combat in terms of goals or casualties and group their cognitions into other systems. A single cognition is influenced by its larger frame of reference. This suggests that we may not fully understand a perception unless we know some of the properties of the system surrounding it. Stereotypes are a good example. These are sets of general traits attributed to every individual in the group. For example, "Asians are inscrutable," "blacks are lazy," "Germans are aggressive," and "Jews are arrogant." When we meet someone from any of these groups, the "part-whole effect" of cognitions comes into play. We perceive the person (the part) in terms of the perceived attributes of the group (the whole).

How Goals and Wants Affect Beliefs

We all change our ideas about things from time to time. According to many social psychologists, changes in thinking usually are related to continuing changes in wants or goals. Motivations not only initiate but also determine the results of learning and thinking. Suppose, for example, a student fails an important exam. The failure blocks successful completion of the course—his goal. What kind of cognitive change will enable him to remove this block and achieve his goal? This depends on a number of factors, including the strength of his desire and his perceptions of the block. David McClelland contends that a weakly motivated person engages in wishful thinking.[3] Let's say that our student doesn't need the course to graduate. In this case, his failure may lead him to think more about passing the course. There may be images of academic honors, satisfied professors, and proud parents. But very little time is spent considering ways to cope with the failure of the exam—the block. McClelland contends that being more strongly motivated brings about a "push to reality"; that is, the person begins to focus on the obstruction and thinks of various ways of removing it. The student may change his method of problem solving and the way he looks at the course material, or he may begin to distort his view of his performance. McClelland goes on to argue that if the want becomes too intense, the individual will abandon the goal-directed behavior and engage in further defensive imagery. The student, for example, may come to believe that it is the instructor's fault; in a more bizarre scene, he may think, "The prof is out to get me." Of course, sometimes an individual perceives the block incorrectly, or not at all. Our student may not know why he is failing, or he may attribute it not to his study habits but to something inherent in the material; it is too difficult, abstract, or confusing. In such cases, instead of dealing with the block, he simply may change his thinking about himself (e.g., "I am really not cut out for this course").

Changes in our perceptions are not determined solely by wants and goal blockage. As we have suggested previously, the characteristics of the cognitive system (its complexity, interconnectedness, and "consonance") may also be important. These factors, coupled with certain personality traits, such as intolerance and the mobility to accept new information, also play a role in cognitive change.[4]

In the earlier discussion of perception we suggested that information extraction is enhanced in the course of social learning. There are many assumptions about learning that psychologists employ in their study of the formation and growth of ideas. One of the most important of these is that before we can understand the ideas and behavior of adults, we must analyze the knowledge that children have of their world.

The Nature of Conflict

EARLY VIEWS

Let us assume that adult thinking about the world is based upon an evolution of cognitions from childhood. In this case, to analyze conflict, we must first explore the research on children's views about this subject. How do children perceive interpersonal, intergroup, and international conflict? How do they define conflict? What do they see as its causes? How are thoughts about conflict related to other thoughts, and what are the sources of these ideas? Let us consider some research findings of children's views on war and peace.

DEFINING CONFLICT

Studies in several countries indicate that by the age of eight, children have fairly well-defined ideas about war and peace.[5] The majority of their thoughts deal with concrete aspects of conflict. An American and a Japanese child might describe war in terms of weapons; the Swedish child might focus on fighting; the English child might perceive war as soldiers of one country killing those of another country. In all these cases, no matter what the nationality, beliefs about conflict are selectively organized around the tangible and the physical. This is not too surprising, argues Peter Cooper, because the young child's environment is filled with physical objects that become cognitively linked with conflict (1965: 174). Books show many pictures of war planes and guns, and a lot of playtime is often devoted to "playing war" and fighting. Among English children, in fact, war is often defined as "the big fight." War games and fighting (imaginary and real on the playground) are familiar to children as they usually have engaged in them from an early age. At the age of eight, however, children reject the idea that conflict must occur. Although they can fight, coexistence is the norm in their social world. As long as everyone knows his own strengths and weaknesses, conflict can be deterred. They believe, in other words, that the social order has an inherent equilibrium which precludes conflict. However, this equilibrium can be disturbed. Disruption may stem from an ignorance of the rules of coexistence (failure to keep one's feeling in check), unprovoked aggression by "outsiders" (older children and/or "bullies"), and changes in the order as children grow up. The observations of personal playing and fighting are generalized to group and national situations.

For the yound child, beliefs about personal, social, and international conflict are almost identical. Relations between nations involve cheaters, bullies, courage, meanness, friendship, and all other aspects of the child's world. This view of conflict appears to be the same in all countries. On the subject of peace, however, the picture is quite different. Here, children's perceptions vary considerably from culture to culture. Further, they lag far behind conflict in terms of verbal expression. For example, among English children aged eight to fifteen, peace is thought of primarily as a state of mind; very few of them view it as a form of cooperative behavior. In Norway and Japan, on the other hand, children conceptualize peace in terms of sociability and cooperation. Trond Alvik (1968: 191) concludes that as Norwegian children grow up, they adopt a more "pacifist" view of peace than do the English. This appears true for Japanese children as well; between the ages of eleven and fifteen, the idea of respect (a condition central to the philosophy of cooperation) grows quite strong. In this regard, older American children's views of peace seem closer to their Norwegian and Japanese counterparts than to the English. No one has yet determined whether these differences in children's views about peace are attributable to culture, socialization, or some other factor.

THE CAUSE OF CONFLICT

Thoughts about conflict are not only selectively organized, as we have seen, but also are clustered into enduring cognitive systems. One of the most important relationships deals with the causes of conflict. To recognize the causes of conflict, the child must be able to identify and understand the actions of others. This ability, in turn, rests largely upon skill in interpreting other's motivations. For this reason, younger children identify fewer causes of conflict than older children, who have more highly developed interpretative tools. For the eight-year-old, who generalizes from his own experiences, conflict is caused by anything that disrupts his social order. Just as he may be beaten up by the playground bully, so too can one nation "pick on" another. The actual reason(s) why the bully (individual or nation) attacks is unclear. When aggression does occur, the playground law takes reprisal almost for granted. The young child recognizes that he may have to fight to defend himself or some valued object. More important, however, is his belief that conflict is *not* inherent in the social order. Thus there are few causes or reasons for conflict. However, when there is a deliberate disruption of the social order, he must defend himself (which may involve aggression) to restore the "natural balance."

Between the ages of eight and ten, Peter Cooper contends, there is a "profound change in the perception of human psychology," (1965: 178). Now the child begins to identify a wide range of motivations for action in others. As he moves into adolescence, he begins to recognize the desire for power, honor, hate, civic rights, anxiety, tension, and greed as causes of conflict. Furthermore, the correspondence between personal, social, and international conflict begins to weaken. As beliefs about different types of conflict develop, the causal relationships become more differentiated. The narrow perspectives of the playground and personal experience can no longer adequately explain the causes of intergroup and international conflict. Because the adolescent can now understand motives in others, as well as in himself, he also can identify many more causes of conflict. As this process grows in range and subtlety, conflict becomes more justified. Adolescents appear to think either that deterred coexistence is not the order of things or, if it is, it is simply too difficult to maintain, given the many human motivations that disturb the rules of equilibrium and order.

We have been discussing the *cognitive* component of perception—the development of beliefs and the acquisition of knowledge. Learning is an important process; through it, the individual can refine and enlarge his or her "cognitive map." As that map grows in complexity and fullness, the individual learns how to perceive and think in more subtle ways.

There is another side to perceptual orientation—the *affective* component. This has to do with attitudes, emotions, and judgments regarding good and bad or right and wrong. Next, we will examine two of the most important affective elements—attitudes and values. As we shall see, certain combinations of cognitive and affective styles are important in analyzing conflict behavior.

The Nature of Attitudes

"Attitude" is probably one of the most widely used and indispensable terms in the social sciences. As one might expect, it has come to mean many things to many scholars: "a mental and neural state of readiness, organized through experience, exerting a directive or dynamic influence upon the individual's response to all objects and situations with which it is related" (Allport, 1935: 10); a "relatively stable affective response to an object" (Rosenberg, 1956: 367); a "tendency or disposition to evaluate an object or the symbol of that object in a certain way" (Katz and Stotland, 1959: 428); and "enduring systems of positive or negative evaluations, emotional feelings, and pro and con action tendencies with respect to social objects" (Krech et al., 1962: 139). This last definition is appropriate for our purposes. It is inclusive enough for us to see the interrelationships among cognition, response disposition, and behavior, and to examine how these interrelationships form enduring evaluative systems.

COMPONENTS OF ATTITUDES

Let us consider the above definition of attitudes. As Krech and his colleagues point out, there are three basic components: the cognitive, affective, and action tendencies.[6] The cognitive dimension refers to impressions or ideas we have about our social environment; they are evaluations of some aspect of reality. For example, your ideas about totalitarianism might include knowledge of specific political ideologies and impressions about the histories of certain totalitarian regimes, such as the Nazi government of Germany in the 1930s. Your affective component consists of the way you feel about this knowledge. You might believe that totalitarianism enslaves people, is basically aggressive, and hinders personal freedom. In this case, then, you have negative affect for totalitarianism. It is this emotional dimension of thought that gives attitudes their motivational character. A number of experimental studies have shown that when attitudes are aroused, they are accompanied by strong emotions.[7] Emotions can even take the form of physiological changes (i.e., galvanic skin responses) (J. B. Cooper, 1959).

An action tendency is a readiness to respond to persons and objects; we are impelled to act on our feelings. For example, if you like someone, you are probably disposed or ready to support, aid, or reward him or her. Attitudes affect not only behavior in general but specific action tendencies as well. Thus, for example, if a college student likes fraternities or sororities, he or she will have an action tendency to seek them out, join them, and give them high social status. Thus, evaluative cognitions and emotions influence overt behavior by predisposing us to action.

ATTITUDE FORMATION

Although knowing the components of attitudes is useful if we are to examine the impact of attitudes over time we need to know how attitudes are formed and changed. There are many theories regarding attitude formation. In this section we will examine some of them, particularly those related to the formation of the three attitude components discussed above.

To cope with the millions of stimuli that bombard us daily, we group them into arbitrarily designated categories. These categories are defined by specific attributes or qualities that are required for membership. What qualities does a liquid need to belong in the category "vodka"?[8] The liquid must be colorless, have a certain alcohol content, have no additives other than water, and be purchased in a bottle labeled "vodka." As Klaus Scherer and his colleagues point out, we must be careful to distinguish between the attributes that define a category and those associated with the category through social convention or personal experience (1975: 124). For example, vodka has no aftertaste; it is commonly mixed with fruit juices; Russians are famous for their vodka.

Racial Attitudes: Stereotypes

More than fifty years ago, Walter Lippmann coined the term "stereotype." Lippmann contended that individuals develop certain beliefs to aid them in simplifying the cognitive world. These beliefs, or fixed impressions, are not based on direct observation. Rather, they are mental images of the world. People act and react to a world that they imagine, and for them this "reconstructed world" is real. It may not be the "real world"—and it usually is not—but if it is imagined as real for the individual, then it is real in its consequences. (That is, if you *believe* that someone you have never met is hostile toward you, whether or not he or she really *is* hostile, you are likely to behave defensively, if not belligerently, should you ever meet that person. Such behavior is the result of a belief that may have no basis in fact.) Stereotypes are fixed impressions or images which may conform very little to the facts they claim to represent; they result from our tendency to define our environment first and observe it later. Prejudice, for example, consists of the stereotypes we have about people of other races and classes. Since stereotypes are believed to be a key factor in explaining prejudice, and since prejudice is basic in racial conflict, let us examine the major findings on the subject. Our discussion will be based on a survey of the literature by Nelson R. Cauthen and his colleagues. Their review analyzes three important dimensions of stereotypes: the *content* of the stereotype (i.e., the various traits associated with the image), the *uniformity* of the stereotype (i.e., how much individuals agree on the content of the image), and the *direction* of the stereotype (i.e., whether the belief is favorable or unfavorable, positive or negative) (Cauthen et al., 1971: 103–125).

LABELING: THE CONTENT OF STEREOTYPES

In the 1930s, Daniel Katz and Kenneth Braly were the first to research the link between verbal stereotypes and racial prejudice. How, they asked, could people in various parts of the United States agree as to their relative likes or dislikes for different racial groups? What troubled them was "that there are wide individual differences within any nationality group—that is, not all Englishmen are alike, nor are all Frenchmen, nor are all Russians" (1933: 281). Thus Katz and Braly hypothesized that this uniformity of beliefs represented prejudices developed from stereotypes of racial groups: "We have learned responses of varying degrees of aversion or acceptance to racial names and where these tags can be readily applied to individuals, as they can in the case of the Negro because of his skin color, we respond to him not as a human being but as a personification of the symbol we have learned to look down upon" (1933: 281). This tag, or verbal symbol, is a stereotype.

Since the time of Katz and Braly's study, *stereotype* has come to be defined "as a psychological construct that singles out an individual as sharing assumed characteristics on the basis of his group membership" (Cauthen et al., 1971: 103). Racial prejudice is therefore more than a conditioned response to a racial label. It is an evaluative reaction to all of the traits associated with that label. The intent of various stereotypical labels are found in Table 2.1. These findings give us some idea of the content of various racial stereotypes that were prevalent more than forty years ago. An important question is raised by these findings: Do stereotypes change over time?" The answer to this question will tell us something about the uniformity of stereotypes.

UNIFORMITY OF STEREOTYPES

Since stereotypes reflect our perception of the world, they might be expected to change as the world changes. In other words, as our environment changes, so does our experience; therefore, our perceptions may change as well. If this is the case, then it is logical to assume that stereotypes may change.

Research findings on uniformity of stereotypes are mixed. Ehrlich

Table 2.1 THE TWELVE TRAITS MOST FREQUENTLY ASSIGNED TO EACH OF VARIOUS RACIAL AND NATIONAL GROUPS IN 1933 BY 100 PRINCETON STUDENTS

Traits Checked, Rank Order	Number	Percent
GERMANS		
Scientifically-minded	78	78
Industrious	65	65
Stolid	44	44
Intelligent	32	32
Methodical	31	31
Extremely nationalistic	24	24
Progressive	16	16
Efficient	16	16
Jovial	15	15
Musical	13	13
Persistent	11	11
Practical	11	11
ITALIANS		
Artistic	53	53
Impulsive	44	44
Passionate	37	37
Quick-tempered	35	35
Musical	32	32
Imaginative	30	30
Very religious	21	21
Talkative	21	21
Revengeful	17	17
Physically dirty	13	13
Lazy	12	12
Unreliable	11	11
ENGLISH		
Sportsmanlike	53	53
Intelligent	46	46
Conventional	34	34
Tradition-loving	31	31
Conservative	30	30
Reserved	29	29
Sophisticated	27	27
Courteous	21	21
Honest	20	20
Industrious	18	18
Extremely nationalistic	18	18
Humorless	17	17
JEWS		
Shrewd	79	79
Mercenary	49	49
Industrious	48	48
Grasping	34	34

(continued)

Traits Checked, Rank Order	Number	Percent
Intelligent	29	29
Ambitious	21	21
Sly	20	20
Loyal to family ties	15	15
Persistent	13	13
Talkative	13	13
Aggressive	12	12
Very religious	12	12

AMERICANS

Industrious	48	48
Intelligent	47	47
Materialistic	33	33
Ambitious	33	33
Progressive	27	27
Pleasure-loving	26	26
Alert	23	23
Efficient	21	21
Aggressive	20	20
Straightforward	19	19
Practical	19	19
Sportsmanlike	19	19

NEGROES

Superstitious	84	84
Lazy	75	75
Happy-go-lucky	38	38
Ignorant	38	38
Musical	26	26
Ostentatious	26	26
Very religious	24	24
Stupid	22	22
Physically dirty	17	17
Naïve	14	14
Slovenly	13	13
Unreliable	12	12

IRISH

Pugnacious	45	45
Quick-tempered	39	39
Witty	38	38
Honest	32	32
Very religious	29	29
Industrious	21	21
Extremely nationalistic	21	21
Superstitious	18	18
Quarrelsome	14	14
Imaginative	13	13
Aggressive	13	13
Stubborn	13	13

(continued)

Traits Checked, Rank Order	Number	Percent
CHINESE		
Superstitious	34	35
Sly	29	30
Conservative	29	30
Tradition-loving	26	27
Loyal to family ties	22	23
Industrious	18	19
Meditative	18	19
Reserved	17	17
Very religious	15	15
Ignorant	15	15
Deceitful	14	14
Quiet	13	13
JAPANESE		
Intelligent	45	48
Industrious	43	46
Progressive	24	25
Shrewd	22	23
Sly	20	21
Quiet	19	20
Imitative	17	18
Alert	16	17
Suave	16	17
Neat	16	17
Treacherous	13	14
Aggressive	13	14
TURKS		
Cruel	47	54
Very religious	26	30
Treacherous	21	24
Sensual	20	23
Ignorant	15	17
Physically dirty	15	17
Deceitful	13	15
Sly	12	14
Quarrelsome	12	14
Revengeful	12	14
Conservative	12	14
Superstitious	11	13

SOURCE: Daniel Katz and Kenneth W. Braly, "Verbal Stereotypes and Racial Prejudice," in Martin Fishbein (ed.), Attitude Theory and Measurement (New York: Wiley, 1967), pp. 34–35.

and Rhinehardt demonstrated that in 1965 the stereotype of Jews still contained the same assigned traits (shrewd, mercenary, industrious, grasping, etc.) as Katz and Braly found in 1933. Studies by Seago (1947) and Gilbert (1951), however, show significantly less agreement on the attributes assigned to "Japanese," "Germans," and "Chinese" over time. Gilbert's study is often cited as evidence of a decline in the uniformity of stereotypes over time. And yet, a 1969 study by Karlins et al., revealed a resurgence of high uniformity.

To James Jones, these mixed findings indicate that the trait contents of older stereotypes are fading, only to be replaced by new ones—some of which are more positive than their antecedents (1972: 72). The uniformity of the black stereotype is significant. Between 1933 (the Katz and Braly study) and 1969 (the Karlins et al. study), the negative traits assigned by white respondents were balanced by several positive attributes. But the general tendency to stereotype—to assign attributes such as "musical," "happy-go-lucky," "pleasure-loving," "lazy," and "ostentatious" to black people—continues (Jones, 1972: 70).

ORIGINS AND DEVELOPMENT

One usually does not discuss the "direction" of stereotypes, since in popular usage they are often assumed to be unfavorable. Thus, rather than focus on direction (e.g., favorable stereotypes about Americans versus negative ones about Russians), we will discuss the origins of negative racial stereotypes and the reasons most of them are negative. To explore these issues, we must look at the genesis of racial stereotypes in children.

One of the earliest attempts to analyze the origins of racial attitudes was Eugene and Ruth Horowitz's 1938 study of white boys. The Horowitzes found that prejudicial attitudes about blacks began very early in the child's development—sometimes by the age of three. One three-year-old commented, "I don't like black boys." Blake and Dennis (1943) also found early prejudicial attitudes among children. On the basis of these studies, it appeared that racial awareness developed early in childhood. But the important question raised by these studies were, What was racial awareness? and Why was it associated with negative attitudes toward other racial groups? Some of the most important studies that sought to answer these questions were done by Kenneth Clark (1955) and Kenneth and Mamie Clark (1939, 1940).

In researching racial identification and preference among black children, the Clarks defined "racial awareness" as "a consciousness of the self as belonging to a specific group which is differentiated from other observable groups by obvious physical characteristics which are generally accepted as being racial characteristics." (cited in Newcomb and Hartley, 1947). Some of the most common physical traits identified were skin color, hair color, and facial characteristics. The most controversial Clark studies focused on skin and hair color in an interesting series of doll-preference experiments. Black children were given four dolls identical in every respect except for skin and hair color. Two of the dolls were brown with black hair and two were white with yellow hair. Each child then responded to eight requests by choosing one of the dolls considered most suitable. The requests were: (1) Give me the doll that you like to play with (like best); (2) Give me the doll that is a nice doll; (3) Give me the doll that looks bad; (4) Give me the doll that is a nice color; (5) Give me the doll that looks like a white child; (6) Give me the doll that looks like a colored child; (7) Give me the doll that looks like a Negro child; (8) Give me the doll that looks like you (Clark, 1955: 19, 23). Requests 1 to 4 were designed to reveal racial preferences; requests 5 to 7 revealed knowledge of racial differences; and request 8 revealed self-identification.

Racial identification among Negro children was found to center not on the label "Negro" but rather on the terms "colored" and "white." These designations of color were the basis of their knowledge of racial differences and thus their perception of racial identification. Was there a link between racial identification and racial preference? Before an answer could be given, it was important to determine what the racial preferences were (i.e., responses to requests 1 to 4). The majority of black children preferred the white-skinned, yellow-haired doll and rejected the "colored" doll. Clark found that 59 percent of these children indicated that the colored doll "looked bad," while 60 percent thought that the while doll was a "nice color." When asked to identify themselves (request 8), some of the children became disturbed and emotional. One child even felt compelled to explain that his "brown skin was the result of a summer at the beach" (1955: 37).

What do studies such as the Clarks' and others tell us about racial stereotypes? Do they suggest that a predominant social stereotype favors "whiteness"? Do they suggest that most children want to be white and therefore form negative attitudes about other skin colors? It is difficult to judge. In a more recent study black children preferred black dolls in the same proportion as those who had selected white dolls in the Clark study (Hraba and Grant, 1970 as cited in Jones, 1972). Does this mean that among black children "black is beautiful"? Possibly, but results from still another study by Asher and Allen in 1969 found results similar to those of Clark (Jones, 1972).

A social psychologist, James M. Jones, has criticized the doll-preference studies that have been conducted in the last forty years. He speculates that there is a poor correlation between doll-color choice and racial attitudes because the findings of the various doll-preference studies are so contradictory (1972: 92–94). As Jones put it, "the simplified methodologies and naive operational assumptions that have guided research in this area have perpetuated relative ignorance in the real-life racial dynamics in this country" (1972: 95). This type of research probably will be the subject of considerable debate and similar criticism in the future. All we have learned is that racial choice does exist, that such choice is influenced by racial self-awareness and preferences, and that among children these choices develop very early in life.

One of the most important components of a child's racial awareness is self-identification with a racial group. It has been shown that self-identification is linked to racial stereotypes. In other words, the child who self-identifies as black or white develops corresponding attitudes toward either race. Why is this the case? One answer emerges from the research on group dynamics.

Groups, as we have noted, are important agents of socialization. In growing up, we tend to internalize the norms and beliefs of the groups to which we belong. This process influences our attitudes and often has a profound effect on our behavior. This is particularly true when we act within our own group(s) or interact with other groups. Since prejudice is composed of both attitudes and behavior, and since group dynamics are crucial in their formation and direction, group dynamics may account for the link between racial identification and stereotypes. In fact, a number of scholars have advanced this thesis. They call it the "group norm" basis of prejudice and they contend:

> The factors leading individuals to form attitudes of prejudice are not piecemeal. Rather, their formation is functionally related to becoming a group member—to adopting the group and its values (norms) as the main anchorage in regulating experience and behavior. (cited in Allport, 1954: 39)

Kenneth Clark also shares this group norm explanation of prejudice. One learns racial identity as well as racial preferences during socialization, where groups play a significant role. Racial ideas, he contends, reflect children's awareness and acceptance of the racial attitudes of their society (1955: 23). As Kenneth Clark puts it:

> The fact that young Negro children would prefer to be white reflects their knowledge that society prefers white people. White children are generally found to prefer their white skin—an indication that they too know that society likes white better. (1955: 24)

However, not everyone accepts this group norm explanation. Gordon Allport, for example, rejects it as the *sole* explanation for the formation of prejudicial attitudes. He contends that prejudice is also influenced by personality formation and development: "No individual would mirror his group's attitudes unless he had a personal need, or personal habit, that leads him to do so" (1954: 41).

The group and personality explanations work together to explain why and how racial stereotypes emerge. Nelson Cauthen and his colleagues, for instance, state that the intensity of stereotyping depends on one's personality (1971: 110), and Allport says that "It is possible to hold the individualistic type of theory [personality] without denying that the major influences upon the individual may be collective [group]" (1954: 41).

SUMMARY

1. Stereotypes, mental constructs that assign traits to an individual who is part of a group, have played a key role in developing a theory of prejudice.
2. The attributed traits do not define the stereotype. Instead, the label (e.g., "Negro") defines the traits that are attributed to the stereotype.
3. The content of stereotypes remains relatively stable over time. However, it can be changed, even if the process is slow.
4. The tendency to stereotype remains even when social experience and the environment change. The uniformity of agreement on stereotypes varies over time.
5. Stereotypes are ways of expressing racial identity and preferences. While stereotypes may not initiate behavior, they do serve as frames of reference for preferences and behavior.

Want Fulfillment and Frustration

According to Milton Rosenberg, we develop favorable attitudes toward people and relationships that help us to achieve valued objectives. Conversely, people or relationships that frustrate us will be negatively evaluated (Rosenberg, 1956). This explanation suggests that many of the factors influencing goal development may affect attitude formation as well. For example, Abraham Maslow has proposed a theory based on a hierarchy of needs. Maslow contends that our wants develop sequentially from "lower wants," such as food and safety, to "higher wants," such as esteem and the desire for self-fulfillment. Until the lower wants are adequately satisfied, the higher wants do not emerge (Maslow, 1943).

The influence of wants in attitude development can be seen in the function of stereotypes, particularly racial stereotypes. What functions do racial stereotypes perform? What wants do stereotypes serve? A partial listing of such functions and wants might include managing repressed wants, enhancing feelings and self-regard, protecting the self-image against threats to self-esteem, providing explanations for status deprivation, and rationalization for displaced aggression stemming from frustrations.[9] A study by Angus Campbell on attitudes toward Jews shows the relationship between want frustration and negative ethnic attitudes. Campbell found that (non-Jewish) people who were dissatisfied with their economic situations were more hostile and negative toward Jews than those who were content. This held true for the rich as well as the poor. The degree of satisfaction with income was the key factor in explaining stereotype formation about Jews (Campbell, 1942; in Allport, 1954: 223–224). Campbell's study shows the correlation between satisfaction of lower-level wants and stereotyping.

In trying to satisfy higher-level wants, such as self-esteem and self-image, people often attempt to find others to denigrate. Thus a low-income, unskilled white laborer might feel superior (enhance his self-esteem and image) by perceiving certain racial groups as beneath him socially. He might think, for example, "I may not be wealthy, but at least I'm not black." The inference is that being black is lower in status than being poor. The desire for status and superiority is thus served by the formation or reinforcement of unfavorable racial stereotypes.

The Nature of Values

SOCIALIZATION OF VALUES

Attitude formation, particularly action tendencies, is closely related to the development of cultural norms and desirable symbols. Sometimes referred to as *values*, these are general concepts of what a society or its subgroups deem desirable.[10] In the United States, for example, research has shown that people value, among other things, a comfortable life, a sense of accomplishment, family security, equality, national security, and self-respect. Among individual qualities Americans value ambition, courage, intelligence, honesty, and self-control (Rokeach, 1973: 57–58). Values are abstract standards indicating desirable or preferred attributes of persons, groups, and social relationships (Rokeach, 1968). Since values have what we might call an "ought dimension," they are influential in pointing out the "correct" or "proper" behavior in approaching or avoiding persons and relationships. It is this moral aspect of values that makes them so important in attitude formation and consequent behavior.

VALUES AND THE SELF-CONCEPT

There are many different kinds of values and norms in any society, and often they conflict. Furthermore, social norms are of different kinds. Some norms are very strict (for example, to obey the law and respect authority). Some values are particularly emotion-laden (for example, those involved in defining the self, group, and national identity). Such feelings are maintained by concrete expressions or attitudes. While many attitudes act to prevent us from revealing to ourselves and others repressed wants and values (as noted in the discussion of stereotypes), other attitudes give positive expression to central values. For example, you may see yourself as an enlightened liberal and thus form attitudes which indicate your liberal values. You might, for example, approve of minority-group causes, support government spending, and become angry when you hear isolationist views on foreign affairs. In each case, you enjoy expressing attitudes which reflect your cherished values. You are rewarded not by gaining social recognition (though this may also occur) but by confirming your self-identity. Just as we find satisfaction in using certain talents, so we are rewarded in expressing values through attitudes and behavior.

VALUES, THE SELF, AND SOCIALIZATION

Socialization, as we have said, is a learning process in which a society (or groups within a society) transmits its values and norms to the individual. In terms of self-image, socialization sets limits on individual development. There are, of course, many different types of socialization. Political socialization, for example, strengthens political identity, national cohesiveness, and affection by creating attitudes that support the political system. In the United States, over 90 percent of those in one sample supported the American political system because it reflected the following values: (1) democracy or government by consent is the *best* type (my emphasis) of political system; (2) the existing constitutional system works effectively; (3) change should occur through legal means (Andrain, 1971: 29). According to Gabriel Almond and Sydney Verba, most Americans associate their national identity with the attachment to democratic political institutions. To help them accept this core value, they develop positive attitudes to representative government, political freedom, and the concept of "democracy" (as cited in Andrain, 1971: 30). In a study by Charles Andrain, children in Southern California were asked, "What makes you proud to live in America?" Over 62 percent of them gave a political reply based on civic values. For example: "America has the most representative form of government in the world" (Andrain, 1971: 33).

Agents of socialization vary. In considering political socialization, a great deal of research has focused on the family and the school (Coleman, 1965; Easton and Dennis, 1969; Hess and Torney, 1967; Piaget, 1950). Which agent is the single most important factor in socialization? No one knows. As Kirkpatrick and Pettit (1972) point out, political socialization continues to develop over the entire life cycle—beyond the influence of parents and formal education. Other dimensions of the self-concept, such as race, religion and ethnicity— as well as their respective agents—also influence attitude formation. We shall see more of this later.

We have shown how the three components of attitudes—evaluations, emotions, and action tendencies—develop under the influence of several factors. Attitudes are *learned* predispositions. Whether we learn them from personal experience or from others, they are necessary if we are to understand and function in our social environment and protect our self-esteem. Attitudes aid us in organizing and simplifying our world. Along with cognitions, they are fundamental to the process of perception.

Attitude Networks

Various types of attitude formation have been described in regard to the components of attitudes. While these components are all interrelated, each develops at a different rate (Triandis, 1971; 118). By the time a person reaches adolescence, these components have become unified into fairly consistent attitude networks. These networks are similar in complexity and structure to cognitive systems. Let us consider how these networks are formed. Of the many available theories, two categories have been selected for analysis: information theories and group theories. The concept of "information" is crucial to perceptions, while groups play a significant role in structuring conflictual and cooperative behaviors.

ATTITUDE FORMATION AND INFORMATION

In addition to acquiring beliefs to satisfy various needs, people also seek information to give meaning to an otherwise chaotic world. As they learn, their attitudes are shaped. Herta Herzog, in a classic study of daytime radio serials (the soap operas of the 1940s), found that to the housewives listening, these dramas were a source of information; they helped to form attitudes about life-styles, personalities, and interpersonal relations. The dramas were popular because they helped explain various dimensions of life (Herzog, 1944; as cited in Schramm, 1965; 50–55). Herzog's study, as well as studies by Cartwright and Harary (1956) and Morrissette (1958), indicates that people use information to form these attitudinal frames of reference. In developing attitudes, we use information not to form new ideas but to support old ones. As Krech and his colleagues point out, "new information is frequently used to form attitudes which are consonant with pre-existing related attitudes. Information is rarely a determinant of an attitude except in the context of other attitudes" (Krech et al., 1962: 187).

Some attitudes, particularly those dealing with racial stereotypes and ethnocentric bias, are particularly resistant to new information (Karlins et al., 1969). Other attitudes, however, are more flexible.

Many social psychologists believe that the effect of information on attitudes is determined by the information source. In the early 1950s, Carl Hovland and Walter Weiss tried to determine the influence of source credibility on communication effectiveness. They found that the trustworthiness of the source had no effect on the acquisition or the retention of factual information. However, when it came to opinions—verbal expressions of attitudes—the story was different. Opinions were significantly related to the perceived trustworthiness of the source, although this factor became less important over time (Hovland and Weiss, 1951).

What is the effect on attitudes when fear or anxiety are aroused? Some information, particularly propaganda, is used to influence attitudes in this way. For example, the propaganda campaigns of the United States and the Soviet Union play up the threat and destructiveness of nuclear war. Each country hopes to influence the other's population to support such programs as arms limitations and peace initiatives. Irving Janis and Seymour Feshbach tried to determine whether the arousal of fear would be effective in influencing attitudes (Janis and Feshbach; 1953). Their answer: definitely not. When fear is strongly aroused and not relieved by reassurances, we are motivated to ignore or minimize the information (Janis and Feshbach, 1953: 92).

Attitudes result from many pieces of information, all of which are interrelated. Given this interdependence, we can never tell for sure which bits of information are valid and which may lead to perceptual distortion and "wrong" attitudes. A "wrong attitude" is one based on a distortion of information that leads to a false interpretation of the environment. In discussing social perception, we will consider the importance of information again.

GROUP DYNAMICS

In discussing socialization and attitude formation, we stated that there were many agents in socialization. One of the most important in transmitting and developing beliefs, values, and attitudes is the group. Every child internalizes the beliefs and values of the largest group to which he or she belongs—the society. This adoption of group principles influences our attitudes. It will often affect our behavior within the group and in interactions with other groups and their members. The central question is, How and why do individuals internalize group attitudes?

Groups have been studied since antiquity. And yet, within the last twenty-five years, our knowledge about groups has expanded so rapidly that it has become a specialized subfield within a number of disciplines. The field of "group dynamics," as it is sometimes labeled, focuses on the nature of groups, the laws of their development, and their interrelations with individuals, other groups, and larger institutions (Cartwright and Zander, 1968: 7). Group dynamics will be considered in the next few chapters. Here we shall examine only one aspect of the group—its ability to influence our attitudes.

T. M. Newcomb's famous study at Bennington College was one of the first to demonstrate that our attitudes are strongly rooted in the groups to which we belong (Newcomb, 1943). Newcomb established that Bennington College was politically liberal and that certain of the freshman women came from conservative homes and had conservative political beliefs and opinions. These attitudes deviated from the prevailing political norms of the college community (which at that time consisted of approximately 250 female students and 50 faculty). Newcomb demonstrated that by their senior year, these political conservatives had become more liberal; they had changed their attitudes to conform to their political culture. Of particular interest was Newcomb's finding that the liberal community rewarded students who adopted the existing norms by identifying them as "good citizens," treating them as favorites, and choosing them to represent the school at intercollegiate gatherings.

What do we mean by the term "group"? The group is an object of everyday experience. All of us can identify a long list of groups to which we belong or with which we interact. Because of its many properties, "group" is difficult to define. According to Cartwright and Zander, a set of people constitute a group when

> (1) they engage in frequent interaction; (2) they define themselves as members; (3) they are defined by others as belonging to the group; (4) they share norms concerning matters of common interest; (5) they participate in a system of interlocking roles; (6) they identify with one another as a result of having set up the same model-object or ideals; (7) they find the group to be rewarding; (8) they pursue promotively interdependent goals; (9) they have a collective perception of their unity; (10) they tend to act in a unitary manner toward the environment. (Cartwright and Zander, 1968: 48)

Some of these attributes will be useful in our later discussion of specific instances of conflict and cooperation. For the present, however, we will focus on those that influence attitudes.

GROUP MEMBERSHIP

Many attitudes are formal and supported by groups. In order to maintain attitudes, most of us must have the support of others who think as we do. By mingling with people who share our views, we gain support for our beliefs and are drawn to the group. A uniformity of attitudes results from the fact that group members share similar norms and beliefs. (See attribute 4 of Cartwright and Zander, above.) Group norms prescribe the "right" beliefs, values, and attitudes. As Asch and others have shown, the pressure to conform to group attitudes and perceptions is great (Asch, 1956).

Anyone who belongs or seeks to belong will find that his or her attitudes are affected by the group. A group that is held together by strong positive attraction is said to be cohesive. Such a group will have a strong impact on the attitudes of its members (Cartwright and Zander, 1968: 50).

In thinking about the individual's relationship to a group, it is important to remember that people usually belong to many different groups. The groups that people use for comparison and to which they relate their attitudes are known as *reference groups*. One of the most important functions of such groups is what Kelly and Thibault call the "normative function." These groups provide a standard by which to evaluate one's environment. The reference group, in turn, evaluates individuals (members and nonmembers) according to their conformity to group attitudes (Kelly and Thibault, 1954). For example, you may identify with the tastes, beliefs, and attitudes of a higher-status group and accept them while belonging to a lower-status group. This situation is common among persons who aspire to greater social mobility (Siegel and Siegel, 1957).

Summary

Throughout this chapter we have examined some of the psychological factors that influence our gathering, extracting, and evaluating of information. We have seen, for example, how our images of other persons are selective. This selectivity can be traced to a number of sources. Our goals, ambitions, attitudes, values, and even our early childhood beliefs all influence how we perceive others and our social environment.

Of particular importance to our understanding of conflict has been the concept of attitudes. The evaluations, emotions, and action tendencies found in our attitudes predispose us to view and act towards people in specific ways. Racial attitudes such as stereotypes may cause us to see specific individuals as sharing certain group traits. If these group traits are seen as negative, we may respond to an individual from that group in a negative manner. Because of the influence of stereotypes on our beliefs and behavior, social scientists have sought to identify their origins and development.

Wants and values also play important roles in shaping our images of others and of our social environment. They, like attitudes, result from a complex interaction between psychological and sociological forces. We have seen, for example, how a person's need to belong can often be met by a group. Within that group, individuals are subject to group values and rules of behavior. The dynamics of the individual's interaction with others in the group are important in shaping his views of himself and others both within and outside of his group(s).

While the psychological factors that we have discussed are important to our understanding of the process of perception, we cannot forget that environmental forces are crucial also. In the next chapter we will examine some of the more important contextual variables that help to shape our perceptions and behavior.

Notes*

1. For one of the earliest discussions of how various factors influence our image of the world, see Kenneth E. Boulding's *The Image*.

2. Social learning theory analyzes these positive incentives that motivate human behavior. Klaus Scherer and his colleagues identify two types of learning that may account for a good deal of behavior: "(1) the shaping of behavior through selective reinforcement, and (2) learning through the observation and imitation of models" (1975: 82).

3. The discussion that follows is based on the general principles identified by David C. McClelland in his works *Personality* and *The Achievement Motive* (with J. W. Atkinson, R. A. Clark, and E. L. Lowell). The examples are the authors'.

4. For a more detailed discussion of the effects of multiplicity, consonance, and interconnectedness on cognitive development, see David Krech et. al., *Individual in Society: A Textbook of Social Psychology*, particularly pp. 30–45.

5. The number of studies that deal with the development of children's views of "war" and "peace" are limited. Fortunately, among those that do exist, several present cross-national findings. Among the studies utilized were: Peter Cooper, "The Development of the Concept of War"; T. Alvik, "The Development of Views on Conflict, War and Peace Among School Children"; and Takeshi Tahida, "Beyond the Traditional Concepts of Peace in Different Cultures."

6. Action tendencies will be discussed only briefly in this section. They will be covered in more detail in chapter 4, in the content of discrimination. We view discrimination as an action tendency resulting from sets of attitudes called "prejudice."

7. Emotions such as anger and hatred are usually considered individual states of mind. Much of the literature on human aggression and violence deals with these emotional states. Many of these studies argue that anger is necessary for frustration to be translated into violence.

8. Klaus Scherer and his colleagues suggested this illustration of cognitive categorization with their description of Scotch whiskey, pp. 67–71.

9. For an excellent survey of the literature on stereotypes, see Nelson R. Cauthen et al., "Stereotypes: A Review of the Literature 1926–1968."

10. For an excellent examination of the difference between personal and social values, as well as a general study of human values, see Milton Rokeach's *The Nature of Human Values*.

*Complete citations for the works mentioned here will be found in the Bibliography, pages 38–40.

Bibliography

ALLPORT, GORDON W. *The Nature of Prejudice.* Reading, Mass.: Addison-Wesley, 1954.

————. "Attitudes." In C. Murchison (ed.). *Handbook of Social Psychology.* Worcester, Mass.: Clark University Press, 1935.

ALVIK, T. "The Development of Views on Conflict, War and Peace Among School Children." *Journal of Peace Research,* 2 (1968), 171–192.

ANDRAIN, CHARLES. *Children and Civic Awareness.* Columbus, Ohio: Charles E. Merrill, 1971.

ASCH, SOLOMON E. *Studies of Independence and Conformity.* Washington, D.C.: American Psychological Association, 1956.

ASCHER, S. R., and V. L. ALLEN. "Racial Preference and Social Comparison Process." *Journal of Social Issues,* 25 (1969), 157–167.

BLAKE, R., and W. DENNIS. "Development of Stereotypes Concerning the Negro." *Journal of Abnormal and Social Psychology,* 38 (1943), 525–531.

BOULDING, KENNETH E. *The Image.* Ann Arbor: University of Michigan Press, 1956.

BULLIS, H. EDMUND, and CORDELIA W. KELLY. *Human Relations in Action.* New York: Putnam, 1954.

CAMPBELL, ANGUS. "Factors Associated with Attitudes Toward Jews." In Gordon W. Allport, *The Nature of Prejudice.* Readings, Mass.: Addison-Wesley, 1954, pp. 223–224.

CANTRIL, HADLEY, and GORDON W. ALLPORT. *The Psychology of Radio.* New York: Harper, 1935.

CARTWRIGHT, DORWIN, and ALBIN ZANDER, (eds.). *Group Dynamics, Research and Theory.* 3rd ed. New York: Harper, 1968.

———— and F. HARARY. "Structural Balance: A Generalization of Heider's Theory." *Psychological Review,* 63 (1956), 277–293.

CAUTHEN, NELSON R., et al. "Stereotypes: A Review of the Literature, 1926–1968." *The Journal of Social Psychology,* 84 (1971), 103–125.

CLARK, KENNETH. *Prejudice and Your Child.* Boston: Beacon Press, 1955.

————, and MAMIE P. CLARK. "Skin Color as a Factor in Racial Identification of Negro Preschool Children." *Journal of Social Psychology,* 11 (1940), 159–169.

———— and ————. "The Development of Consciousness of Self and the Emergence of Racial Identification in Negro Preschool Children." *Journal of Social Psychology,* 10 (1939), 591–599.

COLEMAN, JAMES S. *Adolescents and the Schools.* New York: Basic Books, 1965.

COOPER, J. B. "Emotion in Prejudice." *Science,* 130 (1959), 314–318.

COOPER, PETER. "The Development of the Concept of War." *Journal of Peace Research,* 2 (1965), 171–192.

DAHL, ROBERT A. *Pluralist Democracy in the U.S.: Conflict and Consent.* Chicago: Rand McNally, 1967.

EASTON, DAVID and JACK DENNIS. *Children in the Political System: Origins of Political Legitimacy.* New York: McGraw-Hill, 1969.

EHRLICH, H. J., and J. W. RINEHART. "A Brief Report on the Methodology of Stereotype Research." *Social Forces,* 43 (1965), 564–575.

FISHBEIN, MARTIN (ed.). *Readings in Attitude Theory and Measurement.* New York: Wiley, 1967.

GILBERT, G. M. "Stereotypes Persistence and Change Among College Students." *Journal of Abnormal and Social Psychology,* 46 (1951), 245–254.

HERZOG, HERTA. "Motivations and Gratification in Daily Serial Listeners." In Wilbur Schramm (ed.), *The Process and Effects of Mass Communication.* Urbana: University of Illinois Press, 1965, pp. 50–55.

HESS, ROBERT D., and JUDITH V. TORNEY. *The Development of Political Attitudes in Children.* Chicago: Aldine, Atherton, 1967.

HOROWITZ, E. L., and RUTH HOROWITZ. "Development of Social Attitudes in Children." *Sociometry,* 1 (1938), 301–338.

HOVLAND, CARL L., and WALTER WEISS. "Changes in Attitudes through Communication." *Journal of Abnormal and Social Psychology,* 46 (1951), 424–437.

HRABA, J., and G. GRANT. "Black Is Beautiful: A Reexamination of Racial Preference and Identification." *Journal of Personality and Social Psychology,* 16 (1970), 398–402.

INSKO, CHESTER A. *Theories of Attitude Change.* New York: Appleton, 1967.

JANIS, IRVIN L., and S. FESHBACH. "Effects of Fear-Arousing Communications." *Journal of Abnormal and Social Psychology,* 48 (1953), 78–92.

JONES, JAMES M. *Prejudice and Racism.* Reading, Mass.: Addison-Wesley, 1972.

KARLINS, M., et al. and "Underfading of Social Stereotypes." *Journal of Personality and Social Psychology,* 13 (1969), 1–16.

KATZ, DANIEL, and EZRA STOTLAND. "A Preliminary Statement to a Theory of Attitude Structure and Change." In Sigmund Koch (ed.), *Psychology: A Study of a Science,* vol. 3. New York: McGraw-Hill, 1959, pp. 423–475.

———, and K. W. BRALY. "Racial Stereotypes of 100 College Students." *Journal of Abnormal Social Psychology,* 28 (1933), 280–290.

KELLY, H. H., and J. W. THIBAULT. "Experimental Studies of Group Problem Solving and Process." In G. Lindzey (ed.), *Handbook of Social Psychology,* vol. 1. Cambridge, Mass.: Addison-Wesley, 1954.

KIRKPATRICK, SAMUEL A., and LAURENCE K. PETTIT. *The Social Psychology of Political Life.* Belmont, Calif.: Duxbury, 1972.

KRECH, DAVID, RICHARD S. CRUTCHFIELD, and EGERTON L. BALLACHY. *Individual in Society: A Textbook of Social Psychology.* New York: McGraw-Hill, 1962.

LAZARSFELD, PAUL F., and F. N. STANTON (eds.). *Communications Research.* New York: Harper, 1944.

MASLOW, A. H. "A Theory of Human Motivation." *Psychology Review,* 50 (1943), 370–396.

McCLELLAND, D. C. *Personality.* New York: Holt, 1951.

————, et al. *The Achievement Motive.* New York: Appleton, 1953.

MORRISSETTE, J. O. "An Experimental Study of the Theory of Structural Balance." *Human Relations,* 11 (1958), 239–254.

NEWCOMB, T. M. *Personality and Social Change: Attitude Formation in a Student Community.* New York: Dryden Press, 1957.

———— and E. L. HARTLEY (eds.). *Readings in Social Psychology,* New York: Holt, 1947.

PIAGET, JEAN. *The Psychology of Intelligence.* London: Routledge and Kegan Paul, 1967.

ROKEACH, MILTON. *The Nature of Human Values.* New York: Free Press, 1973.

————. *Beliefs, Attitudes and Values.* San Francisco: Jossey-Bass, 1968.

ROSENBERG, MILTON J. "Cognitive Structure and Attitudinal Affect." *Journal of Abnormal Social Psychology,* 53 (1956), 367–372.

SCHERER, KLAUS, et al. *Human Aggression and Conflict.* Englewood Cliffs, N.J.: Prentice-Hall, 1975.

SEAGO, D. W. "Stereotypes: Before Pearl Harbor and After." *Journal of Psychology,* 23 (1947), 55–63.

SIEGEL, ALBERT E., and S. SIEGEL. "Reference Groups, Membership Groups, and Attitude Change." *Journal of Abnormal Social Psychology,* 55 (1957), 360–364.

TAHIDA, TAKESHI. "Beyond the Traditional Concepts of Peace in Different Cultures." *Journal of Peace Research,* 2 (1969), 150–159.

TRIANDIS, HARRY C. *Attitude and Attitude Change.* New York: Wiley, 1971.

3 | THE CONTEXTS OF VIOLENT CONFLICT

Conflict, as we have said, occurs when one actor pursues objectives incompatible with those of other actors. But values, beliefs, and attitudes change; and as they do, the prospects for violent and nonviolent conflict may increase or decrease. In this chapter, we will examine some circumstances conducive to violent conflict, focusing on those conditions that emerge primarily from the society and the culture. Our perspective, however, is not purely sociological and anthropological. Psychological factors are also important in studying social phenomena such as revolutions and war.

Group Conditions and Violent Conflict

In the preceding chapter, we mentioned group influences in the formation of beliefs and values. For example, groups forge psychological bonds among their members. This bonding creates a uniformity of norms. We also considered some of the conditions that affect group formation and intragroup functions. Let us now examine certain conditions within groups that influence intergroup perceptions in such a way as to promote conflict.

GROUP SOLIDARITY AND ETHNOCENTRISM

One of the most important characteristics of any group is its cohesiveness—the degree to which its members are bound together. This cohesiveness influences the group's perceptions and relations. Let us examine one type of extremely close group, and the effects of solidarity on its perceptions and actions.

In 1906, William Sumner introduced the concepts of "ingroup," "outgroup," and "ethnocentrism." He argued that within any society, distinctions arise between ourselves and everyone else. We refer to ourselves as the "we-group" or "ingroup" and everyone else as the "other group" or "outgroup." This distinction is accompanied by positive sentiments toward the ingroup—a willingness to sacrifice for it, feelings of comradeship and peace, and negative feelings to-

Table 3.1 FACETS OF ETHNOCENTRISM

Attitudes and Behaviors Toward Ingroup	Attitudes and Behaviors Toward Outgroup
1. See selves as virtuous and superior	2. See outgroup as contemptible, immoral, and inferior
3. See own standards of value as universal, intrinsically true	
4. See selves as strong	5. See outgroups as weak
	6. Social distance
	7. Outgroup hate
8. Sanctions against ingroup theft	9. Sanctions for outgroup theft, or absence of sanctions against murder
10. Sanctions against ingroup murder	11. Sanctions for outgroup murder or absence of sanctions against
12. Cooperative relations with ingroup members	13. Absence of cooperation with outgroup members
14. Obedience to ingroup authorities	15. Absence of obedience to out group authorities
16. Willingness to remain an ingroup member	17. Absence of conversion to outgroup membership
18. Willingness to fight and die for ingroup	19. Absence of willingness to fight and die for outgroups
	20. Virtue in killing outgroup members in warfare
	21. Use of outgroups as bad examples in the training of children
	22. Blaming of outgroup for ingroup troubles
	23. Distrust and fear of the outgroup

SOURCE: Robert A. Levine and Donald T. Campbell, *Ethnocentrism: Theories of Conflict, Ethnic Attitudes and Group Behavior*, (New York: Wiley, 1972), p. 12. Reprinted with the permission of the authors.

wards the others—even hatred, hostility, and contempt. The closer or more cohesive the ingroup, the more intense its sentiments.

The technical term for this view of things is *ethnocentrism*. It refers to the sentiments and relations within and between groups where "one's own group is the center of everything, and all others are scaled and rated with reference to it; [where] . . . each group nourishes its own pride and vanity, boasts itself superior, exalts its own divinities, and looks with contempt on outsiders" (Sumner, 1906: 13).

There has been considerable elaboration of Sumner's work in the last seventy years. Many summaries of this literature are available. One of the most recent, by LeVine and Campbell (1972), is the basis of many of the comments that follow. In their review, these social psychologists identify and discuss twenty-three facets of ethnocentrism, which are presented in Table 3.1.

Two obvious generalizations emerge. First, there appears to be a division between the perceptions of "ins" versus "outs." For example, if a group sees itself as strong, then it sees others as weak; if ingroup members cooperate among themselves, they do not cooperate with outsiders. Ralph White (1970) and others have called this "black and white thinking." This mental "set" is illustrated in White's study of the Vietnam War. From the American perspective, the North Vietnamese and Vietcong were the outgroups, with a "diabolical enemy" image; the United States was the ingroup, with a virile and moral self-image (White, 1970: 242). The Vietcong and North Vietnamese, on the other hand, viewed themselves as courageous defenders of a just cause against ruthless American aggressors (White, 1970: 106).

The second thing we notice about ethnocentrism is the relationship between ingroup solidarity and outgroup hostility. Black-and-white thinking is the perceptual expression of this hostility; it can appear in behavior as well. One of the first scholars to measure these manifestations was Emory Bogardus (1925). He contended that ingroups show how they feel about outgroups by maintaining *social distance* between them. This is done by preventing others from establishing ties with them. The ingroup can erect barriers to kinship by marriage, restrict housing, discriminate in employment, and forbid citizenship. When the ingroup is the predominant racial group in a country, these restrictions become institutionalized, and government policies toward the outgroup(s) are segregationist and discriminatory. Bogardus's measure of social distance has been used throughout the world. The findings suggest that "all ingroups, as judged by the average member, hold most outgroups at some degree of social distance, even if not that all ingroups hold all outgroups at some social distance" (LeVine and Campbell, 1972: 15).

Hostility toward outgroups may also be expressed as aggression. This aggression results from the ingroup's need to release the tensions that are usually caused by the pressures of group life. These pressures, which may take a number of forms, all tend to frustrate some of the individual members' objectives. As frustration builds, the ingroup's ability to function and exist is threatened. Rather than let this continue, the leader may try to release the tension through intergroup hostilities. For example, following a military coup d'état in Indonesia in 1965, the new regime found it difficult to solidify its hold on the government. Faced with the resulting political and economic instability, the regime launched a massive campaign of discrimination against the Chinese minority living in Indonesia. Thus the government sought to relieve tension by causing Indonesians to displace aggression by turning it against the Chinese. The intergroup hostilities eventually became so violent that thousands of Chinese were killed. Any outgroup could provide a highly visible target. As MacCrone states:

> The existence of the outgroup covers the ingroup against the risks of internal conflict and aggressiveness. If we could imagine a state of affairs

in which such a group did not exist, it would become necessary to invent one, if only to enable members of the ingroup to deal with conflicts, internal and external, without wrecking their own group. (cited in LeVine and Campbell, 1972: 117)

If this notion is correct—if group life does create aggression that must be displaced outside the group—then conflict cannot be avoided. There exist only alternative targets of this aggression. Intergroup hostilities will inevitably occur.

THE THREATENING ENVIRONMENT

Although there is a definite relationship between group solidarity and outgroup hostility, is solidarity the cause or the result of hostility? Those scholars who view it as a result have identified certain properties that are believed to help induce conflict. One of these properties is *group goals*. LeVine and Campbell refer to this view as the "realistic group conflict theory" (1971: 29–42).

This theory states that intergroup conflicts often arise when one group prevents another group from attaining its goal. The frustrated group will estimate potential gains if it decides to aggress. If intergroup conflict does occur, it results from the rival goals of the antagonists and not from any need to release tensions in order to preserve group solidarity (Coser, 1956: 49).

Such conflict of interests operates in an environment characterized by threat. Successful achievement by one group may threaten to block the goals of another group. Where the contention is between "ins" and "outs," feelings of distrust and fear about each other's intentions already exist. If the goals are highly valued, distrust and threat are intensified and conflict becomes certain. In preparing for confrontation, each group increases its cohesiveness, sharpens its identity, and generally intensifies its ethnocentrism (LeVine and Campbell, 1972: 30–33).

Does a "real" conflict of interests necessarily lead to violence? According to Lewis Coser, the answer is no. The frustrated group may find equally satisfying ways to achieve its goals (1956: 50). For example, antagonists may decide to compromise or trade off goals that may be more useful for their long-range interests. In such a situation, intergroup violence may be averted. Today we have ample illustrations of how superpower confrontations over foreign policy objectives stop far short of violence. Groups and individuals, like nations, often express conflict as protests or other less violent forms of behavior. Probably in the last analysis, the less valued the goal, the less likely that intergroup violence will occur.

Our discussion of the effects of group goals on intergroup conflict began by analyzing the relationship between group solidarity and intergroup hostility. It seems appropriate to conclude with a related observation. There is considerable evidence that group cohesiveness and intergroup hostility both cause and affect each other. The technical term for such a relationship is *bidirectionality*. In everyday usage, this means that intergroup conflict can stimulate group solidarity. As group solidarity increases, ethnocentric sentiments tend to emerge, promoting intergroup hostilities (Deutsch, 1973: 76–77). This "spiral effect" can and usually does result in aggressive conflict.

GROUP STATUS AND SOCIAL REWARDS

In every society, some types of behavior are admired and others are punished. If a group promotes values and norms which are highly valued in the society, it can gain status. We are all aware of the advantages in holding a high-status position. In some cases, this takes the form of privilege, together with the social, economic, and political rewards. In their attempts to achieve or maintain high status, people adopt values and engage in behavior that they have learned are status-conferring. Society begins to reinforce (reward) such behavior early in life. Patterson, Ludwig, and Sonada have demonstrated that children who are praised for hitting increase their attacks more than those who receive no approval (1961). Adults, too, can become more hostile when their conflictual behavior is rewarded with social praise (Green and Stonner, 1971).

Societies differ in what they value, and within any single society, value differences exist among groups. In part, these differences are reflected in social structures, and they affect the ways these structures change.

Various groups within a society, ranging from the family to political parties to social classes, are interrelated through what are known as *social structures*. The exact nature of these social structures varies depending on the closeness of one group to another (e.g., the ties between various families within an ethnic community) or the distance between groups (e.g., the alienation of the various socioeconomic classes from one another as they strive for social rewards) (Deutsch, 1973: 77–78). Some theorists contend that intergroup conflict often arises because of the nature of these structures (e.g., Dahrendorf, 1959) and the changes that occur within them (e.g., Davies, 1962). To test both of these ideas, we need to consider how structures exert pressure upon groups, pushing them toward conflict. To illustrate, let us examine group access to social status and rewards and how this process may lead to intergroup conflict. Many of these notions will be expanded in chapter 4.

According to Johan Galtung, we can classify social positions by dividing society into four parts: a decision-making *nucleus*, surrounded by a *center*, which is surrounded by a *periphery*, which again is surrounded by an *extreme periphery* (1965: 207). Thus Galtung's model of social structure consists of four concentric circles. If we extend a line from the center of the "nucleus" circle to the outside edge of the "extreme periphery" circle, we have a continuum of social positions within the structure. Depending upon the level of analysis and the kind of structure being analyzed, we could locate individuals or groups along the continuum and have a rough idea of their social positions. Galtung contends that in each structure "the social center occupies positions that are socially rewarded, and the social periphery positions that are less rewarded and even rejected" (1965: 208).

On the basis of this model and other theoretical analysis, Galtung has developed a "structural theory of conflict." Tension, he believes, forms when social positions occupy different statuses in different structures. When this happens, a state of imbalance exists, and conflict arises to bring the structures into equilibrium (Deutsch, 1973: 81, citing Berger, Zelditch, and Anderson, 1966). One form of conflict is violence. Take, for instance, the position of blacks in the United States in the early 1960s. Throughout the 1950s, social legislation had moved their social and economic positions from the extreme periphery to the periphery. In the political structure, however, they remained on the extreme periphery. According to Galtung's theory, this imbalance created a movement to raise their political status. When faced with opposition, they resorted to conflict and, in some cases, violence. It is debatable, of course, whether status equilibrium is ever achieved between the various positions. This may be particularly true for minority groups who only recently have gained equality under the law. Furthermore, status disequilibrium alone may not generate either conflict or violence. For instance, one could argue that violent conflict emerged only because of the violent opposition of central groups (e.g., many white groups in the South) to black advancement. The turmoil in the early 1960s surrounding black voter registration drives in the Deep South is a case in point.

The social structure theory, although incomplete, has been applied in various ways. One of the most important variations deals with the notion of relative deprivation among groups and its effect on the potential for revolution (Coser, 1967; Davies, 1962; Gurr, 1970).

Relative Deprivation

Relative deprivation refers to the tensions that develop when individuals or groups perceive a discrepancy between what they feel they deserve and what they actually receive. As Gurr states:

. . . people may be subjectively deprived with reference to their expectations even though an objective observer might not judge them to be in want. Similarly, the existence of what the observer judges to be abject poverty of "absolute deprivation" is not necessarily thought to be unjust or unremediable by those who experience it. As Runciman puts it, "If people have no reason to expect or hope for more than they can achieve, they will be less discontented with what they have, or even grateful simply to be able to hold on to it." (Gurr, 1970: 24)

This deprivation is not the result of an absolute amount of frustration. Groups in either the periphery or the extreme periphery of a social system may be deprived of status and rewards and not even be concerned. In the (former) caste system of India, the lower castes were aware of their deprivation but accepted it as being legitimate for religious reasons (Coser, 1967: 59). Relative deprivation arises when groups in the peripheries compare their lot in life with those of others nearer to the center. If they use these higher-status people as their reference group, they become more aware of the unequal distribution of the goods and conditions of life. A resulting sense of relative deprivation may then emerge. Minority groups have a strong sense of relative deprivation in societies that promote upward social mobility in theory but block it in reality. American children, for example, are taught in school that everyone can aspire to higher status and a "better" life. Yet they often find that this upward mobility is blocked by one type of discrimination or another. They then have a greater tendency to compare themselves with others of higher status. Hence, among various minority groups relative deprivation is likely to be high. This sense of relative deprivation may have been at the core of the civil rights movement in the United States in the 1950s and 1960s. The same might also be said about other societies such as South Africa, where lower-status groups believe that the unequal distribution of rewards is illegitimate. Where such relative deprivation becomes intense, intergroup conflict and violence may result. In chapters 4 and 5, we will describe some of the conditions that turn relative deprivation into conflict. For now, let us summarize our observations.

We have examined group conditions that lead from frustration to conflict. The pressures of group life (i.e., the tensions of group solidarity or ethnocentrism) often produce so much internal frustration that intergroup conflict is necessary to release tension before it destroys the group. Further, clashes of interest between groups can often result in conflict. Again, ethnocentrism seems to influence this relationship, particularly when perceptions of hostility create a threatening environment. Finally, peripheral groups are more likely to suffer structurally induced frustrations than others. Under conditions of clear inequality and intensified feelings of relative deprivation, these groups may express their feelings through conflict.

The situations we have examined so far deal with conditions that emerge from the immediate environment of the individual or group. However, broader sociological and anthropological conditions may also be important in influencing attitudes, beliefs, and behavior. In the following sections, we will examine some of these conditions and their effects.

Punishment and Violent Conflict

Conflict, as we have seen, often occurs because it produces desired results. These results may include the release of intragroup tension, the realization of group goals, the securing of status equilibrium, and the elimination of relative deprivation. Albert Bandura suggests that violence can be reduced by either removing the offending conditions or by curtailing the rewards of these conditions (1973: 221). Since the conditions leading to either conflict or violence are not susceptible to easy or rapid change (e.g., restructuring various status systems), groups—particularly governments—usually attempt to prevent violence by curtailing its rewards. One way to do this is through punishment or coercion.

When there is a clash of interests, the group views conflict as one way of realizing its frustrated goals. Whether violence is selected as the weapon depends in part upon its utility. If the negative consequences of violence outweigh the positive gains, then violence may be averted. These negative consequences may be increased by punishment. As Bandura points out, "Behavior that produces aversive effects is generally performed less frequently, if not discarded altogether" (1973: 221). The influence of punishment on the use of violence involves a number of factors. Let us examine some of these.

Much research on the effects of punishment has focused on society's efforts to control criminal behavior. Punishment is administered (usually by institutionalized groups, such as the police and the courts) as a deterrent. The effectiveness of punishment is widely debated. Legal sanctions were once thought to be most effective among persons of high status. For these persons, the social costs of engaging in prohibited conflict were supposedly quite high. Faced with the possibility of losing status through punishment, they were less likely to become violent. The Watergate affair and the general rise in "white collar" crimes has done much to challenge these claims. It is still thought that peripheral or extreme peripheral groups have nothing to lose by engaging in violent behavior. With these groups, the threat of punishment as a deterrent is considerably weakened.

Punishment—or the threat of it—has been widely challenged on the grounds that often it doesn't work, or more importantly, that it promotes violence rather than deters it. This argument has gained widespread support among scholars studying violent conflicts, such as riots and other civil disorders. In such cases, several factors are important. First, in collective situations (such as riots), group norms may prevail over threats of coercion. When group members see other members engaged in violence and group ties are strong, the deterrent effects of punishment may be reduced or even eliminated (Berk, 1972).

Crowd behavior may also be important in nullifying the effects of punishment. Where the crowd is large (as in a riot), an individual may be willing to risk violence, believing that he can lose himself in the crowd and thus escape punishment. If one believes that one cannot be personally identified in the turmoil of the crowd, the feeling of personal threat is reduced (Hundley, 1970). Other elements of crowd behavior that affect conflict will be discussed in chapter 4.

When a riot occurs, punishment often does not deter violence. In fact, punishment can actually stimulate violence or intensify it once it has begun. Ted Gurr has examined these circumstances in his research on civil disorders such as revolutions (1970). Groups which experience a feeling of relative deprivation, he believes, perceive punishment by the central authorities as reinforcing deprivation. In addition to feeling deprived, the group may also believe that its very security is threatened by this punishment. When this happens, the use or threat of force becomes an additional frustrating condition that may stimulate intergroup conflict. Gurr points out, however, that the crucial factor is the intensity of the force and the government's willingness to use it. When a regime is willing to employ such extreme measures as wholesale arrests and indiscriminate executions (e.g., in Haiti, Uganda, and more recently Cambodia), relative deprivation—no matter how intense—will not flare into open conflict. Any repression short of this, however, may intensify the relationship between relative deprivation and intergroup conflict (Gurr, 1970: 236–260).

Cultural and Subcultural Norms

Most people have opinions about the extent to which and the conditions under which violence is justifiable. One might believe, for example, that violence is justified only to protect oneself from physical violence. If people believe that violent conflict is proper, are they more likely to engage in it? Sociologists have found that violence within a society often results from the presence of norms that support it. Ted Gurr has considered the potential for political violence. He concludes that it is more likely to occur when violence in general is widely justified (1970: 156). These and other findings suggest, therefore, that conflict is often influenced by norms. These norms are found in a society's culture.

The term *culture*, as used here, refers to an organized body of rules concerning the ways in which persons in a society communicate with one another, think about themselves and their environment, and behave. These rules usually differ among societies, and they are not universally or constantly obeyed. Often variations on the themes of the dominant culture will emerge. When this occurs, we say that a *subculture* has developed. These subcultures form distinct clusters of rules, which are usually associated with particular groups within the society. While they share many rules of the parent culture, subcultures will also create new principles or modify existing norms (Wolfgang and Ferracuti, 1967: 95).

THE LEGITIMATION OF VIOLENCE

Cultural norms, as we have said, prescribe and proscribe certain types of social behavior. They confer legitimacy because they reflect society's judgment of what constitutes good, moral, and right behavior. For example, most middle-class Americans hold that individualism, initiative, and hard work are legitimate means for securing their interests.

Legitimacy is a powerful tool that strongly influences the way individuals and groups treat one another. Both the police and the military, for example, operate in cultural contexts that not only support the use of violence but view it as morally acceptable (Westley, 1966: 121–126). As Sandra Ball-Rokeach points out, legitimated violent behavior is actually rewarded by a grateful community or nation with praise and social status. Policemen and soldiers are decorated and promoted. They come to see themselves as good, moral people because their behavior is so regarded by others (1972: 102).

Rarely, however, is violence clearly legitimate. In most cases, this depends on the perspective of the dominant group and whether this group has the power to enforce its judgment. There is more than a grain of truth in the cliché that "might makes right." Thus, a key question regarding intergroup conflict is: Does the dominant group have the right to employ "establishment violence" (Von der Mehden, 1973)? Whenever there is a lack of consensus or a dubious justification for violence, efforts will be made to rationalize it in one way or another. Governments, for example, have tried to justify war and repression using such notions as necessity, the right of vengeance, the character of the opposition, and national defense (Von der Mehden; 1973: 48–52).

In some societies, certain kinds of violence are accepted without question. Such acts may not even be viewed by their perpetrators as illegitimate. If a "violent act" is not viewed as illegitimate, there is no need to justify it. Perhaps the most common instance where we are given a license to use violence is during war. When a soldier kills an enemy, it is considered an act of violence but is not viewed as illegitimate by his nation. We "get away with" the violence of war because, in part, our opponents are "devalued" by us.

Throughout history, people have been devalued and dehumanized. The most extreme case was that of the six million Jews who were dehumanized and exterminated by the Nazis. Japanese soldiers were commonly referred to as "monkeys" by U.S. soldiers during World War II. More recently during the Vietnam War, dehumanization took the form of referring to military actions against "gooks." The tragedy of the My Lai massacre resulted in part from such dehumanization. Such dehumanization is deliberately planned so that people can kill with a minimum of moral reservation. Once dehumanization is successful, there is no need to justify violence (Ball-Rokeach, 1972: 100–111; White, 1970: 312–313).

THE SUBCULTURE OF VIOLENCE

Suppose there arose a situation where violence was not justified, but was later legitimated by the norms of the dominant culture. Where might people turn to support their violent actions? It has been argued that in such situations, people resort to subcultural norms that glorify violence. Sociologists see these norms as emerging from a *subculture of violence*.

A subculture of violence may exist within a society. This is not to imply, however, that all the values, norms, or attitudes of the subculture deal exclusively with violence. Rather, there is a potent theme of violence in the subculture, and this theme is more prevalent than that of the dominant culture. Most importantly, when a subculture of violence exists, individuals may employ violence and use their subculture to justify it. The subculture, then, legitimates the violence that might be illegitimate in the dominant culture.

It has been argued that many subcultures of violence exist in the United States. The evidence, however, is inconclusive. Blumenthal and her colleagues have shown that the working-class subculture is more prone to violence than the middle-class subculture (1972). A 1972 survey, however, found no social-class differences in attitudes and norms justifying violence (Erlanger, 1972). Some sociologists contend that there is a subculture of violence in the Southern United States and that southerners are more prone to violence that non-southerners (Blumenthal et al., 1972: 41–71; as cited in Scherer, 1975: 202). Yet, the data of Scherer and his colleagues do not show that a Southern culture of violence exists (1975: 203).

Probably the most clear-cut evidence for the subculture of violence thesis emerges from studies by Cloward and Ohlin on criminal subcultures and that by Wolfgang on criminal homicides among Philadelphia street gangs (1958). Wolfgang points out that groups with the highest homicide rates and greatest delinquency had the strongest subculture of violence. In such a subculture:

> . . . the significance of a jostle, a slightly derogatory remark, or the appearance of a weapon in the hand of an adversary are stimuli differentially perceived and interpreted by Negros and Whites, males and females. [In such situations] . . . a male is usually expected to defend the name and honor of his mother, the virtue of womanhood, and to accept no derogation about his race (even from a member of his own race), his age, or his masculinity. Quick resort to physical combat as a measure of daring, courage, or defense of status appears to be a cultural expression . . . when such a culture norm response is elicited from an individual engaged in social interplay with others who harbor the same response mechanism, physical assault, altercations, and violent domestic quarrels that result in homicide are likely to be common. (1958: 188)

While the subcultures that Wolfgang and Cloward and Ohlin describe focus on a "mystique of violence," no subculture can be totally divorced from the parent society. For instance, American literature which reflects the values, norms, and attitudes of the dominant culture, has shown a peculiar fascination with homicide. The "Western hero" symbolized the rugged individualist, whose aggressive self-reliance was seen as a constructive and wholly natural force. While the focus of American literature has changed often in the last 150 years, a popular genre today shows the same preoccupation with murder, rape, and deadly combat that began with James Fenimore Cooper in the 1800s (Davis, 1966: 29–36). This literary fascination with violence is part of the dominant American culture. The subculture of violence, particularly its stress on the violent, individualistic hero, is a variant of these themes.

The use of violence in a subculture may be viewed as legitimate if subcultural norms, values, and attitudes put a premium on violence. Individuals or groups sharing these basic norms will not express violence in all situations. When they do, however, they will not have to deal with feelings of guilt about their aggression because violence has become part of their life-style. Furthermore, when both the victim and the assailant belong to the same subculture, violent retaliation is readily legitimized by the norms they both share (Wolfgang and Ferracuti, 1967: 161).

TRADITIONS AND THE JUSTIFICATION OF VIOLENCE

Societies vary widely in their justification of violence. This variation might be based on each society's experience with violence. When a society has a history of extensive and successful violence, its members come to expect future violence and to justify it on the basis of previous experience.

One act of violence is not likely to create either a precedent or a tradition to justify it. Where violence is persistent, however, expectations of future violence emerge. A self-fulfilling prophecy is created. As people come to expect violence, they begin to prepare for it. In preparing for it, they often create the circumstances necessary for violence. Consider two groups with a history of intergroup conflict— the Catholics and Protestants of Northern Ireland. Both perceive themselves as threatened by the other; both engage in "defensive" preparations against the other. These preparations are viewed by both sides as evidence of genuine threat, and each increases its defensiveness to a point where the slightest misconduct by the other usually precipitates violence.

Even if we expect violence, however, we do not necessarily justify it (Gurr, 1970: 169). Violence is most likely to be justified where there is either an absence of norms or a disagreement on norms governing its use. That is, a vacuum exists. Sociologists refer to such situations as *anomic*. When expectations of violence coincide with anomic situations, norms justifying violence are likely to emerge. As Ted Gurr puts it.:

> Angry people are likely to initiate others' violence, especially if they get the impression that violence is justified; such an impression is conveyed either by the fact that violent models "get away with it" or by others' intimations that violence is justifiable. . . . The more common collective violence is in a society, the more likely it is that some individuals will find it rewarding and hence be prepared to engage in it in the future. (1970: 172)

The cycle of violence-expectancy-justification-violence tends to perpetuate itself. Each round escalates to increasing levels of violence, greater expectancy, more resolute justification, and more damaging conflict. One has only to look at the recent history of violence in Northern Ireland to see how quickly these cycles can build. Although these spiral processes are self-perpetuating, environmental conditions can reinforce or retard their growth. Many of the ideas we have discussed elsewhere in this chapter, such as the importance of group dynamics, can reinforce or retard the growth of traditions and justifications of violence.

Competitive and Cooperative Situations

Certain group and cultural circumstances are thought to be more conflict-prone than others. When certain combinations of these circumstances are present, we say that conflict-promoting and conflict-retarding *situations* exist. Generally speaking, a *situation* is a "relative combination of circumstances at a particular moment in time" (Hermann, in Rosenau, 1969: 410–11). While each situation is unique, it is possible to describe general situations, identify their particular combination of circumstances, and analyze their effects on behavior. We can also identify many combinations of group and cultural circumstances that might induce conflict and set the stage for the possible use of violence. Two combinations that have received the most attention are those dealing with competition and cooperation. We will focus on the works of Morton Deutsch (1973) and Muzafer Sherif (1956). Deutsch's work on the effects of cooperation and competition upon intragroup processes, and Sherif's famous "Robber's Cave" study on intergroup processes, are now considered classics in this area of research and thus merit our attention.

SOME DEFINING CHARACTERISTICS

A competitive situation is one in which the goals of the actors are negatively linked, so that goal attainment by one involves frustration of the other. Two individuals trying to gain a single promotion, two street gangs trying to gain control over one neighborhood, and political parties out to elect their candidates are all in a competitive situation. As Deutsch (1973: 20) and others point out, in a case of "pure" competition, the actors can attain their goals if, and only if, the others with whom they are linked are blocked. In a cooperative social situation, the goals of the actors are positively linked; neither can win unless each actor promotes the interests of the other.

Competition and cooperation can occur at all levels of interpersonal and intergroup relations, from two-party situations to those involving many different groups and nations. Unlike several of the factors that we have discussed, competition and cooperation are not defined by our level of analysis. Competitive and cooperative situations can reinforce or retard conflict behavior among families, communities, and nations.

Few real-life situations correspond perfectly to the definitions of competition or cooperation given above. As Deutsch points out (1973: 22) most everyday situations involve a complex set of goals. Individuals may cooperate to reach one goal while competing for another. In most team sports, for example, team members cooperate to win but may compete for status and rewards. Thus competition and cooperation are not mutually exclusive. They can occur simultaneously, and often do when a persistent pattern of interaction is established between actors. The United States and the Soviet Union, for example, compete internationally for prestige and power while cooperating in joint ventures in outer space.

In summary, in a cooperative situation the actor tries to further his chances of goal attainment by increasing the chances of others with whom he is linked. In a competitive situation, the actor attempts to increase his own chances of goal attainment by reducing those of others. Violence may be used to affect the outcome (Deutsch, 1973: 22). To further illustrate competitive and cooperative situations, particularly their effects on behavior, let us turn to Muzafer Sherif's "Robber Cave" study (1956).

THE ROBBER'S CAVE

Using a "natural" experimental setting—a summer camp called Robber's Cave—Sherif brought together boys of eleven and twelve years of age and placed them into two groups, the "Rattlers" and the "Eagles." Over a period of time, the boys in each group developed friendships and came to view themselves as members of distinct groups. The next stage was to establish intergroup relations. The Rattlers were then set against the Eagles in a series of competitive games (e.g., tug-of-war) where there could only be one winner. Tension and conflict quickly developed between the two groups, escalating into verbal abuse, fights, and retaliatory raids on each other's campsites. Meanwhile, peace and harmony reigned within each group. Group solidarity and cooperativeness increased as Rattlers came to identify with Rattlers and Eagles with other Eagles.

The next stage in the experiment was designed to test various methods for reducing the intergroup conflict that had been generated. Two methods were tried. In one case, the Rattlers and Eagles were brought together in a series of pleasant, noncompetitive situations. There was no attempt to create interdependence between the groups. These supposedly pleasant communal activities (special dinners and joint celebrations on the Fourth of July) quickly degenerated into open conflict (e.g., insults at the Fourth of July celebration and a free-for-all one evening at dinner). The second approach at reconciliation involved creating situations of intergroup dependency, where the same outcome was desired by both groups but could be achieved only by cooperation between them. Through a series of joint projects that required their cooperation, the Rattlers and the Eagles reduced their previous hostility to each other. As conflict was reduced, friendly interactions developed between both groups. Most importantly, from our perspective, each group's attitudes towards the other became more positive, friendly, and ultimately even trusting. This attitude of trust, which had existed before only within each group, predisposed the boys to react favorably and helpfully to each other's goals and actions.

SUMMARY

Using the Sherif study and a summary of similar studies by Deutsch (1973), we can now identity some additional characteristics and effects of competition and cooperation. Competition will be considered first.

The pervasive effect of group and cultural factors on social interaction has been described. Competition accentuates and reinforces the effects of many of these factors. In the Sherif study, the first task was to create the groups and give them an identity. When competition was introduced, these group identities became almost ethnocentric. Perceptions of ingroups and outgroups were created and developed into black-and-white thinking.

In his summary of the competition literature, Deutsch suggests that the competitive situation has a marked ability to sensitize the group to differences in the other group while minimizing the similarities between them. The possible goal attainment by the outgroup poses a real threat to the ingroup. Because of this, the threatening environment and hostile attitudes within both groups are reinforced as competition accelerates. While we have no specific evidence, it also appears that these hostile attitudes are converted into group norms which highlight group differences and increase the social distance between them. Such norms may be used to justify conflict and even violence. As competition increases the social distance, communication links between groups are either broken or the quality of the information passing along existing links is diminished. As the groups move further and further apart, competition tends to increase. The result is to further highlight and reinforce the factors conducive to conflict.

In cooperative situations, the pursuit of goals creates no threatening environment. While group identities are maintained, the cooperation tends to increase group sensitivity to similarities rather than differences. Common interests are more easily identified, and divergent interests are played down. Group identity is not likely to manifest itself in terms of "ins" versus "outs"; as a result, it is extremely difficult for black-and-white thinking to emerge. In this situation, the social distance between the groups will be minimal. After repeated cooperative interaction, social distance is even further reduced. Since the environment is perceived as neither threatening nor hostile, group attitudes necessary to support conflict are either absent or unimportant. Instead, there are more positive attitudes of intergroup trust and friendship. Like competitive situations, cooperative situations tend to be self-perpetuating. With minimal social distance, increasingly positive attitudes, and enhanced communication between participants, "a benign spiral of increasing cooperation" occurs (Deutsch, 1973: 31).

Bibliography

BALL-ROKEACH, SANDRA J. "The Legitimation of Violence." In James F. Short, Jr., and Marvin E. Wolfgang (eds.). *Collective Violence.* Chicago: Aldine-Atherton, 1972, pp. 100–111.

BANDURA, ALBERT. *Aggression: A Social Learning Analysis.* Englewood Cliffs, N.J. Prentice-Hall, 1973.

BERGER, J., M. ZELDITCH, JR., and B. ANDERSON. *Sociological Theories in Progress.* Vol. 1. Boston: Houghton Mifflin, 1966.

BERK, RICHARD A. "The Emergence of Muted Violence in Crowd Behavior: A Case Study of An Almost Race Riot." In James F. Short and Marvin E. Wolfgang (eds.). *Collective Violence.* Chicago: Aldine-Atherton, 1972.

BLUMENTHAL, MORICA D., et al. *Justifying Violence: Attitudes of American Men.* Ann Arbor, Michigan: University of Michigan Press, 1972.

BOGARDUS, EMORY S. *Making Social Science Studies.* 3rd rev. ed. Los Angeles: J. R. Miller, 1925.

CLOWARD, RICHARD A., and LLOYD E. OHLIN. *Delinquency and Opportunity: A Theory of Delinquent Gangs.* Gencoe, Ill.: Free Press, 1960.

COSER, LEWIS. *Continuities in the Study of Social Conflict.* New York: Free Press, 1967.

————. *The Functions of Social Conflict.* Glencoe, Ill. Free Press, 1956.

DAHRENDORF, RALF. *Class and Class Conflict in Industrial Societies.* London: Routledge and Kegan Paul, 1959.

DAVIES, JAMES C. "Toward a Theory of Revolution." *American Sociological Review,* 6 (1962), 5–19.

DEUTSCH, MORTON. *Conflict Resolution.* New Haven: Yale University Press, 1973.

ERLANGER, H. S. "An Empirical Critique of Theories of Interpersonal Violence." Paper presented at the 67th Annual Meeting (1972) of the American Sociological Association. Cited in Klaus R. Scherer et al. *Human Aggression and Conflict.* Englewood Cliffs, N.J.: Prentice-Hall, 1975, p. 201.

GALTUNG, JOHAN. "Foreign Policy Opinion as a Function of Social Position." *Journal of Peace Research,* 11 (1965), 206–230.

GREEN, R. G., and D. STONNER. "Effects of Aggressiveness Habit Strength on Behavior in the Presence of Aggression-Related Stimuli." *Journal of Personality and Social Psychology,* 17 (1971), 149–153.

GURR, TED R. *Why Men Rebel.* Princeton, N.J.: Princeton University Press, 1970.

HERMANN, CHARLES E. "International Crisis as a Situational Variable." In James N. Rosenau (ed.). *International Politics and Foreign Policy*. Rev. ed. New York: Free Press, 1964, pp. 409–421.

HUNDLEY, JAMES R., JR. "The Dynamics of Recent Ghetto Riots." In Richard A. Chikota and Michael Moran (ed.). *Riots in the Cities*. Rutherford, N.J.: Fairleigh Dickenson University Press, 1970.

LEVINE, ROBERT A., and DONALD T. CAMPBELL. *Ethnocentrism: Theories of Conflict, Ethnic Attitudes and Group Behavior*. New York: Wiley, 1972.

PATTERSON, G. R., et al. "Reinforcement of Aggression in Children." cited in Albert Bandura. *Aggression: A Social Learning Analysis*. Englewood Cliffs, N.J.: Prentice-Hall, 1973, p. 354.

SCHERER, KLAUS R. et. al. *Human Aggression and Conflict*. Englewood Cliffs, N.J.: Prentice-Hall, 1975.

SHERIF, MUZAFER. "Experiments in Group Conflict." *Scientific American*, 195(5), (1956), 54–58.

SUMNER, W. G. *Folkways*. New York: Ginn, 1906.

VON DER MEHDEN, FRED R. *Comparative Political Violence*. Englewood Cliffs, N.J.: Prentice-Hall, 1973.

WESTLEY, WILLIAM A. "The Escalation of Violence Through Legitimation." In Marvin E. Wolfgang (special ed.). *Patterns of Violence. The Annals*, 364 (1966), 120–126.

WHITE, RALPH K. *Nobody Wanted War; Misperceptions in Vietnam and Other Wars*. Garden City, N.Y.: Doubleday, 1970.

WOLFGANG, MARVIN E. *Patterns in Criminal Homicide*. Philadelphia: University of Pennsylvania Press, 1958.

—— and FRANCO FERRACUTI. *The Subculture of Violence: Towards an Integrated Theory in Criminology*. London: Tavistock Publications, 1967.

4 | PATTERNS OF RACIAL CONFLICT

The Report of the National Advisory Commission on Civil Disorders (1968) argued that the racial turmoil of the 1960s was caused by deep-seated prejudice and discrimination. Race prejudice is one of the most potentially explosive conditions facing this country. Rather than simply decrying instances of racial violence, however, we must strive to understand them. What are their causes, and what patterns of behavior do they reflect? These questions require careful analysis, not only because of their inherent importance but also because of their complexity.

Pervasive discrimination and segregation in employment, education, and housing contribute to a social environment that encourages racial strife. Interracial violence, however, involves more than group interactions or the environment. It also includes people's perceptions about race and their conditions of life. These contribute not only to frustrated hopes and despair but also to heightened self-esteem and pride.

In this chapter, we will first examine one instance of racial violence and determine what actually happened. Next, we will try to determine why such incidents of racial violence occurred during the mid-1960s in certain American cities. We will examine a number of theories that try to answer this question, and one of them—dealing with urban violence—in some detail. We will also examine the general and immediate preconditions of racial violence. This discussion will be interwoven with the major concepts discussed in the preceding chapters. Most importantly, we will show how perceptions of self, others, and the conditions of life can influence behavior.

Profile of a Riot: Detroit, 1967

Some people called it a disturbance, others a riot; a few even referred to it as a rebellion. During the summer of 1967, the undercurrent of racial discrimination that had long separated blacks and whites surfaced in Detroit with a series of violent racial disorders. For some the memory of the Detroit riot of 1967 is sharp; for others, it is only part of the historical record. What follows is a profile of the events that made up the Detroit riot. The description seeks to identify how the riot happened, how it was viewed by various people, and what were some of its important decisions and incidents.

RAIDING A "BLIND PIG"

At approximately 3:45 A.M. on the morning of Sunday, July 23, 1967, twelve police officers raided an illegal after-hours drinking club chartered as the United Community League for Civic Actions (UCLCA), on 12th Street in a predominately black section of downtown Detroit. The raid had been planned for some time as part of a general police program to close after-hours bars (called "blind pigs") where narcotics sales and prostitution were flourishing. Unlike previous "blind pig" raids, however, this action resulted in the arrest of some eighty individuals. Unprepared to take so many people into custody, the police called in additional patrol cars and vans. By the time these units had arrived and the patrons of the "blind pig" had been herded inside them, a crowd of about 200 had gathered. As the police left, many of the bystanders began to taunt the police and throw bottles at the departing police vans.[1] Smaller groups of teenagers quickly fanned out from the arrest site, moving up and down 12th Street, breaking store windows, throwing litter baskets and bricks, and looting. A riot had begun in America's fifth largest city.[2]

Police quickly set into motion preplanned procedures for notifying key civil authorities, such as Detroit Mayor Jerome Cavanagh. Within two hours, Detroit's police strength was increased from 193 to 369 men. County sheriff's personnel were alerted, and liaison with the state National Guard was established. All units of the city's fire and public works departments were put on standby status as all available police personnel were dispatched to the troubled Tenth Precinct. Their immediate goal was to cordon off the riot area, isolating it from key commercial and residential areas as well as utility installations.

"LOOK AT HIM—HE AIN'T NEVER BEEN HUNGRY"

While police units were being mobilized, efforts were also underway to persuade well-known leaders of the predominantly black 12th Street community to defuse the explosive situation. After being briefed, the leaders moved to the eight-block stretch of 12th Street where the violence was most intense. By this time (mid-morning), the police had mobilized an estimated 1,122 men. A seventeen-man police commando unit had already attempted to sweep 12th Street of the crowds, but just as the police had mobilized, so too had the number of rioters grown. By now, an estimated 3,000 persons roamed the riot zone, which was spreading along the 12th Street thoroughfare and its many side streets. By noon, three groups had converged on the riot scene: the metropolitan police, reinforced with paramilitary units, the rioters, and the twenty or so black community leaders. As the community leaders, such as Congressman John Conyers, Jr., moved down 12th Street, they met with limited success scattering the crowd. Some bystanders and rioters went home, but others actively rejected attempts to disperse them. The following account by Sauter and Hines (1968) shows the mood that black leaders such as Conyers faced.

> "We don't want to hear it," someone shouted before Conyers even began to speak. Undaunted, Conyers climbed onto a car and promised the milling Negroes that if they would go home, the white police concentration in the area would be reduced. . . . "No! No! No!" the crowd protested. "We don't want to hear it, Uncle Tom. Get down, Uncle Tom!" the people shouted at the man some considered the "most popular Negro leader in Detroit.[3]

Even as these unsuccessful dispersal efforts were being made, a police commando unit moved into a space adjacent to the riot area. Their presence further antagonized local residents, and they were withdrawn. Simultaneously, acts of arson and stone throwing accelerated in the riot areas.

Most accounts of the Detroit riot seem to agree that up to this point, Detroit officials believed that (1) the "disturbance" would eventually dissipate after the people had "blown off steam"; (2) even if the crowds did not disperse, the police "could put it down"; and (3) the "disturbance had nothing to do with either civil rights agitation or race in general—the disorder was the work of a small minority fed by criminal elements" (Gordon, 1971: 123; Report of the National Advisory Commission, 1968: 84–108).

DANCING AMID THE FLAMES

As the intensity of the looting and arson heightened, Mayor Cavanagh was forced to concede that the situation was deteriorating badly. At about 2 P.M. the first call for outside reinforcement was made. State police were quickly mobilized and moved toward Detroit. The city's police forces, which were now being used to protect firemen from threatening crowds at the scenes of fires, were becoming dangerously overextended.

By late Sunday afternoon, firemen without police protection were being withdrawn from an area of approximately 100 square blocks on either side of 12th Street.[4] As police units dispersed one crowd, another one would form several blocks away, along one of the side streets that fanned out from 12th Street. The riot thus began to spread throughout the city, with the side streets spilling havoc into the downtown commercial districts. In less than an hour, looting had spread from 12th and Lindwood to areas covering approximately twenty-five square miles of the city (Locke, 1969: 33).

Throughout Sunday afternoon, violence continued to intensify in spite of growing police strength reinforced with state units. According to Sauter and Hines, Mayor Cavanagh is quoted as saying, "If you call out the guard, you have a riot" (1968: 21). By 4:30 P.M., the mayor and other city officials were forced to concede that their "civil disturbance" was in fact a riot. At 4:20 P.M., Cavanagh had requested that the Michigan National Guard be committed to Detroit. By 7 P.M. the first troops were on the streets, while over 1,600 additional troops were in transit from Grand Rapids and Flint, Michigan. Not only had Detroit's "disturbance" not been dissipated, but it also was becoming increasingly obvious that local forces could not contain the violence. Local leaders' definition of the situation had therefore proven incorrect on at least two counts, and they recognized that fact. Interestingly, however, they persisted in the belief that the riot was motivated by lawlessness, promiscuity, and hoodlumism. Detroit's riot was still not racial. The *Detroit Free Press* would state in an editorial on Tuesday (three days into the riot):

> This is not Negroes against "Whitey"—a hoodlum uprising became a riot and then integrated anarchy as Negro looters were joined by whites and guardsmen were joined by Negro vigilantes. . . . The time has come in the civil rights movement to draw finer and clearer lines . . . to separate . . . the basically good people . . . from the hoods and punks. Hoodlums, whatever their color, must be separated from society.[5]

Why community leaders persisted in this view of the situation is important; it will be discussed later.

In spite of a 7 P.M. to 5:30 A.M. curfew, thousands still roamed the riot scene. To the growing reports of looting and arson were added the first instances of sniping. Like so many other types of violence in Detroit that day, the sniping soon spread. By 9:30 P.M., firemen were coming under heavy rifle and pistol fire. As they withdrew from these areas, the unattended fires spread. When Governor George Romney flew over the city that night, he said, "It looked like the city had been bombed on the west side and there was an area two-and-a-half miles by three-and-a-half miles with major fires, with entire blocks in flames" (*Report of the National Advisory Commission*, 1968: 92). Shortly after his return to police headquarters in Detroit, Governor Romney proclaimed a state of public emergency in the city. Herbert Locke, then an administrative assistant to Mayor Cavanagh, later wrote that between 11 P.M. and midnight, reports of looting and arson were coming into the police command post at the rate of more than three per minute. Locke goes on to document the spreading havoc that was gripping Detroit: "By the end of the first 19 hours of rioting, the police department had logged over 900 calls . . . over 10,000 people had surged through the streets of Detroit . . . over 300 fires had been set, with more than 40 still raging out of control." The loss of life and damage had only begun in a city which had previously liked to reassure itself that racial conflict could not happen there.[6]

AN APPEAL FOR FEDERAL ASSISTANCE[7]

After one day of rioting, city officials developed a more pessimistic view of their situation. In their view, the situation was likely to get much worse before it got better. As Michigan National Guard troops began appearing on Detroit's streets in increasing numbers, the violence intensified.[8] Arson and looting continued throughout the early morning hours of Monday, July 24, and reports of the first riot deaths started to come in. Between 1 A.M. and 2 A.M. the first in a series of calls was made by Mayor Cavanagh to federal officials in Washington. In conversations with Vice President Hubert Humphrey and Attorney General Ramsey Clark, Cavanagh was cautious in evaluating the situation, but he did imply that federal troops might have to be committed if conditions worsened. There is still much controversy over the ensuing events. In his conversation with Attorney General Clark, Mayor Cavanagh was supposedly informed of the gravity of requesting federal troops. According to testimony before the National Advisory Commission on Civil Disorders, popularly known as the Kerner Commission, Attorney General Clark stated that federal statutes were strict in defining the conditions under which federal troops could be sent into the city. Clark apparently informed Cavanagh that before the bureaucratic machinery could be set into motion, Governor Romney would have to declare that the situation in Detroit had so deteriorated that it could not be controlled by either local or state authorities. Most accounts now agree that Governor Romney was unwilling to make such a statement at that time.[9]

By 9 A.M. the violence in Detroit showed no signs of abating, even with 1,200 National Guardsmen in the streets. Governor Romney could no longer postpone his declaration. In separate telegrams to President Lyndon Johnson and Attorney General Clark, he requested the immediate dispatch of 5,000 federal troops. It would be some fourteen hours before any of these troops would be committed to Detroit.

A few minutes after noon on Monday, federal officials converged on Selfridge Air Force Base just outside of Detroit. Among the officials present were Lt. Gen. John L. Throckmorton, commander of the federal troop task force, and Cyrus R. Vance, the president's personal envoy and former deputy secretary of defense. Almost immediately upon their arrival, briefings began. State and local officials contended that their resources were almost depleted and rioting was still out of control. Most city officials conceded that the situation would likely worsen as night approached. Mayor Cavanagh, for one, thought that it was crucial to have federal troops on the streets by dark. Federal officials, in general, particularly Vance, did not accept this assessment of the situation.[10]

For the next ten hours, while federal paratroopers arrived at Selfridge Air Force Base, Vance and Throckmorton sought to develop their own assessment of the situation. By 8 P.M. Vance had concluded that paratroopers were unnecessary and so informed President Johnson. Governor Romney agreed with Vance's decision, much to the chagrin of Mayor Cavanagh and assembled community leaders.

No sooner had night fallen than the looting, arson, and sniping increased. In light of this new development, both Vance and Throckmorton advised President Johnson that federal forces should now be committed. At 11:20 P.M., some fifteen hours after the initial call for troops, President Johnson federalized the Michigan National Guard, placing it under General Throckmorton's control, and authorized the use of regular army paratroopers.

"YOU ARE NOT FIGHTING THE VIETCONG— YOU ARE FIGHTING YOUR NEIGHBORS"

Some twenty-two hours after the first request was made for federal troops, elements of the 82nd and 10th Airborne Divisions appeared on the streets of Detroit. These troops would patrol the riot area east of Woodward Avenue until Thursday, when they would be withdrawn. The now-federalized Michigan National Guard would concentrate their patrols in the area west of Woodward Avenue, where the rioting would later become the most intense. General Throckmorton's decision to divide his forces in this manner would prove to be fateful.[11] As the *Report of the National Advisory Commission* would later state:

> . . . there were nearly 5000 Guardsmen in the city, but fatigue, lack of training, and the haste with which they had been deployed reduced their effectiveness. Some of the Guardsmen traveled over 200 miles and then were on duty for 30 hours straight. Some had never received riot training and were given on-the-spot instruction on mob control. . . . [I]n the resulting confusion some units were lost in the city. Two guardsmen assigned to an intersection on Monday were discovered still there on Friday (1968: 97).

Into the worst of the rioting were sent men who were tired, undisciplined, and plainly frightened. The result of this act was to add to the havoc that the Guardsmen were sent to control. Their lack of restraint, coupled with already trying circumstances, would cause a number of tragic events in the ensuing hours. Two such incidents convey something of the atmosphere that prevailed in Detroit at this time.

Carl Smith was a member of Ladder Company 11 in Detroit's fire department. According to Sauter and Hines's account of this incident (1968), Smith was an eager fireman, anxious to perform his duties. On Monday night, just before the paratroopers came onto the streets, Smith joined another engine company that had been pressed into service to cope with the numerous fires. Escorted by police and National Guard units, Smith's engine was believed to have come under sniper fire as it approached the intersection of Mack and St. Jean Streets. According to Sauter and Hines the National Guardsmen gave return fire, shooting out the street lights and plunging the whole area into darkness. In the resulting chaos of rifle fire, Smith was separated from his fire engine. Later Police Sergeant Roy Snyder testified that he saw Smith run between the Guardsmen and the area where the sniping was thought to have originated. Smith was believed to have reached cover; as the shooting continued, however, witnesses saw Smith fall to the street. To this day, no one knows whether he died from a shot by a sniper, or a Guardsman, or even a Detroit policeman.[12]

The second incident concerned John LeRoy. He, like so many other Southern blacks, saw Detroit as a place of opportunity. Employed by the Chrysler Motor Company, LeRoy had recently bought a home in Detroit's East Side, which was in the riot zone. A number of LeRoy's friends had gathered at his home Tuesday night to talk. According to several accounts, one of them, Ronald Powers, noticed that it was late and asked a friend to take him home. Everyone decided to go along for the ride. LeRoy joined the group, and they all set out in Charles Dunston's car. No one apparently realized that they were violating the curfew. The Dunston station wagon was stopped almost immediately at a National Guard roadblock two or three blocks from LeRoy's house. According to Dunston's account, the Guardsmen told them that there was sniping in the area and to proceed, but to choose another route. Dunston later said that he complied. At Lycaste Street, according to testimony in the National Advisory Commission report, Dunston saw a jeep sitting in the street. Believing this was another roadblock, Dunston stopped his car. At about that moment, "a shot rang out. A National Guardsman fell, hit in the ankle. . . . Shot after shot was directed against the vehicle, at least 17 of them finding their mark" (*Report of the National Advisory Commission*, 1968: 97–98). Everyone in the car was hit. John LeRoy was pronounced dead at the hospital several hours later, the victim of three gunshot wounds.[13]

In an attempt to reduce tension, General Throckmorton ordered his paratroopers to establish cordial contact with the people in their areas by engaging in such action as cleaning up debris. More importantly, the paratroopers were ordered not to fire unless they could clearly identify their target. Under no circumstances was mass undirected fire permitted. These orders proved effective. As later evidence would show, "no paratrooper was shot, only one person was shot by a paratrooper and the 2700 Army troops expended only 201 rounds of ammunition" (Gordon, 1971: 62).

Unfortunately, this was not the situation in the western section of the riot zone, patrolled by National Guardsmen. On the east side of Woodward, the paratroopers unloaded their weapons; on the west side of the street, the Guardsmen did not. Paratroopers removed street barricades; Guardsmen added to their number. Street lights were turned on in the southeastern districts; in the west they were shot out by Guardsmen.[14] To this day, no one knows whether Guardsmen were ignorant of Throckmorton's directives or whether they chose simply to ignore them. By late Tuesday night, the grim pattern of previous days' violence had reemerged. First in one precinct and then another, in a checkerboard pattern across Detroit, police command posts, National Guard units, and firehouses came under renewed sniper fire. In the last twenty-five minutes of Tuesday alone, the police department records show fifteen reports of sniper fire, four looting incidents, and four firebombings (Locke, 1969: 43).

THE RIOT SUBSIDES

Throughout Wednesday, July 26, the Detroit riot built to its climax. Probably its most intense period, however, was early Wednesday morning, when seven persons died. It was also during Wednesday that such controversial incidents as the one at the Algiers Motel took place.[15] Charges of police brutality, misconduct, and violence would emerge during this time as police were put under increasing stress.

As arson and looting abated, Detroit officials took steps to reopen the city. Businesses were urged to reopen, the curfew was modified, and limited gasoline sales were permitted. No sooner had this happened when sniping broke out again in various parts of the city. Once again, police stations and fire houses were the targets. Most observers at the time agreed, however, that as night came on Wednesday, the scope and intensity of the chaos were diminishing. The tasks of emergency relief and the prosecution of the more than

7,200 persons arrested during the riot would now have to begin. By Thursday, the problem of processing and housing prisoners had reached a crisis of its own. More than 4,000 persons were crowded into makeshift detention centers scattered throughout the city. The city's booking procedure was swamped by the staggering number of arrestees.

While the judicial system was becoming overburdened with the enormity of the riot, the paratroopers were quietly being withdrawn to command centers outside the city, leaving only token infantry patrols to walk the streets. By noon on Thursday, the curfew was lifted and normal public services were resumed. That night, however, Governor Romney reimposed the curfew at dusk. Even on Friday, July 28, some isolated cases of sniping occurred. By this time, federal troops and National Guardsmen were moving out of the city, and more and more police efforts were redirected to transporting and maintaining the more than 7,000 individuals in their custody.

When did Detroit's riot end? According to Mayor Cavanagh's assistant at the time, no one can really say. In terms of intense violence, it probably was over on Friday. Federal troops and National Guardsmen left the city on Sunday—exactly one week after the riot began. Curfew restrictions, however, remained until Tuesday, August 1, and then they too were lifted. Detroit was then free to reemerge from its nightmare.

The costs in lives and resources were staggering: forty-three persons were killed during the riot—thirty-three black and ten white. Most of the deaths, according to the official report, were accidental, but homicide could not be ruled out in some cases. Property damage was estimated at between $22 million and $45 million. The cost of the riot on individual lives, personal attitudes, and group relations is impossible to calculate.

IMMEDIATE REACTIONS: THE WHITE PERSPECTIVE

After Detroit's riot there was a general feeling of anxiety, alarm, and tension among white suburban residents. Donald Warren's survey of Detroit suburbanites found that in the nine communities sampled, more than 48 percent felt that renewed rioting was likely in coming months (1971). Within this sample, 27 percent knew of neighbors and friends who had purchased firearms as a result of the riot. On the average, 30 percent of the respondents in communities such as Dearborn and Royal Oaks experienced growing tension (1971: Tables 1, 2, 3; pp. 127–129). Interestingly enough, these general local reactions could be found in similar white communities throughout the country. As these perceptions spread and became entrenched, the social and psychological distance between white and

Table 4.1 ORDERING OF RESPONSES TO TEN CAUSES OF THE 1967 DETROIT DISORDERS FOR ALL SATELLITE COMMUNITIES

"Which of the following do you think is the most important reason that the disorders occurred?"

	FIRST-CHOICE RESPONSES	TOTAL FIRST-, SECOND-, AND THIRD-CHOICE RESPONSES
Black nationalism	16.0%	40.5%
Poverty	15.7	37.5
Criminal elements	10.8	31.2
Lack of jobs	9.1	31.7
Failure of white public officials	7.0	25.6
Powerlessness	6.9	20.8
Poor housing	6.7	25.4
Too much welfare	6.6	26.0
Teen-agers	4.7	24.0
Police brutality	0.7	3.1
Don't know	10.8	—
Other	4.1	—
Not ascertained	1.0	—
	100.1% (N=788)	

SOURCE: Donald I. Warren, "Community Dissensus: Panic in Suburbia," in Leonard Gordon (ed.), *A City in Racial Crisis* (Dubuque, Iowa: William C. Brown, 1971), p. 130. Reprinted with permission.

black Americans increased in the late 1960s. Nowhere was this distance more apparent than in both groups' perceptions of the causes of the riots. As Campbell and Schuman concluded, these divergent perceptions made it "difficult for either race to form an accurate picture of the other and makes it easy for each to develop misunderstanding, apprehension, and mistrust" (1968: 29). Let us examine these divergent perceptions.

CAUSES OF THE DETROIT RIOT:
WHITE AND BLACK VIEWS

Approximately one year after Detroit's riot, white suburbanites were asked to identify the most important reason why it had occurred. Their responses are presented in Table 4.1. As we can see, the vast majority of the respondents identify "black nationalism," "poverty," and "criminal elements" as either their first, second, or third choices. Warren concludes that "for the vast majority of persons in satellite communities the Detroit riot was as likely to be the work of social undesirables or agitators as it was to be attributed to more enduring social forces" (1971: 130).

When Warren compared these perceptions with those of black and white respondents who lived in the inner city, the results indicated quite different views regarding what the riot was about and what conditions had caused it (see Table 4.2). Whites, in both the suburbs and the inner city, generally saw the riot as stemming from either social conditions that affected only a small percentage of the black community or from purely criminal causes. Black images were generally reversed in order, with specific social grievances heading the list. The forces that whites saw as central to the riot were perceived by blacks as being almost unrelated.

Nowhere were perceptions more polarized than in each group's views of the police. Riot area blacks in Detroit listed "police brutality" as the main cause of the riot. Whites in Detroit and in the suburbs unanimously agreed, however, that "police brutality" was the least likely cause.

Whites' views of the police are generally more supportive than those of blacks. In Campbell and Schuman's comparative analysis of black and white attitudes, 60 percent of the whites felt that police responded quickly to their calls. Among the blacks sampled, however, this figure dropped to 34 percent. With respect to "police brutality" (e.g., act of verbal disrespect, frisking, and rough behavior), Campbell and Schuman found that "relatively few white people felt that this sort of thing happened in their neighborhood and even reported it had happened to them or to people they know" (1968: 42). The psychological gap implicit in these responses can also be seen in each group's beliefs about social change in general and race relations in particular.

RACE RELATIONS: WHITE PERCEPTIONS

Looking back, we probably should not be surprised to learn that a substantial number of white urbanites in the mid-1960s did not feel that widespread racial discrimination existed. In the previous discussions of the white perspective, our focus was primarily on Detroit. In this section, our analysis is more broadly based, relying on samples in fifteen cities, with Detroit among them. Campbell and Schuman found that "nearly four out of ten white people apparently believe that few if any Negroes are subject to discrimination in hiring or promotions" (1968: 29). While many whites did perceive discrimination in housing and education, they did not believe it affected all black citizens.

A number of studies have found that general white attitudes toward black people are stereotyped. In one survey, whites were asked to explain the fact that "many Negroes as a whole" suffered discrimination in employment, housing, and social services. Their responses are representative of white views about black people. Three-fourths of Campbell and Schuman's white sample stated that the "fault" lay with blacks and their low motivation for "better" jobs, housing, and

Table 4.2 Selected Riot Causes as Perceived by Detroit Area Negroes and Whites (Rank Ordered)

	Negro Respondents in Detroit			White Detroiters		
Rank	RIOT AREA NEGROES (AUGUST 1967)[a]	NORTHWEST DETROIT (DECEMBER 1967)[b]	DETROIT MIDDLE-INCOME SURVEY (MAY 1968)[c]	NORTHWEST DETROIT (DECEMBER 1967)[d]	DETROIT MIDDLE-INCOME SURVEY (MAY 1968)[e]	Satellite Suburbs (JUNE 1968)[f]
1	Police brutality	Poor housing	Police brutality	Black nationalism	Teenagers	Black nationalism
2	Poor housing	Lack of jobs	Poor housing	Poverty	Black nationalism	Poverty
3	Lack of jobs	Poverty	Lack of jobs	Poor housing	Too much welfare	Lack of jobs
4	Poverty	Police brutality	Poverty	Lack of jobs	Poor housing	Poor housing
5	Disappointment with white public officials	Disappointment with white public officials	Disappointment with white public officials	Teenagers	Poverty	Too much welfare
6	Teenagers	Teenagers	Teenagers	Too much welfare	Lack of jobs	Teenagers
7	Black nationalism	Black nationalism	Black nationalism	Disappointment with white public officials	Disappointment with white public officials	Disappointment with white public officials
8	—*	Too much welfare	Too much welfare	Police brutality	Police brutality	Police brutality

[a]437 respondents
[b]188 respondents
[c]392 respondents
[d]213 respondents
[e]208 respondents
[f]788 respondents
*"Too much welfare" not listed in this survey.

SOURCE: Donald I. Warren, "Community Dissensus: Panic in Suburbia," in Leonard Gordon (ed.), A City in Racial Crisis (Dubuque, Iowa: William C. Brown, 1971), p. 145. Reprinted with permission.

education. Such phrases as "Negroes' . . . laziness, lack of ambition, or unwillingness to take advantage of opportunities" were frequently used (Campbell and Schuman, 1968: 30–31).

To this generally negative image of blacks should be added white fear and hostility. According to the fifteen-city survey:

> . . . two-thirds of our white respondents sense some degree of negative feeling towards Negroes as widespread among the white population and their sense of Negro dislike of whites is if anything even stronger. A simple cross-tabulation of the answers to the two questions ("Do you think that only a few white [Negro] people in the [city] area dislike Negroes [white people], many dislike Negroes [white people], or almost all dislike Negroes [white people]?") reveals a substantial association between white perception of widespread dislike of Negroes among whites and their perception of widespread dislike of whites among Negroes. (Campbell and Schuman, 1968: 31)

These images of hostility reinforce the social distance that is already maintained by whites in their generally negative attitudes about blacks. When these attitudes are coupled with white perceptions about the causes of the riot, the psychological distance between the races is shown to be considerable. Interestingly enough, however, after the riots, there was no "white backlash" (Bellisfield, 1972–1973: 579–584). Whites, particularly the college-educated young, continued to support specific forms of racial integration just as they had before (Campbell and Schuman, 1968: 32–36), and while tension and anxiety did grow, the general pattern of interracial communication did not worsen. Instead, more and more people attempted to explain what they had lived through and to answer the question, Why did these disturbances occur? Many social scientists, too, sought answers. Let us now turn to their theories.

Theories of Rioting

At the height of the Detroit riot, Vice-president Hubert Humphrey reportedly told Mayor Cavanagh that "if it can happen in your town, then it can happen anywhere." Similar feelings of dismay followed the other civil disorders of the 1960s. Concerned citizens asked themselves whether such events could happen again. No one could answer that question until the reason for the disorders could be explained. What were the causes of the urban riots?

Many explanations have been offered, most of them based on theories of collective behavior and crowd action. These theories usually fall into three categories: (1) those stressing the social and psychological makeup of rioters, (2) those emphasizing social conditions, and (3) those contending that a combination of psychocultural and social forces were at work. In the first category are theories that rioters are incorrigible mischief makers who are "naturally" prone to violence. Theorists in the second category would counter by arguing that ghetto life created such frustration that aggression occurred. In the third category are theories that ghetto conditions have created a "new ghetto man" who uses violence as a legitimate means of redressing social ills.

Within each of these major categories are further distinctions that reflect the theorists' political perspective. For example, within the first category a political conservative might emphasize the rioters' emotional instability and label them "riffraff." A liberal might stress the rioters' unemployment or lack of education and refer to them as part of the "underclass." Such political distinctions have important implications, as we shall now see.

THE RIFFRAFF VERSION

At the start and finish of the Detroit riot, civil authorities (both white and black) and white suburbanites tended to categorize rioters as "riffraff"—destructive, irrational social misfits, criminals, unassimilated migrants, and psychopaths. This riffraff theory portrayed the rioter as forming a minority of the society, with few if any social or political ties or concerns (Caplan, 1970: 59). He is usually seen as part of the criminal element of the inner-city ghetto, deeply involved in narcotics, thefts, and criminal violence (Sears and McConahay, 1973: 20). Such an individual can be easily frustrated in his "selfish desires," and when he resorts to violence, it is because of his own personal failure. No broader social or political significance, therefore, can be attached to his actions (Fogelson and Hill, 1968).

According to the riffraff theory, when individuals such as these came together, they formed a crowd based on opportunistic impulse. It was unpredictable, unrestrained, and without purpose (Marx; 1972: 48).[16] It was also thought that such rioters were extremely dangerous to the social order and difficult to control. Society, however, could deal with them. Because they were social deviants, the solution lay in inducing them to conform to the status quo, through either psychotherapy or social work. If these measures failed, harsher treatment would be used, such as physical coercion, confinement, or other forms of punishment.

Did the riffraff theory have many supporters? The answer is an unqualified yes. Variations of this theory will be found in public statements by Detroit Mayor Cavanagh, Michigan Governor Romney, and the editors of the *Detroit Free Press*. Detroit authorities were not unique in their support. Richard Fogelson and Robert Hill (1968) found that every mayor of every city hit by racial disorders in the

Table 4.3 ATTITUDES EXPRESSED BY NEGROES RELATING TO RIOTS

Attitudes Expressed	Study Sample	Locale and Source
RIOT SYMPATHY		
Do not view riots as "essentially bad"	50%	Nationwide, *Fortune*, 1967 (Beardwood, 1968)
In sympathy with rioters	54	Fifteen American cities (Campbell and Schuman, 1968)
Believe riots are helpful	30	Houston, 1967 (McCord and Howard, 1968)
Believe riots are helpful	51	Oakland, 1967 (McCord and Howard, 1968)
RIOT PARTICIPATION		
Active participation in Watts riot	15	Watts (Sears and Mc-Conahay, 1970a)
Active participation in Detroit riot	11	Detroit (Caplan and Paige, 1968a)
Active participation in Newark riot	45 (males, age 15–35)	Newark (Caplan and Paige, 1968a)
Active participation in riots	20	Six major riot cities, 1967 (Fogelson and Hill, 1968)
Willingness to participate in riots	15	Nationwide, *Newsweek* poll (Brink and Harris, 1966)
Advocated use of violence	15	Fifteen American cities (Campbell and Schuman, 1968)

SOURCE: Nathan Caplan, "The New Ghetto Man: A Review of Recent Empirital Studies," *Journal of Social Issues,* 26 (1970), 61. Reprinted with permission.

1960s cited the riffraff theory. In California, the McCone Commission even went so far as to attribute primary responsibility for the Watts violence to riffraff.[17] Similar beliefs have been found among Detroit suburbanites as well.

What are some of the social, political, and individual implications of the riffraff portrayal of the rioters? First, by attributing the riots to the personal shortcomings of the rioters, blame was removed from the social institutions. In other words, nothing much was wrong with the society. Such a belief is reassuring to persons who wish to maintain the status quo. The theory also suggested that the ghetto violence had no political significance. There was no emerging ideological foundation for black action—no black political protest and no "new dimension" of the civil rights movement. In short, there was no threat to the existing political system.[18] Finally, and possibly most importantly, the riffraff theory robbed civil disorders of any legitimacy by branding them the work of criminals who were a tiny fraction of the population. Since the action reflected criminal intentions, it was fundamentally and unconditionally illegitimate.

Did evidence support the riffraff theory? Table 4.3 indicates that it did not. Further, these data suggest that many ghetto residents actually supported or at least sympathized with the rioters. Not only did they believe that the riots were socially relevant, but they also admitted participating in them.

THE UNDERCLASS INTERPRETATION

In contrast to the riffraff theory, this one takes a sympathetic view of the rioter. Here the rioter is not villain but rather victim. He suffers from the social injustices common to ghetto life. He is probably uneducated, unemployed, living on welfare in substandard housing. He is, in other words, part of the lowest class in the social hierarchy—the underclass. As a member of this underclass, this person is subject to the stress and strain of abject poverty. Being uneducated, he is barred from employment; because he is unemployed, he and his family must receive welfare payments; because these payments are limited, his family is committed to poor living conditions. A cycle of despair is created. Without hope, the potential rioter sees himself consigned to the bottom of black society—"the poorest of the poor." In frustration he strikes out at society.

The purpose of riot behavior, according to this theory, is to protest the injustices of ghetto life. Viewed in this light, riot behavior is both rational and political. The crowd may be unpredictable and unrestrained, but it lacks neither goals nor purpose. Robert M. Fogelson goes so far as to suggest that "rioters chose their targets with a consistency which suggests that a look at the violence will reveal the nature of the grievances and thereby clarify the meaning of the riots" (1970: 144).[19]

An obvious question is, How does society cope with such persons? The National Advisory Commission report (which ascribed in part to this underclass theory) suggests several remedies. They include: more and better education, revitalizing inner-city housing and transportation, and finally, political reforms that ensures political rights.[20] As the reader will no doubt notice, there is a significant difference between these remedies and those prescribed by the riffraff theory. The implication is that these persons have not been rejected by society (i.e., have opposed conformity) but rather have been bypassed by it. Redistribution of benefits, not stricter law enforcement, is offered as a remedy. The more humane and temperate tone of these prescriptions made them appealing to many.[21] However, the evidence supporting the underclass theory appears to be mixed.

If the underclass thesis is correct, rioters should rank lower in income, education, and employment than other ghetto residents. In fact, data collected in Detroit, Los Angeles, and Newark indicate that there is no significant difference in the income (both real and relative) of rioters and nonrioters. Not surprisingly, evidence shows that those at the very bottom of the income ladder are the least likely to protest, much less riot (Murphy and Watson, 1970, cited in Caplan, 1970: 62). Similarly, no significant difference in participation was found that could be related to education. In fact, the rioters were, if anything, slightly better educated than other ghetto dwellers (Sears and McConahay, 1973: 23–24). The only support for the underclass theory appears to be in a strong correlation between unemployment and riot activity. In both Los Angeles and Newark, the unemployment rate among rioters was significantly higher than among nonrioters. This relationship was even stronger when the variables of sex and age were controlled. Young (under thirty) black unemployed males in both cities were most likely to riot.

On the whole, however, existing data do not support either the riffraff or underclass theories. With the exception of age and unemployment, none of the other major arguments of either theory seems convincing. Nor are other theories that emphasize such factors as the breakdown of ghetto family life or black immigration from the rural South.[22] Explanations that blame the riots on outside agitators or black nationalist conspirators also seem to have no foundation. Obviously the civil disorders of the mid-1960s were so complex that single-factor explanations such as these could not provide valid answers to the question, Why did these people riot?

THE NEW URBAN BLACKS[23]

Certain findings, however, suggest the outline of an answer. It has been noted that the rioters tended to be younger than nonrioters. Further, a large percentage of these persons had grown up in middle-size or large cities (e.g., Tomlinson, 1970: 97). As young, urban-reared blacks, they held a strong positive image of themselves, taking pride in their black identity. At the same time they exhibited hostile attitudes toward whites and particularly such, white institutions as the police (e.g., Caplan, 1970).

These younger, better-educated blacks did not compare their social status to that of other blacks but rather to their white counterparts in the working and middle classes. Their resulting sense of relative deprivation was a powerful source of dissatisfaction.[24] Regardless of these perceptions or their background, these individuals had to cope with the day-to-day problems of ghetto life—problems such as poor education, ponderous welfare systems, confusing government rules and regulations, substandard housing, and exploitative businesses.[25] Confronting such real and specific grievances, these people believed that they lacked access to conventional channels of protest (e.g., Marx, 1972: 58). When people perceive that the usual means of redress are blocked, they may come to believe that violence (such as riots) will bring needed social change and ultimately redress.

In sum, these separate findings suggested that the rioters were persons whose background, environment, and psychological makeup caused them to identify situations in certain ways and predisposed them to riot under certain conditions.[26] Such a person has been called the "new ghetto man" (Caplan, 1970); collectively they are referred to as the "new urban blacks" (Sears and McConahay, 1970, 1973).

A General Theory of Urban Rioting

The portrayal of the "typical" rioter as the new urban black is the basis of a general theory of urban rioting. The most complete statement of this "politics of violence" theory is Sears and McConahay's study of Watts (1973). The theory consists of three sets of variables: (1) certain demographic changes in urban areas of the North and West, which have affected black socialization; (2) mediating racial attitudes, political values, and definitions of situations resulting from population changes, socialization, and specific ghetto conditions; and (3) actual riot participation. These three sets of factors are interrelated by two key hypotheses. One hypothesis links population changes to certain psychological states, and another links these states of mind, in combination with certain contextual factors (e.g., specific ghetto grievances), to riot action (1973: 54).[27] Since this theory illustrates the general psychological, contextual, and perceptual principles discussed in chapters 1, 2, and 3, let us examine it in detail.

GOING NORTH: THE ORIGINS OF THE POTENTIAL RIOTERS

A number of studies have shown that persons reared in the strife-torn cities were more likely to have rioted than recent migrants. In Detroit, for example, 74 percent of the rioters identified the North as their region of origin. Furthermore, almost 60 percent of the Detroit rioters were born in that city. In Detroit and across the nation, these findings reflected some changes in the demographic profile of the black population.

One of the most important of these changes has been the increased black migration from the rural South to the cities of the North and West. This geographical redistribution is dramatic. In 1910, only 9 percent of the black population lived outside the South; by 1968, this figure had risen to almost 45 percent. This geographical movement was not only to the North and West but to the cities. Fully 70 percent of the black population lived in cities by 1968, compared to only 28 percent fifty years earlier (*Report of the National Advisory Commission 4*, 1968: 237).[28] As Sears and McConahay point out, in the riot areas of the mid-1960s the black population was almost entirely urban (1973: 36–37).[29]

The black population is not only more urbanized than the white population but is also significantly younger. In 1968, about one out of every six children under five and one out of every six babies born in this country were black. The median age among blacks today is twenty-one years. Among whites the median age is also young (twenty-nine years in 1966), but its rate of change is significantly less than that of blacks.

As blacks have migrated to the North and West, they have settled in predominantly black and older sections of the central city. For a number of reasons—primarily discrimination in housing—wave after wave of black immigrants have been forced to settle and remain in the inner city. The resulting pattern of residential segregation is illustrated by the fact that the proportion of blacks in all central cities rose from 12 percent in 1950 to 20 percent in 1966, while the metropolitan areas outside the core remained about 95 to 96 percent white.[30] Thus in the last two decades, one generation of black immigrants has been replaced by a new wave of younger, more literate, and urban-socialized blacks.

GROWING UP IN THE NORTHERN CITY[31]

The political socialization of the new urban blacks is different from that of their older, less educated, and/or Southern counterparts in several important ways. Politically they have been socialized to expect the same political rights and powers as white children. While the evidence is scant, it does suggest that these children initially accepted political values of equality, civil rights, and responsibilities (Sears and McConahay, 1973: 44). Later, when confronted with discrimination and social injustice, these chidren were understandably more disappointed.[32] These children have also learned to express their dissatisfaction more openly. They associate discrimination and social injustice with whites who hold political and economic power— usually in their own communities. While protest can take many forms, the potential for open hostility is great.

One important result of northern socialization is the strong black racial identification.[33] Today's black children are more likely to view their race positively, and to express racial pride and superiority (for an earlier statement, see Caplan and Paige, 1968). This "black consciousness" can be seen in the preference for the term "black" rather than "colored" or "Negro" (Caplan, 1970: 66).

All of these differences stress the consequences of Northern urban socialization. Little has been said about the climate of this socialization. The term most often used is "radicalism" or "militancy." This militancy has been expressed in a number of ways. At one extreme, there was growing sympathy for the Black Muslims, who preached aggressive defiance of white society (Tomlinsón, 1970: 94). At the other extreme was a gradual shift from legal to direct action among civil rights activists. By 1963, for example, civil rights protests had assumed an urgency and a demand for completeness. Yet in many cases, these demands were met by brutal white resistance in some areas of the South and intransigence throughout much of the North. As a result, blacks felt increasingly frustrated. As this frustration grew, a more militant ideology was formed. Ghetto youths became more aware of this ideology and its slogans of "Black Power" and "Black Is Beautiful." This exposed them to such "unconventional" techniques of social change as street demonstrations, boycotts, and even violence that were either implied or openly advocated by militant groups.

The substance, impact, and climate of northern socialization have created a distinctive set of attitudes, values, and views of the world. Let us examine some of them.

POLITICS AS VIOLENCE

The new urban blacks held distinctive attitudes about a number of issues. Most of the studies of black views have focused on such issues as "racial integration," "black separatism," "social-economic-political dissatisfaction," "social change," and "the uses of violence" (Caplan and Paige, 1968; Campbell and Schuman, 1968). Since the specific findings of each of these studies cannot be discussed here, let us summarize their results under three important categories, comparing the views of new urban blacks with those of the general black community.[34]

Attitudes About Self Black self-esteem is high throughout the racial community. Black self-esteem is often referred to as "black consciousness." It is an active attempt to recognize and promote black achievement both inside and outside the black community. This cultural emphasis on blackness has wide appeal within the urban black population. In the Campbell and Schuman studies, "96 percent of the sample affirmed that 'Negroes should take more pride in Negro history' or that nearly as many agreed 'there should be more Negro businesses, banks and stores' " (1968: 19–21). Other dimensions of "blackness" have also emerged. There is a greater predisposition toward Afro-American styles—and, most significantly, a growing belief that blacks have a unique racial characteristic, usually referred to as "soul," that separates them from whites.[35] In one study 54 percent answered "Yes" to the question, "Do Negroes have a special soul that most whites have not experienced?" In that same sample, 74 percent also agreed that "black is beautiful" (*Report from Black America*, 1969: 20–21). As Caplan indicates (though there is no evidence), this celebration of blackness is substantially higher among young northern-socialized blacks than any other group (1970: 66–67).

Attitudes About Whites It has been suggested, particularly among whites, that this black consciousness might lead to antiwhite attitudes. However, data from the black community, both inside and outside cities and in all sectors of the country, suggest that blacks "hold strongly, perhaps more strongly than any other element in the American population, to a belief of nondiscrimination and racial harmony." The Campbell and Schuman survey found that "only one Negro out of eight" favored residential segregation. Using follow-up questions to measure commitment to racial integration, these authors concluded from their data on education, friendship groups, and neighborhoods that "the majority of Negro respondents not only favor integration, but that they do so because of either a commitment to racial harmony or a conviction that racial consideration should be transcended entirely" (1968: 15–16). Other studies also show that the black community as a whole is not markedly antiwhite. Nathan Caplan notes that "the Negro community is probably far less antiwhite than most whites are prepared to believe" (1970: 68). Several surveys among whites, particularly in the suburbs, support Caplan's view.

Among the more militant young urban blacks the picture is somewhat different, though not notably so. Tomlinson found that, when asked "if they had any good friends who were white," the majority (of militant, uncommitted, conservative Los Angeles blacks) answered "No." In general, according to Tomlinson, there was a "significant relationship between militant attitudes and attitudes about racial contact, militancy being associated with greater social distance and reduced social contact" (1970: 103–105).[36] How widespread are these attitudes? It is difficult to say. Tomlinson's sample of Los Angeles blacks showed some distaste for interacting socially with whites, but Sears and McConahay contradict even these findings. They did not find a "very high level of antiwhite prejudice in South Central Los Angeles, even in the aftermath of Watts" (1973: 72–73). We can only conclude that an antiwhite attitude in this group is not pronounced, but it does exist. In the words of Gary Marx, "they don't hate (whites), but they don't like them either" (as cited in Caplan, 1970: 67).

ATTITUDES ABOUT RACE RELATIONS: GENERAL DISSATISFACTION

Black attitudes on race relations during the mid and late 1960s were a mixture of optimism for the future and dissatisfaction with the present scope and pace of civil rights. Fully 70 percent (in one major survey) believed that blacks had made substantial progress. Yet in that same survey, 59 percent—a rise of 16 percent in three years—thought that the pace was too slow; only 22 percent were satisfied with their gains ("Report from Black America," 1969: 19).

This dissatisfaction was perplexing to many whites at the time. Campbell and Schuman expressed this when they asked: "Considering the improvements for Negroes over the past 15 years—visible in Supreme Court decisions, in civil rights legislation, in appointment to high offices . . . —why weren't black Americans more satisfied?" (1968: 21). Their data suggested two answers. First, most of the blacks interviewed believed that much discrimination still exists in such areas as employment and housing. Second, about 60 percent believed that "city officials" paid less attention to a request from a black than a white person. This belief is important because it may underlie the black view that improvement in their condition of life may be barred by white discrimination. In fact, on the basis of Campbell and Schuman's data, one might conclude that the best blacks could hope for was white indifference to their goals (1968: particularly Table II-q, p. 26).

Among younger Northern blacks, this sense of dissatisfaction was greater (e.g., Sears and McConahay, 1973: 72–73). As a *Newsweek* magazine poll found, almost 51 percent of this group believed that whites were consciously trying to "keep Negroes down" ("Report from Black America," 1969: 20–26). Thus it was not surprising that almost 25 percent of this ghetto sample believed that they should "give up working with white Americans entirely," and that a majority of those expressing this belief wanted "black separatism."

Political Disaffection The notion of "black separatism" reflects the feeling among many blacks that the American political process does not serve their interests well. Sears and McConahay found that the new urban blacks distrust elected officials, particularly when they are white (1973: 74–76).[37] This suspicion also exists to a lesser extent in the general black community. Even here, the conventional political process is often seen as irrelevant. A growing percentage of blacks feel that it makes no difference which political party holds power ("Report from Black America," 1969: 21).

Even with these beliefs within both black groups, however, there is no evidence of a deep or broad-based rejection of the political system (Caplan, 1970: 69). In fact, blacks in general have if anything grown more sophisticated and more experienced with the political system. Among new urban blacks, however, the picture is different. Because of their deeper disaffection, their growing political sophistication, and their exposure to more unconventional methods of social change (protest and/or violence), they have been less likely to view the political system as a means of improving their life. They tend to see protest and violence as a more attractive and usable tactic. Campbell and Schuman found that 6 to 15 percent of their respondents viewed violence in this way (1968: Table V-j, p. 52).

Grievances: Focus on the Police Our discussion will not document black grievances about ghetto life; this has been done elsewhere (*Report of the National Advisory Commission*, 1968: 251–278). We will focus instead on certain black attitudes about the nature of these grievances. What do they see as the source of their problems, and whom do they blame? One of the biggest local grievances deals with the police. This grievance and its accompanying attitudes will be described in detail.

Black attitudes toward the police are generally quite negative. Campbell and Schuman concluded that "Negroes are less satisfied than whites with the protection they receive from the police and they are much more likely to report unfavorable experiences in their personal contact with the police (1968: 45). Particularly in the ghettos, there is deep hostility between the police and residents (*Report of the National Advisory Commission*, 1968: 299–332). Sears and McConahay's study of blacks in Watts found that 39 percent had seen the police show disrespect and use insulting language to blacks; 20 percent stated that they personally had been frisked and rousted by the police for "no good reason" (1973: Table 4.1, p. 56). Sears and McConahay point out that "antagonism toward the police [in Watts] was so complete throughout the community that almost everyone supported additional controls upon the police" (1973: 57).

The obvious question is, Why do blacks in general, and young Northern blacks in particular, harbor such intense hostility toward the police? The *Report of the National Advisory Commission* suggested (p. 299) that the police symbolize the "entire system of law enforcement and criminal justice." In that system, there are some real grievances— inadequate police services, overcrowding in jails, and disparities in sentencing. Blacks feel that they suffer from these inequalities more than any other group. When police enter the ghetto neighborhood, they symbolize a great deal that is wrong in the system—often through no fault of their own.

In some cases, however, the intense hostility is based more on beliefs about police misconduct than on symbolic presence. According to *Newsweek's* "Report from Black America" (1969), the belief that police are guilty of severe misconduct and discrimination is widespread. In Harlem, 43 percent of those interviewed believed that police were guilty of "police brutality."[38] A 1966 survey found that 60 percent of Watts blacks (aged fifteen to nineteen) believed that there was some police brutality. And in Detroit in 1967, almost 82 percent "believed there was some form of police brutality" (cited from *Report of the National Advisory Commission,* 1968: 302). Similarly, there was a widespread belief among blacks that police are racially prejudiced. Vincent J. Rinella, Jr., has tried to ascertain if there is any relationship between police abuse of blacks and racial prejudice. He found that prejudice is rarely a component or cause of police brutality. Still, from the black vantage point, police abuse is inexcusable, and it is usually perceived as a sign of prejudice whether it is or not (*Report of the National Advisory Commission,* 1968: 313). This is not to say that police are not prejudiced. What Rinella's findings suggest is that as long as blacks see the police as prejudiced, whether they actually are or not is unimportant. The National Advisory Commission report actually documents some discriminatory police practices and procedures. So there is some support for the argument that blacks' negative attitudes toward police are based on real and/or perceived discrimination. Whether these intensely negative attitudes are based on beliefs or fact, they do exist and are thought to be both a powerful precondition and a triggering mechanism of a riot.

General Preconditions of a Riot: Perceptions

Earlier we discussed the characteristics of the new urban blacks. We have examined several studies identifying this group's origin, upbringing, attitudes, goals, and grievances. Taken together, such factors of environment and psychology create in these people a unique view of their world. Let us integrate these factors and discuss their perceptions—perceptions that are thought to exist before a riot can occur.

RELATIVE DEPRIVATION

Perceptions have been defined as subjective images of reality. These images are analogous to a mosaic mural—each image being composed of separate beliefs, attitudes, and values. When these separate psychological states are joined together, they create a unique perceptual lens through which individuals or groups view their world. One of the most important of these shared by the new urban blacks is their perception of relative deprivation.

Relative deprivation has been used to explain civil disorders ranging from riots to revolution.[39] As stated earlier, this is a state of discontent that develops when people perceive a discrepancy between what they think they should have and the actual satisfaction of these aspirations.[40] The concept of relative deprivation is central to a number of theories of violence. According to Gurr, "the potential for collective violence varies strongly with the intensity and scope of relative deprivation among members of a collectivity" (1970: 24).

Sears and McConahay hypothesize that "one motivating force for the violent upheaval in Watts was an unfavorable comparison between the actual attainments of the New Urban Blacks and the outcomes that they expected or felt they deserved on the basis of what others were receiving and what they had received in the past" (1973: 48). They refer to this motivating force as "subjective status deprivation." In many ways, this motivation to violence is similar to the one that Gurr and others have described.[41]

We already have examined this perception of relative deprivation among new urban blacks. It includes rising optimism, growing expectations, a general sense of dissatisfaction, and some political alienation. Taken together, these factors create a sense of relative deprivation.

Collectively, new urban blacks felt discontented. They had higher aspirations and greater optimism than their older ghetto and rural Southern counterparts. Raised in the urban North during the civil rights decade (1954–1964), they came to believe that they were entitled to the same economic, political, and social status as whites. Better educated and politically more aware, their expectations were constantly rising. Yet, these expectations were not met with corresponding increases in jobs and income, political power, or social status. What blacks were actually able to attain did not correspond to what they aspired to. What they wanted was the egalitarian principles of white America that they had been exposed to through early socialization. These principles demanded a higher rate of success to maintain the same level of satisfaction (Sears and McConahay, 1973: 87). When the civil rights movement slowed, and when blacks were confronted with deteriorating ghetto conditions, discontent and dissatisfaction resulted.[42]

BLOCKAGE OF GOALS

Relative deprivation depends on a number of factors, one of which is the group's perceived ability to alleviate its discontent. Gurr hypothesizes that if a group feels that it has alternative means to satisfy its expectations, it is likely to defer its discontent over immediate failures (1970: 73–79). Gurr calls this mediating factor "value opportunities." The more opportunities a group believes it has or will have in the future, the less intense will be its feeling of relative deprivation. These opportunities may take a number of forms; the chance to redress specific grievances may be one of them.

From the evidence we have examined, it appears that new urban blacks did lose faith in such conventional tactics as individual striving, bureaucratic procedures, political action, and nonviolent protest. A significant proportion of blacks believed that such mechanisms were so ineffective that, practically speaking, they had ceased to exist as an alternative value opportunity. Confronted with white indifference to their grievances and overt white opposition to their aspirations, black frustration intensified. As they searched for viable alternatives, they became increasingly committed to their aspirations. When they eventually perceived that conventional means were exhausted, their perceived relative deprivation was more intense than it would have been if no such perceived opportunities had existed. Further, they became more receptive to exploring more unconventional means. One such unconventional opportunity is the political use of violence.

RIOTS

Given their disenchantment with the system, the new urban blacks were likely to explore new forms of redress, such as riots. Protest and violence, as we have said, are seen by new urban blacks as more attractive and usable tactics. At the time, no one asked, Why do they perceive riots in this way? Several studies cast some light on this question.

In their study of black attitudes in fifteen large cities, Campbell and Schuman discovered that over 33 percent thought that riots had aided the black cause in America, while only 25 percent thought they had been harmful (1968, table V-e, p. 49). What, according to blacks, had the riots accomplished? Among the answers were: (1) tangible responses to some of their grievances, (2) a white awakening to black concerns, and (3) a demonstration of black power (Campbell and Schuman, 1968, table V-e, p. 49). On the whole, blacks saw riots as spontaneous—and useful—protests against their grievances. Interestingly, however, while the majority saw these protests as justified and useful, they neither recommended them nor said that they themselves would riot.

Among younger Northern blacks there is a particularly strong view that the riots were symbolic protests. In Tomlinson's study of militant, conservative, and uncommitted blacks in Watts, 70 percent of the militants, 61 percent of the conservatives, and even 55 percent of the uncommitted saw the riot as "Negro protest" (1970: 108). Even more interesting, 34 percent of the militants, 20 percent of the conservatives, and 16 percent of the uncommitted claimed to have taken an active role in the Watts riot (1970: 109). And yet, "there was a common feeling among all the respondents about the negative features which transcends ideological positions. The riot had features that pleased the militants, but it also had features which instilled fear in most of the citizenry regardless of their orientation to grievance redress" (1970: 111).

One major thesis of the Sears and McConahay study was that the new urban blacks saw riots as symbolic protests against their condition in life. For this group, riots became the equivalent to working through the system.[43] If the white-dominated institutions were indifferent to them, rioting might shake this indifference. If whites were consciously denying redress to blacks, then riots might overcome this opposition. If whites were unaware of the emerging black consciousness, then riots might dramatize "black power." Widespread research evidence showed a belief among blacks that protests and riots are viable alternatives to the blockages they must confront. Most importantly, these unconventional techniques were seen as having a positive effect on black life.

SUMMARY

We began with the question, Why did the racial disorders of the mid-1960s happen? Several single-factor explanations, such as the riffraff and underclass theories, were rejected. We then turned to multifactor explanations, such as that of the new urban blacks. This theory stated that the disposition to riot was due to a complex interplay among people's psychological status, their environment, and their perceptions of changes in that environment.

This theory of urban rioting was examined in detail. We profiled an emerging group within the ghettos of large Northern and Western cities—a group which was young, Northern reared, and better educated than their Southern and rural counterparts. These people, furthermore, were proud of their black identity, disenchanted with conventional politics, and more racially prejudiced. Certain socially determined psychological states interacted with specific conditions within the ghetto to produce perceptions of relative deprivation, frustration, and alternative mechanisms for social change.

Taken together, these factors explain how a particular group could become discontented enough to participate in a riot. This "politics of violence" theory identified the following general preconditions of a riot: a crisis in aspiration deprivation; a closing (real or perceived) of channels for bringing about social, political, and economic change; and the belief in the reemergence of hope through violence.

Immediate Preconditions of a Riot

The intense discontent of the new urban blacks created an unstructured potential for riot participation. This discontent was found in a number of ghettos where rioting did not occur. This suggests that even when the general preconditions of rioting are present, violence is not inevitable. It also suggests a set of immediate preconditions which interact with general preconditions to cause riots. These immediate preconditions have been widely studied.[44] There are several important factors that appear to be present just before a riot begins: crowd formation, precipitating events, and resolution of discontent. We will examine each of these, with particular reference to the Detroit riot.

CROWD FORMATION

Before a riot can occur, a crowd must form. Ghettos are a natural setting for a riot. One can expect more crowds in the high-density areas of the inner cities. In Detroit, for example, the density of the 12th Street area was 21,000 people per square mile. This figure is almost twice the citywide average. Crowded into this area, the people are in constant close social contact. Particularly during the summer months, ghetto residents spill out into the streets. This results in a lot of what residents call "street action." The sights are the same in almost every ghetto—groups of young children playing in and along the streets; small crowds of young men gathered in front of stores or along street corners; families of elderly men and women sitting on steps or in windows. This picture—by now almost a stereotype—stresses the fact that these small groups, crowds, and families provide the numbers and close contact necessary for crowd convergence later on.

Not only is there physical and social contact in the ghettos, but substantial communication as well. Much "street talk" goes on in these neighborhoods. What many white Americans—particularly middle-class suburbanites—do not realize is that the ghetto streets are important communications networks. In most cases, these informal networks may pass along information much as do other, more formal, media.[45] Ghetto residents are often more willing to accept this information than the news from the white-dominated media.

In terms of crowd behavior, this physical grouping and chatting is called "milling." When milling, individuals and groups search for information in relatively unstructured social situations, like those in the ghetto streets. Most of us are familiar with the notion of milling. We think of people moving about, with small groups forming, dispersing, and reforming into other groups, where bits of information are exchanged. Many people, of course, think of milling in more dramatic terms. They liken it to the behavior of animal herds, seeing it as filled with tension and anxiety. In the ghetto context, we believe that a far less dramatic characterization is appropriate. Milling is a necessary word-of-mouth process by which information is passed along and evaluated. The streets are an obvious and useful means of communicating within the ghetto.

PRECIPITATING EVENTS

We have already discussed the grievances of the ghettos against specific white-dominated institutions and practices. Many believe that these grievances are usually given a sharper focus just before a riot. A specific situation or incident occurs that clearly emphasizes or intensifies the general discontent and frustration. Such incidents have been called "precipitating events," "typifying incidents," or "triggering mechanism" (Hundley, 1968: 142; *Report of the National Advisory Commission*, 1968: 117). Such events have certain clear characteristics.

First of all, the precipitating event is usually perceived quite differently by whites and blacks. Whites tend to see it as "usually relatively minor, even trivial, by itself substantially disproportionate to the scale of violence that followed" (*Report of the National Advisory Commission*, 1968: 117). Among blacks, however, the event typifies a grievance at the heart of their discontent. As Hundley points out, the specific nature of the event varied from city to city—a police raid in Detroit, a traffic incident involving a black cab driver in Newark, and so on. Although the incidents varied, they were all perceived by blacks in a similar way. The incident was a tangible manifestation of their discontent, a discontent that could now be focused on a specific act. The resulting violence was caused not by the event itself but because it symbolized a long history of grievances that had gone unanswered.

Second, precipitating events usually involve a confrontation between white authorities and black citizens. The actual authorities involved have varied—in some cases civil authorities and in many others (Newark, Detroit, and Watts) the police. Black people, we have noted, tend to have negative attitudes about the police. Given these attitudes, it is not surprising that police involvement may give precipitating events much of their symbolic content.

A third characteristic of precipitating events has been identified in the National Advisory Commission report. These events are usually part of a *series* of incidents that have occurred frequently in the same area. Often the event was of a type that had occurred several times in the preceding weeks. The report states that "most cities had three or more incidents; Houston [for example] had 10 over a five-month period . . . with each such incident, frustration and tension grew until at some point a final incident, often similar to the incident preceding it, occurred and was followed almost immediately by violence" (*Report of the National Advisory Commission*, 1968: 118). In Detroit, a near riot had been averted in August 1966, in the Kercheval section of the city; the report lists at least two other previous incidents in Detroit. Thus precipitating events are part of a general pattern of increasingly disturbing experiences. As the report concludes:

As we see it, the prior incidents and the reservoir of underlying grievances contributed to a cumulative process of mounting tension that spilled over into violence when the final incident occurred. In this sense the entire chain—the grievances, the series of prior tension-heightening incidents, and the final incident—was the "precipitant of disorder. (*Report of the National Advisory Commission*, 1968: 118).

Finally, the precipitating event causes the convergence of a crowd at the site. As Hundley points out, the crowd may be drawn to the scene for a number of reasons. They may already live there and be motivated by a grievance. Others may be curiosity seekers or passersby. Finally, some people, such as police, firemen, and civil authorities, are drawn to the scene in order to monitor potential disorders. Whatever their reasons, the actors in the impending violence are attracted by the precipitating event.

RESOLUTION OF DISCONTENT

Let us return to Detroit on July 23, 1967. The police were raiding a "blind pig" on 12th Street. Small crowds of young black men converged on the arrest site. A reinforced group of Detroit police were hurriedly loading black arrestees into waiting police vans. From about 3:45 A.M. (when arrests began) until about 5:10 A.M. (when the violence began), a large crowd of more than 200 persons formed.

Approximately ninety minutes elapsed before violence broke out. We will never know exactly what went on in the minds of those 200 individuals during that period. On the basis of many studies and reports, however, we can attempt an "ideal" reconstruction. The following narrative is meant to represent a number of experiences, not Detroit's alone. It is a "model" developed from the common elements found in many similar experiences.

For the crowd gathering on 12th Street, the scene was initially ambiguous and unstructured. There were some preexisting expectations as to how the observers should behave. It was expected, for example, that a lot of "cool talk" would go on. Police would be called names, teasing would occur, and there would be some light pushing and shoving.

Among many of the observers, particularly the new urban blacks, there began to develop a mood and a vague image of what was occurring. Their mood was one of discontent coupled with urgency. They "felt" that they must "do something" now—respond in some way to what they "saw." According to the politics-of-violence theorists, what this group saw was a symbolic act unfolding. It typified many of their grievances and provided a specific and immediate focus for their discontent. According to scholars of crowd behavior, the group began to think about what kinds of actions might be appropriate to redress grievances when conventional channels were blocked. These conceptions emerged as the crowd milled about and interacted.[46] Some individuals were already predisposed to use violence. Some young men spontaneously mentioned it as a way of resolving the mood of urgency and discontent.

As violence began to be seen as a useful weapon, word was passed through the crowd. At the same time, as more and more people discovered that they shared similar feelings, they also came to believe that everyone in the group should feel the same. The belief in violence as a solution may now have become a group norm. As a norm, it became a criterion for group membership and a powerful determinant of group solidarity and conformity.

At the group level, riots were being considered as one solution. On the individual level, there was a heightened personal suggestibility. This suggestibility was neither unfocused nor indiscriminate. If favorable predispositions toward rioting existed, these attitudes and norms would now tend to be reinforced along generational lines. As Sears and McConahay point out, "attitudes toward the riot had to develop on the spot in the immediate social environment, rather than being simply deduced from childhood attitudes" (1973: 48). Individuals began to align their feelings with those in the group to whom they were attracted. As group solidarity increased and individual suggestibility heightened, the crowd became more *permissive* in its thinking and behavior.

Definite courses of action began to emerge, increasingly suggesting the use of violence. As more and more individuals accepted these beliefs, their actions became increasingly governed by group norms. If these norms favored the use of violence (as we have suggested they might), then the individual was more likely to be guided by them than be inhibited by society. One of the most important aspects of this stage of social unrest is that it is both a breaking up of the established perception of life (governed by social norms) and a preparation for new collective action governed by new group norms and attitudes. Before this point, individual behavior and attitudes were guided largely by society. Laws, procedures, and rules inhibited, modified, and limited black expression of discontent. Once individuals reached the stage of heightened group solidarity and permissiveness, however, they came to accept another form of control—that of the group, which sanctioned attitudes and behavior that the larger society would never permit.

At this last stage before violence erupted, we see in the street a microcosm of a broader cultural conflict—a conflict between the attitudes, values, and beliefs of white society and those of a certain segment of blacks within that society. For many individuals, particularly the new urban blacks, the subculture had won. Individual behavior was now guided by group sanctions and norms. Both the individual and the group were moved to violence.

In Detroit, as the police left the scene, smaller groups of young persons quickly fanned out, moving up and down 12th Street, breaking store windows. An attempt to resolve discontent through violence had begun.

SUMMARY

For a ghetto riot to occur, many important factors are necessary. These antecedents are the catalysts of the riot, interacting with general psychological properties and ghetto conditions to produce violence. Among these factors are: (1) social contact through milling, (2) a precipitating event that symbolizes general grievances and discontent, (3) the convergence of a crowd at the site, (4) the formation of a crowd-within-the-crowd with its own values, attitudes, and beliefs, (5) the establishment of a belief in the legitimacy and utility of violence, and (6) the breakdown of societal controls as the crowd becomes more permissive and begins to engage in group-sanctioned violence.

Patterns of Racial Conflict

Having examined the causes and consequences of racial violence, let us relate these observations to some of the general comments about conflict and violence found in the first three chapters of the book.

SOCIAL CONFLICT: DEFINING CHARACTERISTICS

Social conflict arises when actors are opposed to other actors because they are striving for what are, or appear to be, incompatible goals. Thus, social conflict (1) is based on motive behavior, (2) represents an integrated act, and (3) implies some type of blocking behavior. How did the racial violence of the mid-1960s share these characteristics?

Consider the black ghetto grievances: police mistreatment, merchant exploitation, inadequate public services, and discriminatory housing, education, and employment. New urban blacks were motivated to find solutions; that is, their actions were goal-directed. Their grievances represented frustrated ambitions and goals. Blacks were placed in opposition to whites because whites dominated the social, political, and economic institutions that frustrated black goals of equal police protection, fair retail practices, and nondiscriminatory social practices.

Later, when blacks sought to redress these grievances, they found that they had to confront whites who controlled the establishment.

When appeals for administrative review, conventional political actions, or negotiation and protest failed, blacks became further frustrated as not only their goals but also their redress were thwarted.

Our definition of social conflict assumes that conflict is an integrated act reflecting the various influences of the actor's wants and goals upon his attitudes, thoughts, and values. Our examination of the politics of violence contended that a group's disposition to participate in a riot was due to a complex interplay among its socially determined psychological states, its environment, and its perceptions of changes in that environment. Among the psychological states noted were an intensely positive black self-image, heightened anti-white attitudes, and generally negative beliefs about conventional solutions to problems. Such attitudes, values, and beliefs were traced to particular socialization patterns. This is not to say that conflict begins solely in the mind. Instead, a person's socially determined psychological states interact with situational factors to produce conflict. Racial conflict is not only an instrumental act but an integrated act as well.

As we saw, black discontent and rising frustration resulted from conscious and unconscious white opposition to black goals and/or their demands for redress. This white blocking took many forms; bureaucratic indifference to the plight of inner-city black residents and police misbehavior were only two. A whole spectrum of violent and nonviolent actions marked white opposition.[47]

Black reaction to this opposing behavior generated its own blocking actions. These took the forms of protest movements, marches, demonstrations and other nonviolent actions. A reinforcing cycle of thwarting behavior was generated between white authorities and young urban blacks. This cycle spiraled into increasingly hostile countermoves by both actors that ultimately resulted in violence.

PERCEPTIONS: GENERAL PRECONDITIONS OF A RIOT

Throughout our discussion, we have stressed the importance of perceptions. For example, actors often engage in conflict because they see goal blockage in various situations. This process of "seeing" or defining situations is crucial to our understanding of conflict in general and racial conflict in particular. We have analyzed how certain segments of the black and white communities saw their world in particular ways. Their images reflected the combined effects of their separate attitudes, values, and beliefs as well as the situations they had to confront. Certain images are conducive to transforming racial conflict into violence. These include images of relative deprivation, perceptions of intense frustration, and perceptions about the specific nature of riots.

These images can be likened to mental mosaics, each mosaic being composed of particular sets of attitudes, beliefs, and values. Let us take the perception of relative deprivation as an example. New urban blacks had higher aspirations and greater optimism than either their older ghetto neighbors or their Southern rural counterparts. They believed that they were entitled to the same goods and conditions of life as whites. Because they were better educated and more politically aware, this group experienced constantly rising expectations. However, they also found that there were fewer, not more jobs; lower, not higher incomes; and little, not more tangible social status available to them. When these harsh realities interacted with preexisting beliefs, the result was an image of relative deprivation and a feeling of discontent and dissatisfaction. These perceptions influenced the thoughts and actions of this group. It also interacted with other perceptions, particularly those dealing with conventional and unconventional forms of protest. Riots came not only to represent instrumental and integrated actions but also to be seen as adaptive psychological responses.

COMMUNICATIONS: ANTECEDENT CONDITIONS

To form and change perceptions, information must be transmitted. This information is usually gathered through social interaction. The effects on race relations of interactions between blacks and whites have been discussed. Black socialization, for example, involved a particular type of information transmission. Through this process, young urban blacks learned certain things that later served as a basis for their attitudes and perceptions of themselves and whites.

The quantity and quality of information learned during social interaction can be influenced in many ways. Black perceptions, for example, often led them to "see" symbolic content in precipitating events. Whites, on the other hand, perceived these same events as relatively minor, even trivial. The nature of information transmission is important too. Black dissatisfaction with the white-dominated media has resulted, in part, in informal street communications. Both the quality and quantity of such "street talk" are often higher than the information transmitted by more formal means.

Nowhere has the importance of communications been more clearly shown than in the immediate preconditions of a riot. Among the immediate factors relevant here were: milling, rumor transmission, and volatile crowd interaction. Without a search for information there would be no milling, and without milling we would not find the prerequisite crowds for collective action. Through rumor transmission, the images and discontent of the crowd are intensified and given a specific focus. Communication within the volatile crowd also promotes the belief that violence may be useful and legitimate. Sharing similar experiences and perceptions, believing in the truthfulness of the messages being sent, and availing themselves of the same channels of communication, young urban blacks quickly develop strong bonds of solidarity.

Our discussion began with the question, What are the causes and consequences of racial conflict and violence? Using the 1967 Detroit riot and employing various findings, we were able to make some observations. These observations, in turn, have been useful in understanding certain aspects of social conflict, particularly where this conflict led to violence.

NOTES*

1. Hubert G. Locke, in his study *The Detroit Riot of '67*, contends that police at the scene were not particularly alarmed by these initial violent acts, nor did they perceive that more serious trouble would result. Following standard operating procedure, the reinforced police units simply withdrew from the area.

2. Here, and later in this chapter, we refer to the riot as if it were a single event. Obviously, however, the Detroit riot of 1967, like those in Watts, Harlem, and elsewhere, was a complex series of interrelated events. For similar usage and reasoning, see David O. Sears and John B. McConahay, *The Politics of Violence*, p. 5.

3. Conyers would later say, "I don't think anybody—except maybe the late Malcolm X—could have dispersed that crowd" (Van Gordon Sauter and Burleigh Hines, *Nightmare in Detroit*, pp. 9–10).

4. According to the *Report of the National Advisory Commission on Civil Disorders* (1968), firemen would be withdrawn 283 times from the riot scene. Fire Chief Charles J. Quinlan would later estimate that approximately 70 percent of the structures were destroyed by unchecked fires rather than fires set at the scene. More than 683 buildings would ultimately be destroyed in the Detroit riot.

5. The quotation originally appeared in an editorial in the *Detroit Free Press*, July 25, 1967. It was also cited in Donald I. Warren, "Community Dissensus: Panic in Suburbia," in Leonard Gordon (ed.), *A City in Racial Crisis*, p. 122.

6. In fact, on Thursday, July 20, 1977, Detroit city officials had actually participated in a simulation of a race riot developed by Conrad L. Mallet of the mayor's office. Sauter and Hines state: "There was no air of immediacy about this meeting; it was strictly an intellectual exercise. No one even took notes . . . " (1968: vii).

7. During the Detroit riot it would be charged that local, state, and national officials "played politics in a period of tragedy and riot" over whether the Detroit incident qualified as a state of insurrection. Local and state requests for federal military assistance to quell an insurrection require a number of formal steps, each bound by specific laws. For an excellent discussion of these measures and their history, see Col. L. J. Crume, "The National Guard and Riot Control: The Need for Revision," and Ruthanne Gartland and Richard A. Chikota, "When Will the Troops Come Marching In?" in Richard A. Chikota (ed.), *Riot in the Cities*, pp. 373–391, 391–411, respectively.

8. In the aftermath of the Detroit riot and others, the role of National Guard troops

*Complete citations for the works mentioned here will be found in the Bibliography, pages 98–102.

in controlling violence was widely debated. In some cases, the facts suggested that because of a lack of special riot-control training, the presence of the Guard actually worsened the situation.

9. Various reasons have been given for Governor Romney's hesitancy. Each of these explanations seems to be influenced by the uncertainty, recriminations, and political realities that followed the 1960 riots. Among the major reasons cited for Romney's delay were: (1) Romney believed that declaring a state of insurrection might cause the cancellation of insurance coverage in affected areas; (2) there was a growing personal tension between Romney and Cavanagh; (3) an inevitable tension existed between Republican Governor Romney and a Democratic administration in Washington; and (4) information from the riot scene was so mixed that an intelligent estimate of its scope and potential for control was impossible.

10. Vance's decision to postpone the paratroopers has been the subject of lively debate. His action seems to have been based, in part, on the fact that arson and looting seemed to decline on Monday afternoon. Nine more deaths, however, were reported during this time.

11. According to the *Report of the National Advisory Commission*, the southeastern sector of the city, which was patrolled by paratroopers on Tuesday morning, was then the most active riot area. General Throckmorton's decision to deploy his paratroopers in this region therefore seems logical. By 6 A.M., however, this area was the quietest in the city; it would remain so throughout the week. The general's decision to keep these seasoned troops here, rather than move them into other riot areas, was widely debated.

12. This and the following description of events were reconstructed from testimony before the Kerner Commission and the discussion entitled "Victim No. 21, Carl Smith," and "Victim No. 32, John Le Roy," in Van Gordon Sauter and Burleigh Hines, *Nightmare in Detroit*. We have tried to present both incidents objectively, attributing responsibility for these tragedies to no one.

13. There are several conflicting accounts of the Lycaste Street incident. Le Roy's brother and other survivors believe that they were ambushed by Guardsmen. The *Report of the National Advisory Commission* says only that it was one of many instances of "misdirected gunfire."

14. According to the *Report of the National Advisory Commission*, a number of important lessons learned during the Watts riot (two years before) were ignored. As the report stated, "roadblocks that were ill lighted and ill defined—often consisting of no more than a trash barrel or similar object with Guardsmen standing nearby—proved a continuous hazard. . . . At one such roadblock, National Guard Sergeant Larry Post, standing in the street, was caught in a sudden crossfire as his fellow Guardsmen opened fire on a vehicle. He was the only soldier killed in the riot" (1968: 100–101).

15. Herbert Locke describes each of these incidents in *The Detroit Riot of 1967*, pp. 43–47. *The Algiers Motel Incident* was also the subject of a novel of the same title by John Hersey. Three persons were shot to death at the motel and seven others were beaten. Later, first-degree murder warrants would be issued against three Detroit police officers.

16. Early conservative theorists, such as Gustav Le Bon emphasized in *The Crowd*, the emotional nature of such crowds. For Le Bon, their violent outbursts reflected nothing more than a "herd instinct" motivated by the basest of human desires.

17. Sears and McConahay identified three key elements of the *Governor's Commission on the Los Angeles Riots* (McCone Commission): (1) labeling the riot an "insensate rage of destruction," the commission proposed that (2) participants were a small fraction (2 percent, or 10,000 persons) who were marginally related to the ghetto community as drifters (principally criminals), the unemployed, and school dropouts and that (3) participants were newcomers from the South who had been attracted by California's liberal welfare policies and who turned to violence in disappointment. Original source: *Governor's Commission on the Los Angeles Riot*, 1965, pp. 1, 4–6, 24, 71, reported in David O. Sears and John B. McConahay, *The Politics of Violence*, p. 19.

18. T. M. Tomlinson analyzes the political dimensions of the Los Angeles riot in

"Ideological Foundation for Negro Action: A Comparative Analysis of Militant and Non-militant Views of the Los Angeles Riot."

19. Robert Fogelson argues that rioting in general gave the ghetto residents a sense of accomplishment; they had at least dramatized their grievances to the white society.With looting, their acute and chronic poverty was manifested, and their acts of arson signaled their hatred of unscrupulous ghetto merchants (1970: 147–154). For another version of this thesis, see Peter H. Rossi and Richard A. Berk, "Local Political Leadership and Popular Discontent in the Ghetto," in Short and Wolfgang (eds.), *Collective Violence* pp. 292–308.

20. Many specific recommendations in the fields of employment, education, welfare, and housing are discussed in the *Report of the National Advisory Commission on Civil Disorders* pp. 410–483.

21. Among those who subscribed to some variation of this theory was President Lyndon Johnson (see Appendix C: "Excerpts from President Lyndon B. Johnson's Address to the Nation on Civil Disorders, July 27, 1967," *Report of the National Advisory Commission*, 1968: 541–583). The theory is supposedly appealing to liberals because it does not challenge the goals of their social and political programs—only their application. For a more complete discussion of this perspective, see Sears and McConahay, *The Politics of Violence*, p. 22, and Gary Marx, "Issueless Riots," p. 49.

22. At the core of the "southern newcomer" theory is the thesis that Southern blacks up from rural areas suffered cultural shock in coping with the stress and strain of urban ghetto life. Disillusioned and frustrated, they became more hostile and eventually more aggressive. When an incident occurred, they used it to lash out against the system that they believed had done such violence to them.

23. Sears and McConahay presented the earliest findings (1970) on what they called the "new urban black." As they later pointed out, a number of scholars have portrayed the substance and views of a "new ghetto person"—one who is substantially different from either his older ghetto neighbors or his younger southern rural counterpart.

24. For the most complete statement of the relative deprivation theory of civil disorder, see Ted R. Gurr's *Why Men Rebel.*

25. The studies on ghetto life and violence are numerous. Rather than identify only a few here, we have included many of them in the bibliography.

26. Sears and McConahay's theory (1973) examines the *general* conditions and processes which precede a riot. They do not examine the *immediate* conditions which provide the "triggering mechanism" of a riot. James R. Hundley, Jr., has developed a model of these immediate preconditions (1968: 137–149) We will examine this model later.

27. Sears and McConahay emphasize that only certain grievances are linked to rioting rather than all grievances related to ghetto life.

28. The black population has also been urbanized in the South. Recent data, furthermore, indicate a general shift in population from the Northeast to the "Sun Belt," which includes the South. Here, large urban centers such as Atlanta, Dallas, and Fort Worth have grown rapidly.

29. Between 1960 and 1967 the black population of Detroit, for example, increased from 20 percent to 40 percent of the total population.

30. See Karl and Alma Tacuber, *Negroes in Cities,* for a study of this pattern of "massive neighborhood transition." Today, interestingly enough, there is evidence of an increasing white reemergence in the inner city as the children of white suburbanites move back into the cities that their parents vacated a generation before.

31. Sears and McConahay's "politics of violence" theory differentiates between two stages in socialization—an early stage that generates more positive self-concepts, more generalized dissatisfaction, and greater white hostility and a later socialization-resocialization process that influences views on both comparative satisfaction and rioting.

32. These children are more disappointed than their older or Southern counterparts because they have grown to expect social and political equality. When this equality is denied them, their frustration is greater.

33. The findings on this point are in conflict. On one side we find studies such as those by Caplan (1970), Tomlinson (1970), and Sears and McConahay (1973) that suggest the development of a more positive black self-image. On the other side are studies which contradict the thesis that "black is beautiful."

34. It is as difficult to speak of the "general black community view" as it is to generalize about the "new urban black view." Two major studies, however, have attempted to identify these views. One "Report from Black America," was a set of three surveys conducted by the Gallup organization for *Newsweek* magazine (1966, 1967, and 1968); the other, (in three separate years) drawn exclusively from an urban sample, was completed in 1968 by Angus Campbell and Howard Schuman, entitled "Racial Attitudes in Fifteen American Cities."

35. The spiritual quality of the term "soul" is hard to pin down empirically, much less discuss it objectively. It represents a quasi-mystical notion of racial identification and awareness. Its subjective content includes notions of affection, comparison, stoicism, emotion, and understanding within a racial community.

36. Tomlinson makes an important observation about this relationship between militancy and attitudes about social contact with whites. As yet, he states, no one can tell whether militancy produces the social distance or whether it is the result of differential social access to whites (1970: 105). The reader may wish to refer to the discussion of social distance in chapter 3 for a reexamination of the relationship between racial attitudes and social intercourse.

37. For a detailed examination of new urban blacks' view of conventional electoral politics, see Sears and McConahay, 1968: 62–63. Black dissatisfaction with such institutions as parties and voting, coupled with low opinions of their political efficacy, meant that their perceived chances for redress were quite low.

38. There is no one definition for the term "police brutality." It is a catch-all term that includes actions ranging from verbal to physical abuse.

39. Some of the scholars who have used this concept are John C. Davies, Ted R. Gurr, and Ivo and Rosalind Feierabend. Their works are discussed in chapter 5 of this text.

40. Throughout the remainder of this discussion, we will be referring to Ted R. Gurr's definition of relative deprivation. Gurr's development of this concept and its role in civil violence are found in his work *Why Men Rebel*.

41. This author detects only one substantial difference between Gurr's use of the notion of deprivation and Sears and McConahay's usage. Gurr deals with collective states of mind—for example, how a group might collectively feel; Sears and McConahay focus on the individual's state of mind. Sears and McConahay discuss these differences between their theoretical focus and those of other deprivation theorists in footnote 5, page 48, of their work. Since we are interested more in the sociological meaning of the terms (i.e., intergroup phenomena), we employ Gurr's usage. Sears and McConahay are interested in the psychology of the individual rioter and not in the new urban blacks as a group.

42. Gurr discusses many different patterns of relative deprivation. Among these is one he calls *aspirational deprivation*. It is marked by "an increase in men's value expectations with a concomitant change in value position or potential. Those who experience aspirational RD [relative deprivation] do not anticipate or experience significant loss of what they have; they are angered because they feel they have no means for attaining new or intensified expectations" (1970: 50). We believe this condition characterized new urban blacks in the mid-1960s.

43. Gurr and others have stated that the sources of people's perceptions of political violence are important. Gurr claims that two such sources are socialization and tradition (1970: 155–182). Sears and McConahay, elaborating on socialization, contend that the new urban blacks have either been exposed to unconventional techniques of social change, such as protest and riots, or are generationally predisposed to follow the lead of others who support such techniques. See pages 46–48 of their discussion.

44. The analysis of collective behavior and riot action encompasses work in psychology, sociology, and anthropology. As one might imagine, a substantial body of litera-

ture has emerged. We found the works by Neil Smelser and Jerome Skolnick to be particularly useful. In the discussion that follows, we also draw heavily on the works of James R. Hundley, Jr.

45. The various functions of communication processes were discussed in chapters 1 and 2 of this text.

46. The reader will notice that our discussion moves between individual and group thoughts and behavior. What we are describing is the transmission by rumors of beliefs held by new urban blacks. These beliefs have been discussed previously as general psychological preconditions for riots. They are mentioned again here in the context of an emerging crowd psychology and behavior.

47. Many black goals are still frustrated. In Detroit, for example, 1973 data showed that median income of the core city was 25 percent below the rest of the city; unemployment in 1972 was 10.8 percent, up 2 percent from 1971; welfare recipients increased from 50,000 to more than 145,000 families from 1968 to 1973; black students are three times as likely as white students to drop out of school by ages sixteen and seventeen; and 63 percent of blacks think that the police discriminate in enforcing the law. (*Subcommittee on Equal Opportunities of the Committee on Education and Labor,* "Proposed Elimination of OEO").

Bibliography

ALLEN, RODNEY F., and CHARLES H. ADAIR (eds.). *Violence and Riots in Urban America*. Belmont, Calif.: C. A. Jones, 1969.

ALLEN, U. L. (ed.). "Ghetto Riots." *Journal of Social Issues*, 26 (1970), 1–220.

BARBOUR, FLOYD B. *The Black Power Revolt: A Collection of Essays*. New York: Collier Books, 1969.

"Behind the Riots: A Sociological Study, address by R. V. SMITH." *American Education*, 3 (Nov. 1967), 2–44.

BELLISFIELD, G. "White Attitudes Toward Racial Integration and the Urban Riots of the '60's." *Public Opinion Quarterly*, 36 (Winter, 1972–1973), 579–584.

BLOOMBAUM, MILTON. "The Conditions Underlying Race Riots as Portrayed . . . " *American Sociological Review*, 33 (Feb. 1968), 76–91.

BOESEL, D., and P. ROSSI (eds.). *Cities Under Seige: An Anatomy of the Ghetto Riots, 1964–1968*. New York: Basic Books, 1971.

BOSKIN, JOSEPH, and FRED KRINSKY (eds.). *Urban Racial Violence in the 20th Century*. Encino, Calif.: Glencoe Press, 1969.

BRINK, W., and L. HARRIS. *Black and White: A Study of U.S. Racial Attitudes Today*. Rev. ed. Louisville, Ky.: Touchstone, 1969.

BROWN, RICHARD MAXWELL (ed.). *American Violence*. Englewood Cliffs, N.J.: Prentice-Hall, 1970.

CAMPBELL, ANGUS, and SCHUMAN, HOWARD. "Racial Attitudes in Fifteen American Cities." Survey Research Center, University of Michigan, June 1968.

CAPLAN, NATHAN. "The New Ghetto Man: A Review of Recent Empirical Studies." *Journal of Social Issues*, 26 (Winter 1970), 59–74.

———, and J. PAIGE. "A Study of Ghetto Rioters." *Scientific American*, 219 (Aug. 1968), 15–21.

CHIKOTA, R. A., and M. C. MORAN (eds.). *Riot in the Cities: An Analytical Symposium on the Causes and the Effects*. Rutherford, N.J.: Fairleigh Dickinson University Press, 1970.

COMMAGER, H. S. (ed.). *The Struggle for Racial Equality: A Documentary Record*. New York: Harper, 1967.

CONANT, RALPH W. "Rioting, Insurrection and Civil Disobedience." *American Scholar*, 37 (Summer 1968), 420–433.

CONOT, ROBERT. *Rivers of Blood, Years of Darkness*. New York: Bantam Books, 1967.

CRUME, L. J. "The National Guard and Riot Control: The Need for Revision."

In R. A. Chikota (ed.). *Riot in the Cities*. Rutherford, N.J.: Fairleigh Dickinson University Press, 1968.

DAVIDSON, B. "If We Can't Solve the Problems of the Ghetto Here, God Help our Country." *Saturday Evening Post*. Oct. 5, 1968, 29–33+.

DEMARIS, OVID. *America the Violent*. New York: Scribners, 1970.

"Detroit." *Life*. Aug. 4, 1967, 16–25.

"Detroit: a Riot-torn City Survives and Bounces Back." *Publishers Weekly*. Aug. 28, 1967, 264–267.

"Detroit Gropes Its Way." *Business Week*, Aug. 5, 1967, 25.

"Detroit: Violence in the Urban Frontier." *Transaction*, 4 (Sept. 1967), 57–68.

DONNER, B. T. "A Critical Examination of the Social and Political Characteristics of Riot Cities." *Social Science Quarterly*, 51 (1970), 349–360.

DOTSON, J. "American Tragedy, 1967: Detroit: Eye Witness Report." *Newsweek*, Aug. 7, 1967, 18–27.

DYNES, R. R., and E. L. QUARANTELLI (eds.). "Urban Civil Disturbances: Organizational Change and Group Emergence." *American Behavioral Scientist*, 16 (1973), 305–439.

ENDLEMAN, SHALOM (ed.). *Violence in the Streets*. Chicago: Quadrangle, 1968.

FEAGIN, JOE R., and HARLAN HAHN. *Ghetto Revolts: The Politics of Violence in American Cities*. New York: Macmillan, 1974.

———, and P. B. SHEATSLEY. "Ghetto Resident Appraisals of a Riot." *Public Opinion Quarterly*, 32 (Fall 1968), 352–362.

"Fire this Time." *Time*, Aug. 4, 1967, 13–18.

FOGELSON, R. M. *Violence as Protest. A Study of Riots and Ghettos*. New York: Holt, 1971.

———. "Violence and Grievances: Reflections on the 1960s Riots." *Journal of Social Issues*, 26 (Winter 1970), 141–163.

———. "From Resentment to Confrontation: The Police, the Negroes and the Outbreak of the 1960's Riots." *Political Science Quarterly*, 83 (June 1968), 217–247.

———, and HILL, R. B. "Who Riots? A Study of Participation in the 1967 Riots." In *Supplemental Studies for the National Advisory Commission on Civil Disorders*, 1968, 217–248.

FORD, W. F., and J. H. MOORE. "Additional Evidence on the Social Characteristics of Riot Cities." *Social Science Quarterly*, 51 (September 1970), 339–348.

GARTLAND, RUTHANNE, and CHIKOTA, R. A. "When Will the Troops Come Marching In?" In R. A. Chikota (ed.). *Riot in the Cities*. Rutherford, N. J.: Fairleigh Dickinson University Press, 1968.

GESSCHWENDER, J. A. "Deprivation and the Detroit Riot." *Social Problems*, 17 (April 1970), 457–463.

GORDON, LEONARD (ed.). *A City in Racial Crisis*. Dubuque, Iowa: William C. Brown, 1971.

GRIER, WILLIAM H., and PRICE M. COBB. *Black Rage*. New York: Basic Books, 1968.

GURR, TED R. *Why Men Rebel*. (Princeton, N.J.: Princeton University Press, 1970.

————. "A Causal Model of Civil Strife: A Comparative Analysis Using New Indices." *American Political Science Review*. 62 (1968), 1104–1124.

————. "Psychological Factors in Civil Strife." *World Politics*, 20 (1968), 245–278.

HAHN, HARLAN. "Black Separatists: Attitudes and Objectives in a Riot-torn Ghetto." *Journal of Black Studies*. 1 (Sept. 1970), 35–53.

————. "Civic Responses to Riots: A Reappraisal of Kerner Commission Data." *Public Opinion Quarterly*, 34 (Spring 1970), 101–107.

————. "Cops and Rioters: Ghetto Perceptions of Social Conflict and Control." *American Behavioral Scientist*, 13 (May–Aug. 1970), 761–769.

————. "Ghetto Sentiments on Violence." *Science and Society*, 33 (Spring 1969), 197–208.

————, and J. R. FEAGIN. "Riot Precipitating Police Practices: Attitudes in Urban Ghettos." *Phylon*, 31 (Summer 1970), 183–193.

"How Detroit Gropes Toward Racial Peace." *Business Week*, Nov. 25, 1962, 83–84.

HUNDLEY, J. R., JR. "The Dynamics of Recent Ghetto Riots." *University of Detroit Journal of Urban Law*, 45 (Spring–Summer 1968), 627–639.

HUNTINGTON, SAMUEL P. *Political Order in Changing Societies*. New Haven: Yale University Press, 1968.

JIBON, R. M. "City Characteristics, Differential Stratification and the Occurrence of Interracial Violence." *Social Science Quarterly*, 52 (December 1971), 508–520.

LE BON, GUSTAV *The Crowd*. London: Irwin and Unwin, 1903.

LOCKE, HUBERT G. *The Detroit Riot of '67*. Detroit: Wayne State University Press, 1969.

"LOOTING, BURNING, Now Guerrilla War." *U.S. News and World Report*, Aug. 7, 1967, 23–27.

LUKAS, J. A. "Whitey Hasn't Got the Message." *New York Times Magazine*, Aug. 27, 1967, 24–25.

MARY, GARY T. "Issueless Riots." In James F. Short and Marvin E. Wolfgang (eds.), *Collective Violence*. Chicago: Aldine-Atherton, 1972, pp. 48–59.

MASOTTI, L. H. (ed.). "Urban Violence and Disorder." *American Behavioral Scientist*, 11 (March 1968) 1–55.

McCORD, W. M., and J. HOWARD. "Negro Opinions in 3 Riot Cities." *American Behavioral Scientist*, 11 (March–April 1968), 24–27.

MOINAT, S., et al. "Black Ghetto Residents as Rioters." *Journal of Social Issues*, 28:4 (1972), 45–62.

MOORE, BARRINGTON. "Thoughts on Violence and Democracy." In *Urban Riots: Violence and Social Change*. New York: Academy of Political Science, 1968.

MORGAN, W., and T. CLARK. "Causes of Racial Disorders: A Grievance-Level Explanation." *American Sociological Review*, 38 (Oct. 1973), 611–624.

MOUNT, E. "Last Night in Detroit City," *National Review*, Aug. 22, 1967, 905–908.

MURPHY, B. J., and J. M. WATSON. "The Structure of Discontent." In N. E. Cohen (ed.). *The Los Angeles Riot*. N. Y.: Praeger, 1970.

"Negro Militancy: A Complicating Dimension." *Science News*, Aug. 12, 1967, 152–153.

"Nightmare Journey: Violence Against Negroes During Riots." *Ebony*, October 1967, 121–124.

RAINWATER, LEE. "Open Letter on White Justice and the Riots." *Transaction*, 4, (Sept. 1967), 22–27.

"*Report from Black America.*" *Newsweek*, June 30, 1969.

Report of the National Advisory Commission on Civil Disorders. New York: Bantam, 1968.

RINELLA, VINCENT J., Jr. "Police Brutality and Racial Prejudice: A Close Look." *Journal of Urban Law*, 45 (1968), 773–804.

ROSSI, PETER H., and RICHARD A. BERK. "Local Political Leadership and Popular Discontent in the Ghetto. In James F. Short and Marvin E. Wolfgang, (eds.). *Collective Violence*. Chicago: Aldine-Atherton, 1972.

RUBIN, I. J. "Analyzing Detroit's Riot: The Causes and Responses." *Reporter*, Feb. 22, 1968, 34–35.

SAMUELS, G. "Help Wanted: The Hard-core Unemployed." *New York Times Magazine*, Jan. 28, 1968, 26–27+.

SAUTER, VAN GORDON, and BURLEIGH HINES, *Nightmare in Detroit*. Chicago: Henry Regnery, 1968.

SCHROTH, R. A. "Detroit, 1967." *America*, Aug. 12, 1967, 151–152.

SCHWARTZ, D. "Psychological Factors in Civil Violence: The Long Hot Summer as Hypothesis." *American Behavioral Scientist*, 11 (1968), 24–28.

SCOTT, R. "Summer of Racial Violence." *Round Table*, 57 (1967), 448–454.

SEARS, DAVID O., and JOHN B. MCCONAHAY. *The Politics of Violence*. Boston: Houghton Mifflin, 1973.

———. "Riot Participation." In N. E. Cohen (ed.). *The Los Angeles Riots: A Socio-Psychological Study*. New York: Praeger, 1970.

SHORT, JAMES F., and MARVIN E. WOLFGANG (eds.). *Collective Violence*. Chicago: Aldine-Atherton, 1972.

SINGER, B. D. "Mass Media and Communication Processes in the Detroit Riot of 1967." *Public Opinion Quarterly*, 34 (1970), 236–245.

SKOLNICK, JEROME H. *The Politics of Protest*. New York: Simon and Schuster, 1969.

SMELSER, NEIL. *Theory of Collective Behavior*. New York: Free Press, 1962.

SPILERMAN, S. "Causes of Racial Disturbances: A Comparison of Alternative Explanations." *American Sociological Review*, 35 (1970), 627–649.

Subcommittee on Equal Opportunities of the Committee on Education and Labor. "Proposed Elimination of OEO." United States Congress, *Hearings*, February–March 1973.

TACUBER, KARL, and ALMA TACUBER. *Negroes in Cities*. Chicago: Aldine-Atherton, 1965.

THIMMESCH, M. "Detroit Aftermath." *Life*, Aug. 11, 1967, 54–58.

TOMLINSON, T. M. "Ideological Foundation for Negro Action: A Comparative Analysis of Militant and Non-Militant Views of the Los Angeles Riot." *Journal of Social Issues*, 26:1 (1970), 93–119.

————. "Development of a Riot Ideology Among Urban Negroes." *American Behavioral Scientist*, 11 (March 1968), 27–31.

WANDERER, J. "Index of Riot Severity and Some Correlation." *American Journal of Sociology*, 74 (March 1969), 500–505.

————. "1967 Riots: A Test of the Congruity of Events." *Social Problems*, 16 (Fall 1968), 193–198.

WARD, H. H. "In Detroit, Black Power vs. White Power." *Christian Century*, Mar. 20, 1968, 368–371.

WARREN, DONALD I. "Community Dissensus: Panic in Suburbia." In Gordon (ed.). *A City in Racial Crisis*. Dubuque, Iowa: William C. Brown, 1971.

————. "Suburban Isolation and Race Tension: The Detroit Case." *Social Problems*, 17 (Winter 1970), 324–339.

————. "Neighborhood Structure and Riot Behavior in Detroit: Some Explanatory Findings." *Social Problems*, 16 (Spring 1968), 464–484.

"Watts to Detroit." *National Review*, Aug. 22, 1967, 885.

"Who Is Really to Blame in the Rioting?" *U.S. News & World Report*, (Aug. 7, 1967), 10.

SCHREIBER, F. R. "Why People Riot." *Science Digest*, 62 (October 1967), 56–60.

"Why the Detroit Riots Got Out of Hand." *U.S. News & World Report*, (Jan. 15, 1968), 16.

WIDICK, B. J. "Motown Blues." *Nation*, Aug. 14, 1967, 102–104.

WILSON, J. "Black and White Tragedy." *Encounter*, 29 (October 1967), 63–68.

5 | PATTERNS OF POLITICAL VIOLENCE

In December 1975, militants from the South Moluccan immigrant community in the Netherlands hijacked a train and seized the Indonesian consulate, demanding Dutch help in winning independence from Indonesia for their Pacific island homeland, a former Dutch colony. Eventually four of the hostages were killed. In May 1977, South Moluccan nationalists seized a Dutch elementary school and a commuter train to further dramatize their demands. More than 162 men, women, and children were held as hostages. This time, seven people eventually died—five terrorists and two hostages.

In June 1976, according to newspaper accounts, South African police dispersed more than 100 black students who had smashed windows at a government administrative building in the black township of Soweto. Major antigovernment rioting had broken out in Soweto a year earlier, and before it was brought under control, it had spread across South Africa, claiming a reported 600 black fatalities.

Approximately 2,000 Katangan insurgents invaded Zaire's mineral-rich Shaba region. Followers of the late Katangan separatist, Moise Tshombe, their objective was to consolidate their control over much of southwestern Zaire. The warfare took on international significance when charges were made that the separatists were armed by the Soviet Union, trained by the Cubans, and operated from bases in Angola. They were countered by government forces armed and trained by a collection of Western European powers and supported by a number of black African states.

Whether one is discussing intercommunal violence in Cyprus, independence or separatist movements in Africa, terrorism in the Netherlands, or attempted coups in Latin America, the experiences are broadly similar. In each case, various groups have used violence for political ends. We have already seen how a certain group of urban blacks in the United States used riots for similar political purposes. In this chapter, we will examine the various forms of political violence that are prevalent today.[1] Particular attention will be paid to revolutions and the use of terrorism. We will analyze these causes of political violence, focusing on the interrelationships among political, economic, and social psychological explanations. Finally, we will discuss the stages, processes, and dynamics of terrorism, drawing on contemporary events.

Characteristics of Political Violence

Political violence has been so widely explored that readers can easily be overwhelmed by definitions. Several excellent review essays have analyzed these definitional controversies in detail.[2] Rather than simply summarizing these reviews, let us make some additional observations about political violence,[3] especially its collective nature, its purposive orientation, and its reliance on force.

THE BEHAVIOR OF GROUPS

Political violence is, first and foremost, an act of groups. Collective action is one of the defining characteristics most often cited in the studies of political violence. This is generally accepted by most scholars of political violence, regardless of their individual viewpoints. As Ted R. Gurr states: " . . . political violence refers to all *collective* attacks within a political *community* against the political *regime*, its actors—including competing political *groups*" [emphasis added] (1970: 3–4). Fred Von der Mehden, in his study of comparative political violence, states that it will be discussed "only as a group phenomenon" (1973: 6).

Several problems arise, however, from this tendency to define and analyze only the collective dimension of political violence. It denies, in many ways, the utility of looking at individuals. It also tends to downplay personal attributes as causes of participation. Thus the psychology of political violence is either written off entirely as being too idiosyncratic or is defined in such restrictive terms (e.g., as personality phenomena) that its application becomes immediately controversial.[4] In taking this group focus, scholars also often overlook the importance of individual acts of political violence. Such acts are important not only for the individual but for the society as well.[5] Terrorist acts, in particular, are intended and perceived to be symbolic. In fact, as Thomas Thornton has pointed out, the efficacy and efficiency of terrorism derives from its symbolic nature (Eckstein, 1964: 77). And although some researchers are aware of the importance of personal acts of violence, the vast majority of incidents that are studied deal primarily with groups. Groups have traditionally been given more attention than has individual behavior in analyzing political violence.

MOTIVATION

Before an event can be considered political violence, more than collective behavior is required; motivation and purpose are needed. Political violence is goal-directed behavior. Kramnick states that violence must have a purpose. The purpose of a revolution, for example, is political change. Most of the literature on revolutionary violence, Kramnick points out, cites a complete and novel restructuring of the entire society as its goal (1972: 30). Von der Mehden agrees. He argues that violent political behavior is directed to political ends; in the case of a revolution, this involves novel and widespread change. In defining revolutionary types of political violence, Von der Mehden focuses on the attempt to establish a new state "molded upon a significantly different economic/political model" (1973: 10). Even when scholars have not focused on revolution, they have identified the directions that political violence has taken.

The most striking characteristic of all forms of political violence is their common commitment to change. In riots, for example, violent behavior serves as a critique of the social order. Other forms of political violence contain similar implicit changes. These challenges assume that there are viable alternatives to the existing system. Where there is foreign domination, there could be native rule; where there is communal inequality, there could be democratic pluralism. These objectives, however, cannot be realized without change. Violent political activists believe in the purposiveness of change. Furthermore, they are convinced that violence can bring it about.

Whereas a scholar like Isaac Kramnick points out that defining revolution as political change is too narrow, we believe that a substantial effort has been made to define *all* the dimensions of change—political, social, economic, and psychological. Implicit in all these definitions is the view that the prevailing system is incompatible with the proposed alternative. The intensity and scope of this incompatibility varies according to circumstance; the most intense and widespread are manifested in revolution. It is these incompatibilities that make political violence part of the larger phenomenon of social conflict.

ATTACKING FORCE: VIOLENCE

The "violence" of political violence is extremely controversial. Throughout our discussions violence has been referred to as one way of resolving the incompatibilities caused by conflicting goals. We also have referred repeatedly to the use of violence for political ends. Gurr follows this tradition in the literature, stating that "the concept represents a set of events, a common property of which is the actual or threatened use of violence" (1970: 4). In each of the acts mentioned at the beginning of this chapter, there was a prominent element of actual or threatened use of violence. Bombing, kidnaping, hijacking, guerrilla warfare, rebellion, and demonstrations are all acts of violence.

Violence is not the same as force. It differs from force in its unnecessary intensity, capriciousness, and destructiveness. As a number of scholars have pointed out, violence is often used for its own sake, and its course from beginning to end is usually highly unpredictable. Most people associate violence with aggression, and where the latter term means behavior motivated by a desire to injure or destroy a threatening object, the two terms are similar. In the main, however, both violence and aggression refer to motivated attacking behavior. Violence is the most extreme form of attacking behavior because it usually involves extreme physical force.

In the context of political violence, attacking behavior is thought to be goal-directed. In most cases, it is initiated to remove a threatening or blocking object so that goals can be realized; this tactic is often successful. In this context, acts of political violence often are thought of as instrumental acts *required* to attain various political ends. The danger, as Harold I. Lief points out, is that the original goal "may be lost as it becomes an end-in-itself" (in Endleman, 1968: 51–52). Should this occur, he contends, "it becomes behavior exercised for its own sake" (in Endleman, 1968: 49). Of all the forms of force in political violence, none is more controversial than acts of terrorism. We shall discuss various dimensions of terror and terrorism later in this chapter.

Based on the characteristics discussed above, let us adopt H. L. Nieburg's definition of political violence:

> Acts of disruption, destruction, injury whose purpose, choice of targets or victims, surrounding circumstances, implementation, and/or effects have political significance, that is, tend to modify the behavior of others in a bargaining situation, that has consequences for the social system. (1969: 13)

This definition gives us sufficient latitude in examining the many facets of political violence.

Explaining Political Violence

The causes of political violence are generally divided into two groups—long-run or general preconditions and short-term or precipitant actions.[6] Earlier in the text, a distinction was also made between objective and subjective causes of racial violence; it will be used again here in analyzing political violence. After examining various explanations of political violence, we will explore two of them in greater detail. One, based on a frustration-aggression model, has been advanced by Ted Gurr. A second one, developed by David C. Schwartz, deals with political alienation resulting from a conflict of values.

OBJECTIVE CONSIDERATIONS

Economic Factors Throughout history, political violence has been linked in theory to economic conditions within a society. Aristotle and Tocqueville, and more recently Kenneth Boulding, Bruce Russett, and J. C. Davies, have argued that the distribution of wealth and status, and the general state of economic development within a country, are powerful preconditions of political violence. Under the umbrella of economic explanations, however, are substantial differences in emphasis and interpretation. One of the sharpest differences is between those theorists who contend that violence results from poverty, lack of progress, and imbalance in patterns of distribution and those who contend that it is a product of prosperity, growth, and balanced economic change. As Kramnick points out, "the conventions of economic scholarship have it, then, that revolution is caused by either immiseration or improvement" (1972: 40). However, several recent studies by Russett, Siegelman and Simpson, and others have challenged the relationship between economic inequality and political violence.

Bruce Russett was one of the first scholars to test cross-nationally the thesis that economic inequality was a precondition for political violence. He focused on the monopoly of agricultural land by a few large landholders, arguing that certain land-tenure systems were an acceptable measure of economic inequality. Russett hypothesized that unequal land distribution was related to political instability. He found, however, that this relationship was at best moderate and in most cases quite low. He was finally forced to concede that the impact of land inequality was small (Russett, 1964).

A more recent study by Siegelman and Simpson (1977) also questions the relationship between economic inequality and political violence. Unlike Russett, these authors measured economic inequality in terms of personal income rather than land ownership. Like Russett, they too contended that frustration will be high where a substantial portion of the population does not share equitably in the distribution of a scarce resource. However, even when they controlled for such factors as absolute wealth available for distribution, social mobility, sociocultural heterogeneity, and social change, Siegelman and Simpson found only moderate support for the hypothesis that "the greater the inequality in the national distribution of personal incomes the greater the level of political violence" (1977:

Figure 5.1   NEED SATISFACTION AND REVOLUTION

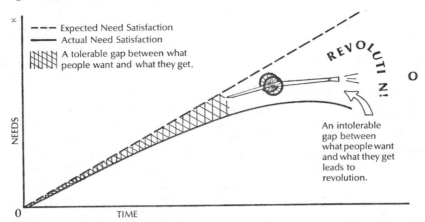

SOURCE: Modified from James C. Davies, "Toward a Theory of Revolution," *American Sociological Review*, 6 (February 1962).

106).[7] These authors, like so many others, are perplexed at their "failure to provide strong empirical support for a relationship so often stipulated in political and social theory" (1977: 124).

Suppose, however, that economic declines or inequalities—or, for that matter, economic advances—are not sufficient to promote revolution. Suppose, instead, that it is some combination of these two trends and forces. James C. Davies's important work, "Toward a Theory of Revolution," advances this thesis (1962). Davies contends that revolutions are most likely to occur when a long period of economic advancement is followed by a short, sudden period of decline. The important motive force is not simply advancement or decline but both, with fear that the hard-won ground gained during advancement will be lost irreparably during the short decline. As Davies states:

> The all-important effect on the minds of people in a particular society is to produce, during the former period [advancement], an expectation of continued ability to satisfy needs—which continue to rise—and, during the latter [decline], a mental state of anxiety and frustration when manifest reality breaks away from anticipated reality. (1962: 6)

Davies's theory is schematized in Figure 5.1. Here, *expected* and *actual* need satisfaction keep pace with each other during periods of economic and social development. Usually there will be some gap between expectation and satisfaction, but such gaps are tolerable and thus do not generate a pressure toward violence. When there is a short, sudden economic decline, the actual need satisfaction line drops sharply, while the expectation line continues to move up. At this point, Davies believes, an intolerable gap exists between what people expect and what they can actually get. This is when revolution can occur. Davies labels this the "J-curve theory of revolution." He contends that Dorr's Rebellion in nineteenth century America, the Russian Revolution of 1917, and the Egyptian Revolution of 1952 all appear to fit the J-curve pattern.

Economic factors probably do play a role in explaining political violence, but most attempts to relate economic conditions directly to violent action have failed. The relationship appears to be indirect and complex. The most we can say on the basis of empirical evidence is that economic factors are one of several objective conditions related to political violence.

The Social System[8] Many sociologists have attempted to identify the social forces conducive to political violence. Generally speaking, they have focused on various "failures" or "dysfunctions" of the social system that produce social strain, tension, and eventual violence.[9] These dysfunctions can result from many forces, but the one force that has received the most attention is *change*. Under certain conditions, almost any change—economic fluctuation, social modernization, political development—can have such widespread effects that it produces social strain. Sociologists are interested in determining how economic, political, and social change generates pressures within a society. Two dimensions of this relationship have intrigued them. The first is change as it strains the structure of society—for example, in creating competition between groups, classes and institutions. The second is change as it affects culture—for example, in the development of incompatible norms and values. These two dimensions are commonly referred to as "structural" and "cultural" changes (Southwood, 1972: 14–20, 21–24).[10]

Structural changes can come about in many ways: the emergence of new groups, the realignment of existing groups, the elimination of groups, and the internal restructuring of groups. A study of national liberation movements, for example, would reveal each of these structural factors. In the preindependence stage of the movement, nationalist groups emerge which must compete for the loyalty of the people. These groups must also challenge the existing colonial authority for ever-increasing political power. Whether the government and various groups can or will accommodate each other's demands will determine the level of strain produced and ultimately the potential for violence. Should national fronts or coalitions be necessary, there might even be a realignment of existing nationalist groups. This, too, may produce strain. Where accommodating coalitions cannot be maintained, not only may strain result but violence may be used to eliminate nonaccommodating members; this occurred in South Vietnam. Even after independence is achieved, there may be strain as the preindependence nationalists take over control of the system, trying to adapt it and themselves to the new demands of nationhood.

Two of the most widely read structural change theorists are Chalmers Johnson (1964) and Johan Galtung (1964). Since both of their theories have been reviewed elsewhere (e.g., Stone, 1966) and since Galtung's theory was discussed in chapter 3, let us briefly highlight Johnson's thoughts.[11] Both scholars contend that political violence arises in situations where there has been little or no adaptation to structural changes within the society. Johnson has identified four sources of these pressures for structural change that produce violence: "exogenous (foreign) value-changing," "endogenous (domestic) value changing," "exogenous environment changing," and "endogenous environment changing." Environmental changes include the introduction of technological advances into developing societies, economic development stimulated by foreign market demands, and changing skills and knowledge among domestic classes. Such innovations— technological advances, for example—may decrease mortality rates and increase the population growth. As the population increases, it may change the relative number and strength of various groups or classes—which, in turn, may affect the division of labor in the society; it may also produce migration from the country to the cities. All of these changes, Johnson argues, have the potential for generating pressures which, if the leaders permit, can produce revolution.

Such changes in the environment (whether from foreign or domestic sources) usually affect the society's values as well. Many developing countries, for example, have recently had to cope with the effects of modern technologies on their traditional value structures. Even some modern societies, such as France, have had to contend with the effects of foreign cultural contact (in this case, American). Similar problems of cultural contact have been faced by the Japanese as well. They have tried to adapt a traditional Asian value structure to the demands of Western technology and innovation.

As stated earlier, the sociology of political violence also focuses on the effects of change in producing incompatible norms and values. Chapter 3 showed how certain group norms and values can stimulate violence both within and between groups. Southwood, in discussing cultural change (or what Johnson calls "value-changing"), argues that violence will not occur unless there is some valued position, resource, or relationship which is believed to be threatened by the pressures of change. Neil Smelser, in examining normative and value strain (1962), considers the effect of change on various roles and sectors within a society. A prime instance of normative strain is the relationship between the peasants and the aristocracy (citing Tocqueville). Here, the obligations of the peasants remained while the feudal responsibilities of the aristocracy declined (1962: 61). Smelser argues that the norms governing the behavior between peasants and aristocrats were changing, and as these norms changed, strain was produced. Tocqueville contended that such normative strain has the greatest potential for violence, and Smelser agrees. To take a more contemporary example, Smelser says, consider a political party that consistently violates norms against the use of coercion to obtain votes. This action not only threatens the political system but also prevents other political actors from attaining their goals. Furthermore, it undermines the power of traditional means for attaining these goals (1962: 62).

Such normative strains affect the values—and therefore the legitimacy—of the political system. Where change initially produced only specific conflicts of interests between groups, these differences may now become generalized as groups probe the basis of each other's divergent interests. According to Smelser, these value strains often bring the very legitimacy of values into question. When this occurs, violent attacks against an "immoral" system or group may result. According to Von der Mehden, the belief develops that because the system or group is immoral or illegitimate, it is moral and legitimate to violently attack it: "almost all defenders of violent politics, whether on the national or international level, have asserted that their acts were moral, or at least that the immorality of the enemy was of such magnitude as to justify violence (1973: 28–29).[12]

Most instances of political violence involve structural or cultural strain. Knowing only that the system is strained, however, is insufficient for predicting whether violence will result. Like purely economic interpretations, sociological explanations alone have proven difficult to sustain. The social setting of individuals, groups, and societies does generate conditions that are conducive to political violence. However, these objective conditions interact not only with each other but with subjective factors as well. As Eckstein and others have pointed out, a wide variety of objective social conditions appear to be capable of creating political violence. What we should avoid is linking any of these social conditions directly to political violence (Eckstein, 1965, as cited in Feierabend et al., 1972: 20).

SUBJECTIVE CONSIDERATIONS

The Revolutionary State of Mind If we cannot link structural change, value stress, and economic considerations directly to political violence, how can we account for their effects? Once again, Eckstein has an answer. He suggests that instead of thinking of the relationship between setting and violence in direct terms—for example, as setting (the stimulus) creating violence (the response)—we should think of the relationship as being mediated by certain psychological factors.[13] In particular, the effects of social setting interact with certain attitudes, values, beliefs, and perceptions to produce a potential for violence. These factors, and the explanations based on them, are referred to as "behavioral hypotheses" (Eckstein, 1964), the "behavioral approach" (Stone, 1966), and "psychological explanations" (Kramnick, 1972; Tilly, 1963). Whatever we call it, this approach argues that certain psychological motivations are important in producing potential political violence. This potential for violence is referred to as the *revolutionary state of mind*. The primary concern of this approach is to identify the motivations that produce violence and the perceptions, hopes, expectations, and frustrations of revolutionary actors. In this approach, states of mind are crucial.[14] Two of the most articulate spokesmen of this "states of mind" approach are Ted R. Gurr and David Schwartz. Since their work illustrates many of the organizing principles discussed earlier in the text, let us examine their work separately and in more detail.

Deprivation and Frustration[15] According to Ted R. Gurr, the most likely social psychological precondition of political violence is the perception of relative deprivation. The basic principles of relative deprivation have already been discussed. Relative deprivation, to review, is a discrepancy between what people think they are entitled to and what they think they actually can obtain. It is a form of collective frustration. This collective state of mind Gurr uses to analyze social phenomena. Several other scholars have also adapted individual psychological concepts such as frustration and deprivation, to social settings (Feierabend et al., 1969 and 1972). They, too, see deprivation or systemic frustration as the basis of most forms of social strife, and they argue that this strife or aggression occurs when people's social needs and aspirations are thwarted.

Gurr's theory of political violence rests on a frustration-aggression hypothesis. Using this hypothesis, Gurr links relative deprivation with political violence. Basically, what happens is this: Certain economic conditions and social relationships block people's social aspirations; relative deprivation results; as this deprivation persists, frustration sets in;[16] this blockage generates anger and social discontent that must be vented; aggression in the form of political violence is one satisfying response.

Relative deprivation can originate in many of the objective preconditions we have identified—such as new modes of life, which strain the structures and values of society, and new modes of thinking, which affect traditional roles and relationships (Gurr, 1970: 92–154).

Let us leave the relationship between relative deprivation and the revolutionary state of mind and deal with frustration-aggression. The central premise of the frustration-aggression theory is that aggression results from frustration. As originally stated, this theory assumed that aggression was *always* a consequence of frustration. Today, this position has been modified. Many different responses can be produced by frustration; aggression is only one of them. This produces some difficulties for Gurr's theory. When does relative deprivation produce frustration that results in aggression (political violence), and when does it create some other response?

Gurr suggests that the relationship between relative deprivation and frustration-aggression is complex. We must also take into account the emotional state of anger. That is, when relative deprivation produces frustration and anger, then aggression usually results. Frustration accompanied by anger is most likely to produce political violence, not frustration alone. Including the emotion of anger, Gurr believes, does not refute the frustration-aggression thesis. As he puts it:

> The basic explanatory element that frustration-aggression theory contributes to the understanding of human conflict, and especially to the analysis of political violence, is the principle that anger functions as a drive. In the recent reformulation of the theory . . . the perception of frustration is said to arouse anger. Aggressive responses tend to occur only when they are evoked by an external cue, that is when the angered person sees an attackable object or person he associates with the source of frustration. (1970: 34)

The new notion of anger is only one of several qualifications of the original frustration-aggression thesis.[17] However, some problems still exist. Elton B. McNeil points out that even when aggressive behavior does occur, it may be disguised, displaced onto nonfrustrating objects or persons, and even delayed. Thus it becomes difficult, if not impossible, to relate frustration to specific acts of aggression (1964). Gurr's model of relative deprivation provides a good solution. If aggression can in fact take various forms of violence, such as a revolution in one case and an act of terrorism in another, how can we trace these forms back to the frustrating state and from there even further back to the specific form of relative deprivation? Gurr suggests some general points that may be useful. For example, civil war is most likely to occur if relative deprivation is intense with respect to a number of political, social, and economic values. Turmoil, on the other hand, is likely when dissidents are poorly organized, where the regime has the resources and is willing to use coercion, where mass relative deprivation affects few economic and political values, and where dissidents are concentrated in areas under regime control. Gurr goes on to identify conditions that also maximize the likelihood of conspiracy (1970: 338–347).

Gurr's model can only link several types of relative deprivation (along with mediating factors) with three types of political violence; still, this is a substantial achievement. Kramnick is concerned, however, that Gurr cannot predict the direction or target of the various types of violence. Kramnick asks why, for example, do the discontented turn their frustration on the government during revolution and not on some other actor (1972: 56)? Gurr offers no answer to this question.[18] This tells us that there are probably important qualifications in the relative deprivation-frustration-aggression thesis. However, this thesis has not been refuted.[19]

Political Alienation The most likely social psychological precondition of political violence, according to David Schwartz, is people's alienation from their political system. Like Gurr, Schwartz contends that political violence can be traced, at least in part, to certain states of mind. Unlike Gurr, however, Schwartz believes it is the perception of estrangement, rather than relative deprivation, that creates a potential for violence. This notion of estrangement or alienation is found extensively in the literature—for example, in Sears and McConahay's theory of new urban blacks and racial violence. The thesis is that people begin by withdrawing their political interest, support, and loyalty; political violence then follows (Brinton, 1938; Huntington, 1968; Schwartz, 1972). Schwartz contends that withdrawal involves people "who no longer share common orientations to the political system" (1972: 60). In other words, people's withdrawal and their eventual active alienation can be traced to a perceived conflict between themselves and their political system. This value conflict develops in several distinct stages, ranging from allegiance (i.e., shared values between self and government) to alienation (i.e., dissimilar values and withdrawal).[20] Each of these stages, and the transitions between them, reflect varying degrees of cognitive balance between personal and systemic values.

STAGES OF POLITICAL ALIENATION

Political alienation begins when people perceive that the values of the government differ from and conflict with their own political values. What causes this perception is not clear. Schwartz is not particularly interested in identifying the causes of value conflict. He is more concerned with the attitudes and behavior that usually result when value conflict occurs.

According to Schwartz, when individuals see that their values are different from those of the political system, they must try to bring these conflicting values into balance because imbalance is a psychologically disturbing state. Schwartz contends that balancing begins when a people start to reevaluate the government and its policies. Behaviorally they can begin to modify their political behavior by becoming more activist (e.g., attempting to reform the system) or by withdrawing (e.g., becoming passively alienated from politics).

Should the value conflict continue, people may either perceive that the political system cannot resolve the conflict or that they cannot operate within the system to bring about the desired value changes (Schwartz, 1972: 63). These perceptions produce feelings of frustration, tension, and anger. Similar cognitive and emotional states (that accompany feelings of political futility) have been discussed in chapter 4. This resulting sense of futility is an important motive force for aggression.

By the time people have experienced this frustration and futility, Schwartz states, they have also withdrawn their attention, affection, and involvement from the political system. Whether they are partly or totally estranged is important in determining whether political violence will result. If they are completely alienated, the potential for revolution is greater (Schwartz, 1972: 64).

The political system, of course, is not a passive actor in this alienation process. The government may, for example, punish even partial and passive political withdrawal. Some countries impose fines if the citizen does not vote. In more extreme cases (as we shall soon see when we examine the uses of political terror), the government may confuse passive withdrawal with active opposition and respond with severe coercion. In either case, threat is generated, and this threat stimulates what Schwartz calls "threat-coping" behavior (1972: 65). Something akin to threat-coping behavior was noted in chapter 4, when we saw how ghetto blacks actively explored alternative means of protest. The search is for some alternative political channel whereby people can feel effective. If these alternatives do not exist, or if they are perceived as being blocked (as in the case of the new urban blacks), then threat is further reinforced. More important, total alienation may set in. "When all the major political institutions relevant to the attainment of the politicized values are seen as closed (both to self and self-surrogates), the threat and frustration generalizes to the system as a whole. . . . " (1972: 65).

Finally, complete and active alienation occurs when frustration can no longer be vented; when the last personal and systemic alternatives have been considered and found useless; when anger and rage become incapacitating. When this stage of alienation is reached, the individual is "cognitively available" for political violence. While Schwartz's theory goes on to examine organizational and tactical factors, we will stop here and summarize his work.

Schwartz's theory is an excellent synthesis of many insights into the nature of political violence. Drawing from the literature of political science, Schwartz focuses on the conflict that can often arise between contending political ideas and values. In this sense, his work is in the tradition of Samuel Huntington, who argues that in explaining political violence one must study the interplay of *political* values and norms. More specifically (and again like Huntington), Schwartz contends that it is a conflict of principles (i.e., values) that stimulates revolutionary behavior. Schwartz unfortunately does not identify the causes of this conflict of principles; this is a serious limitation in his theory. Reading between the lines of his work, however, one might conclude that he would see *change* as the force that causes value conflict. If this interpretation is valid, then his notions of the sociology of value conflict and the causes of these conflicts are similar to those of Neil Smelser, whose work we have already analyzed. In this sense, Schwartz's work relates well to certain sociological findings on the origins and processes of revolution. What distinguishes Schwartz from Huntington (politics) and Smelser (social system), for example, is that he focuses on the political psychology of revolution. Like Gurr, he adapts individual psychological terms to the study of social issues.

It would be a mistake, I think, to put too much emphasis on the different nuances of these psychological theories. Not only is Schwartz's work broadly similar to Gurr's (e.g., they both deal with the social psychological origins of violence), but as Feierabend et al. (1972) point out, they are linked to each other through their use of the frustration-aggression model. For example, Schwartz emphasizes the anger, range, and frustration that accompany the passively alienated person. He goes on to describe how a feeling of futility emerges, reinforces existing frustrations, and further stimulates discontent and anger. As attempts to resolve the conflict fail, as goals continue to be blocked, and as alternative avenues of action are closed, threat perception and tension build up. The potential for violent action emerges. All of these notions can fit clearly into the context of existing psychological terms such as "value inconsistency," "estrangement," and "relative deprivation" that help us to differentiate finer details of complex states of mind. These theories also add immeasurably to our understanding of political violence by developing models that suggest how economic, political, social, and psychological determinants of revolution can be interrelated. Even if we grant that these interrelationships are not always specifically linked, the researchers do serve an important function by emphasizing that their models are complementary rather than mutually exclusive.

Mediating Conditions: Additional Factors

At this point, violence may seem to be directly related to economic, social, political, and social psychological conditions. However, most scholars agree that whether political violence actually occurs (even with the necessary preconditions) depends on a number of mediating factors. These factors, as we shall see, can both inhibit and facilitate the potential for violence.

INHIBITORS OF VIOLENCE

Coercion, Retribution, and Repression One of the most obvious mediating forces in the development of political violence is the government. And since all governments control organized force, most scholars have assumed that a government's capacity and willingness to use repression is related to the likelihood of political violence. Not only can governmental force deter violence, but should violence occur, the government can suppress it. The effectiveness of this suppression is closely related to the likelihood and intensity of subsequent violence (Gurr, 1968b: 269). In a purely revolutionary context, it was Eckstein (1965) who argued that the main target of repression is the revolutionaries (cited in Feierabend et al., 1972: 24).[21]

Under certain conditions, however, repression can actually facilitate violence. Gurr hypothesizes that "if aggression is prevented by fear of retribution or by retribution itself, this interference is frustrating and increases anger" (1968b: 270). In the short run, the very coercion which is being used to stop the political violence may contribute to it. This is never more true, as we shall see, than when terror and terrorist tactics are employed. Repression is generally effective, however, when governments are sensitive in its application.

Institutional Support, Diversions, and Incumbents Repression and counterviolence may, at best, be potentially self-defeating tactics in preventing or controlling political violence. Another strategy that is supposedly less controversial and more effective, in the long run, is providing a "safety valve"—alternative channels for discontent. With this ploy, discontent is minimized, and that crucial sense of futility necessary for generating revolutionary potential is checked. Further, if the alternatives are perceived as being effective, the regime will actually use them to build support. This institutional support, according to Gurr, is more long-lasting than force, because it establishes rewarding patterns of action for those engaged in it (1970: 274). The threat of force, on the other hand, has inconsistent effects.[22] Effective alternative institutions include political parties, labor unions, social organizations, and religious movements. Through such institutions, people not only are able to displace their tensions but often can find alternative means of goal attainment.[23] Whatever functions are served (i.e., displacement or goal attainment), the usual result is that anger is diminished because a sense of futility has been averted.

Another force that can often divert energies from political violence, according to Eckstein, is "diversionary mechanisms." These consist of almost any action or event that "channels psychic energies away from revolutionary objectives—which provide[s] other outlets for aggression or otherwise absorb[s] emotional tension" (Eckstein, 1965, as cited in Feierabend et al., 1972: 24). One of the most supposedly useful diversionary mechanisms is military actions or "adventures." Richard Rosencrance (1963) and Quincy Wright (1965) have stated that within a country, groups seeking self-preservation may be driven to a foreign policy of conflict. This may account for some of the conflict behavior within and between countries. Whereas such foreign adventurism rarely results in war, Rosencrance and Wright believe that regimes often use external military operations as a diversion. They act to displace the attention and hostility of a dissatisfied population onto a foreign enemy and thus prevent domestic revolution. The empirical findings on this relationship, however, are mixed. Tanter has found a small relationship between domestic and foreign conflict (1966: 62), Rummel very little (1963). Additional studies have proved inconclusive. One thing does seem certain: Foreign military adventures must be successful. Only then can this conflict behavior hold the internally troubled society together. If it fails, it can act as a powerful force to intensify the pressures within the nation. Eckstein speculates that Czarist Russia may have entered World War I in part for diversionary reasons. Its military defeat by Germany stimulated revolutionary forces already at work (Eckstein, 1965, as cited in Feieraband et al., 1972: 25). Military diversions, like the threat of force, are not particularly "safe" alternatives for a regime under stress. Their effects are just as likely to facilitate anger as to restrain it. Alternatives, however, seem to be a relatively safe and effective means for displacing anger through peaceful protest.

Terrain and Traditions Land features that might slow down a revolution and inexperience in using violence are two important inhibitors of political violence. Eckstein notes, however, that such conditions usually do not prevent violence if all the necessary preconditions are prevalent. Rather, he argues, these conditions can affect the probability of success once violence has begun (Eckstein, 1965, as cited in Feierabend et al., 1972). Gurr shares Eckstein's view. For example, he sees the terrain and transportation network of a country as only limitating the insurrection, not preventing it from beginning (Gurr, 1970). Open, flat terrain cut off from sources of supply, for example, would not be of much advantage to insurgents. Neither would an area where lack of communications cuts people off from one another. In both cases, revolutionary action is hampered—but the revolution *has* begun.

Certain psychocultural conditions may also enable the regime to control strife. The most important seems to be whether a people has a cultural tradition and historical experience with violent strife. Gurr (1970) points out that a disposition to violence may be deeply rooted in the culture. Such cultural dispositions, in turn, are the result of historical experience and subsequent socialization processes that shape attitudes about the desirability of aggression, the rights and obligations of people, and the responsibilities of the government. These norms, attitudes, and beliefs were discussed in earlier chapters. Our cross-cultural analysis of the definition of war and peace, for example, illustrated how people acquire norms about aggression as part of their history and their daily lives. These enduring psychocultural states can present obstacles to violence when it appears in new circumstances. Just as there are violent societies whose cultural traditions encourage aggression, so too are there peaceful ones whose traditions encourage nonviolence even where there is reason for aggression.[24]

FACILITATORS OF VIOLENCE

We have seen how retribution, diversion, terrain, and tradition can inhibit political violence. However, under certain circumstances, each of these mediating factors could facilitate aggression. For example, a society could develop violent tendencies which would be passed on to its members in the form of socialized attitudes about aggression. For instance, if aggression is rewarding, (i.e., finds social support), people are more likely to resort to it in future social actions. Not all the facilitators of political violence, however, can be accounted for by simply reversing these inhibitors. There are several important facilitators that merit separate discussion. Among these are group dynamics, foreign support for insurgents and incumbents, and lack of regime legitimacy. Let us discuss each briefly.

Group Dynamics We have seen in Chapters 1, 2, and 3 how group structures, norms, and processes help shape the thoughts and behavior of its members. The group provides an important normative support. As we saw in the Robber's Cave experiment, group cohesiveness often promotes intergroup hostilities by supporting aggression through group values and goals.

A group can also facilitate violence by protecting its members from coercive retribution (Gurr). This is done primarily through anonymity but also by its own force capability. As will be pointed out later, one of the primary functions of terrorism is to build morale within the insurgent group, bolstering its cohesiveness while developing the feeling that only through insurgency can members be truly safe.

The group provides the basis for the emergence and growth of the organization. This is probably its most vital facilitating function. As Schwartz points out, if it were not for the emergence of an appropriate organization, "it is conceivable that substantial elements of previously participant population sectors could remain in the stage of initial, passive alienation" (1971: 118). This is an important link between individual alienation and collective anger and subsequent social violence. Space does not permit us to discuss how these organizations emerge. Basically, however, passive political alienation is needed. This alienation, the spur for organization growth, is then turned into more active political behavior (i.e., radicalization). According to Schwartz and others, as the revolutionary organization expands, it is likely to seek outside support. It is to this foreign support that we now shall turn.

Foreign Support A book could be written about the effects of foreign support on the success or failure of political violence. Gurr has found that as foreign intervention rises from the sale of military hardware to the widespread use of foreign "advisors," the level of civil strife increases (Gurr, 1970: 269–271). Karl Deutsch has written a stimulating work on external involvement in civil wars (as cited in Eckstein, 1964: 100–110). He points out that in its later stages, civil war can hardly be distinguished from a "war by proxy," where two countries fight on the soil of a third country. In the latter case, foreign conflict is disguised as a civil war within the third country, where preponderantly foreign goals and tactics are being fought over (1964: 102). Examples of war by proxy abound in history, among them America's recent support of President Mobuto of Zaire against Cuban-backed Shaba insurgents and, possibly, the Vietnam War.

How does this outside intervention affect the course of internal violence? Again, Deutsch suggests some interesting possibilities. For one thing, outside intervention might affect recruitment and attrition rates as one actor or the other is perceived as having the backing of a powerful sponsor. In some cases, the people may feel that with this new support they are more protected from retribution and thus join the "cause." In the group without support, the attrition rate may grow for the same reasons but with the opposite effects. An appeal for foreign support may be misconstrued by the people as a betrayal of their homeland. As Deutsch points out, if the two contending factions in a country have more in common culturally and historically with each other than they do with the intervening country, then outside aid may actually weaken the cause (1964: 109).[25]

Lack of Regime Legitimacy[26] It has long been assumed that a positive view of the government increases its stability. This stability results from two dimensions of support—compliance with the policies of the government and identification with its aspirations and values. These form the basis of the political system's legitimacy. Gurr says that as long as people view their political institutions, processes, and objectives as proper and deserving of support, the system enjoys "legitimacy" (1970: 185).[27]

Gurr has found that regime legitimacy is important in the development of civil strife. For example, legitimacy is linked with coercive potential. Legitimate regimes tend to have large and loyal military and police forces. These capabilities can, in turn be used to limit civil strife and in some cases, as we have seen, to abolish it. High legitimacy, therefore, generates high military loyalty. Low legitimacy, on the other hand, may be associated with high levels of strife. According to Huntington and others, political legitimacy is so desirable that its very absence may create a potential for strife. Gurr appears to agree. He believes that in the absence of regime legitimacy, a sense of deprivation may arise. This may eventually be expressed in either alienation or a predisposition for political violence.[28]

SUMMARY

Many forces hinder the development of social discontent and aggression. Among them are coercion by the regime, alternative channels for discontent, foreign military diversions, physical terrain, and cultural traditions. Under given conditions, these factors can prevent discontent from turning into political violence. On the other hand, there are many facilitators of violence. There include the ability of an insurgent group to protect and advance the interests of its supporters, foreign support, and the erosion of regime legitimacy. No discussion of the causes of political violence is complete without an examination of these mediating factors.

Terror and Political Violence[29]

Of all the forms of political violence, none are more controversial than acts of terrorism. The use of terror is a basic tool of political violence—it is used in coups, secessionist drives, and civil wars. It has become one of the basic weapons of guerrilla warfare. Terrorism is economical; it requires few resources, and the results seem to outweigh by far the resources expended.

Terror and terrorism have various meanings. For our discussion, let us define terror as both an induced state of mind in an individual or group, and as a tool of political behavior employing the threat or use of violence for political objectives. Terror as a psychological weapon is designed to produce anxiety, general disorientation, despair, withdrawal, and fear. As a political instrument, terror is employed or threatened to gain political, economic, psychological, and even military objectives. It is used by a group that is seeking political power or control over the political system.[30]

There are many different forms of terrorism. In general, they are all violent and go well beyond the normal use of force within a society. Terrorism includes torture, assassination, massacre, bombing, and kidnapping.[31] The techniques ultimately selected vary, of course, with the situation and the objective. It has been suggested that the society's level of development helps determine which acts will be used (Aaron, 1974). In Kenya during the Mau Mau uprisings of the 1950s, black terrorists not only massacred their victims but also mutilated the European dead. Russian peasant partisans during World War II were also noted for acts of mutilation, particularly among their own people who had collaborated with the Germans. During Israel's struggle for independence in the 1940s, the Stern Gang and the Haganah (the Israeli defense army) resorted primarily to assassination, arson, and bombings. In the Middle East conflict between the Israelis and Palestinians in the 1970s, the Palestinians have used hijackings, bombings, and assassination. In both the Israeli and Palestinian cases, it has been argued that their selection of more sophisticated types of terror was due in part to the higher levels of development in their societies (Aaron, 1967). Cruder forms of terrorism, such as torture and mutilation, are more common (and probably more effective) in more traditional societies, such as Kenya or agrarian Russia.

THE OBJECTIVES OF TERRORISM

Terrorism, by its very nature, is a highly emotional subject. Because of its excessive violence, terrorism creates strong negative emotions in most observers.[32] Yet, as Brian Crozier rightly points out, we should not permit our emotions to convince us that terrorism is senseless or without motive. Like political violence in general, terrorism is based on goal-directed behavior. Crozier contends that the goals of terrorism determine the techniques selected. He identifies two distinct types of terrorism (1974: 127).

The first type is what he calls "disruptive terrorism." Its primary objectives are (1) to advertise the movement, (2) to build morale within the movement and among sympathizers outside the movement, (3) to demoralize and disorientate civil authorities, and (4) to provoke the authorities into alienating the citizens, either by becoming too repressive in response to terrorism or by causing popular social, economic, and political programs to suffer (1974: 127). The techniques most often associated with disruptive terrorism are airplane hijackings, kidnappings of prominent individuals, and murder of selected persons. If one had to select the clearest illustration of disruptive terrorism, one might choose the kidnapping and massacre of the eleven Israeli Olympic athletes in Munich in September 1972. As Crozier points out, the "Munich Massacre" gained worldwide publicity for the Black September Arab terrorists. It built morale within this faction of the Palestinian movement, and it helped to rally the young in many Arab countries.[33]

The second type of terrorism is what Crozier calls "coercive terrorism." In this case, the primary objectives are (1) to generally demoralize the population, weakening its ties with the government and instilling fear of the terrorist movement, and (2) to enforce obedience to the leaders of the insurgent political movement (1974: 128). Coercive terrorism is used primarily to punish deviation within the movement. "Traitors," "Collaborators," and so on, are terrorized—by torture, for example—to punish their deviation. This punishment, in turn, serves as a vivid reminder to other would-be deviators within the movement. This is a favorite tactic of the IRA in Northern Ireland. Their acts of assassination or torture demonstrate to both insiders and outsiders the IRA's coercive potential. It does not matter whether we call these objectives "disruptive-coercive" (like Crozier) or "proximate" (like Thornton). What is important to remember is this: The ultimate objective of terrorism is to influence political behavior.

To do this, certain psychological responses must be created in both the movement and the general population. Thomas Thornton (as cited in Eckstein, 1964) has examined these psychological objectives of terrorism. Let us explore some of these briefly.[34]

The ultimate psychological response of terrorism is disorientation—the isolation of individuals from their society. Thornton states:

> Disorientation occurs when the victim does not know what he fears, when the source of his fear lies outside his field of experience. . . . By dissociating his victims from structures associated with the incumbents, the insurgent has removed the target from the ranks of the opposition. He has little to fear, for terrorized victims are in a condition associated with anxiety neuroses and are thus unlikely to do much except look to their own security. In searching for safety and reassurance, however, most will attempt to locate new structures of authority that can alleviate their aloneness and give promise of being capable of dealing with the changed situation . . . it now remains for the insurgents to demonstrate that they are capable of infusing meaning into the unstructured environment. (In Eckstein, 1964: 83)

The intermediary psychological responses contributing to this disorientational neurosis include fright, anxiety, and despair (Thornton, as cited in Eckstein, 1964: 80–81). Each of these states in its own way is a powerful weapon. Fright, for example, evokes a state of danger with which individuals must deal. Since, in most cases, this danger is a novel experience, alternative forms of behavior must be explored. In short, fear may cause us to reorder our subjective and behavioral priorities. Interestingly enough, however, this state of fear must be constantly reinforced with increasingly intense experiences. For example, villagers who have witnessed a series of assassinations will cease to be frightened once they perceive that the acts form a pattern. As Thornton points out, once the individual perceives that the terrorist's act "fits into the pattern of his previous experience" he will learn how to deal with this type of action (as cited in Eckstein, 1964: 80).

With either increased violence or acts that fall outside perceived patterns, the terrorist can achieve the next intermediate state: anxiety. As defined by Thornton, anxiety is a psychological state of uneasiness accompanied by fear. Unlike the state of mind that we have just examined, however, this fright is fear of the unknown. This uneasiness over some vaguely defined impending event or action creates psychological discomfort and some disorientation. In crowded cities, something akin to this anxiety is created by random acts of bombing against selected targets. As a primarily disruptive device, the IRA bombings in London in 1975–1976 were successful in creating anxiety because they were unexpected, seemingly random, and occurred in locations where people tended to congregate (e.g., streets in front of crowded shops, shops themselves, historical points of interest, and subways). Many scholars and governments interested in countering terrorism are now finding that cities are highly conducive to generating or intensifying anxiety.[35]

The final state that Thornton identifies is despair. Here, fear and anxiety are so intense that individuals begin to lose hope. This may focus on their own helplessness or on the society's inability to protect them. In either case, when this extreme anxiety occurs, intense disorientation sets in. Individuals may now try to withdraw themselves and their support from existing institutions and practices. Should that occur, the individual is then lost to the existing political, social, or economic systems. The insurgent movement has realized one of its political ends (i.e., detached the target from the opposition) by generating the intermediary psychological states leading to disorientation.

THE PHASES OF TERROR

The use and effectiveness of terror involves many considerations. Most of the existing research on these factors deals with the use of terror in revolutionary or civil wars. But as Crozier rightly points out, terror "has also been used by many groups or movements that do not practice anything recognizable as revolutionary war" (1974: 128). However, since this latter situation has not been widely studied,[36] we will examine the stages, patterns, and dynamics of terrorism as part of a revolutionary civil war.

Stage 1   The need for terror usually develops soon after the insurgent movement is organized. The first priority is to consolidate the movement itself. Terrorism is needed both to protect the movement from counterinsurgent actions and to guard it against infiltration and internal deviation. While this coercive terrorism is going on, disruptive terrorism begins. The use of terror in this initial phase of revolution is important. It is now that the movement must gain publicity, build morale, discredit and demoralize its opponents, and rule the areas and populations it may control. At this stage, timing and subtelty in applying terrorism are crucial.

During stage 1, indiscriminate and uncontrolled terrorism can end the movement even before it has begun to expand. The terrorist is confronted with a number of problems. At this point, for example, the incumbents usually have an immense psychological advantage with the general population. Thornton points out that although the government does not enjoy wholehearted support on all issues, it can count on a general commitment to the existing social system. Insurgents, on the other hand, "represent an alienated factor, which the organism of the society will normally be predisposed to cast out" (as cited in Eckstein, 1964: 74). The objective of the terrorist movement is to disrupt this commitment. The question is: What terrorist tactics are to be employed, how much violence is to be used and how indiscriminate must it appear?

Terror is a double-edged weapon of political violence. Indiscriminate terrorism, for example, may alienate the very target groups it is trying to win over. In the Malayan insurgency of 1948–1951, popular dissatisfaction with the government was replaced by a greater animosity toward the rebels. According to Aaron, when the leaders of the Malayan Races Liberation Army (MRLA) realized their error, they curtailed their action. This move, however, raised another problem. Once the terror was reduced, the Malayans began to think that the MRLA had weakened and ceased to accede to its demands (1974: AS-1–7, 8).[37]

The constant use of terror, however, reduces its psychological effect. Also, when terror continues to be used and the government forces remain strong, the protracted terror appears as the irrational action of a dying movement. But this may not be immediately apparent to the people, who have trouble in perceiving the situation. Usually, they hear only of isolated acts and gain little or no information on terrorist trends. In stage 1 of the revolution, the government may see only uncontrolled terrorism. It is clear at the local level, however, that the terror is conscious and controlled. Here the people see that only certain groups are affected, such as government officials, teachers, and agricultural specialists. Thornton points out that at this point, the discriminate use of terrorism plays an important role:

> Any element that tends to make terror more unknowable and therefore more disorienting contributes to the creation of anxiety. . . . [Most people] do not become anxious in the face of highly discriminate terrorism, but if

they believe they are confronted with seemingly indiscriminate terror, they will experience the required sense of personal involvement . . . the terrorist must always have the distinction between *apparent* indiscrimination and *actual* indiscrimination clearly in mind, if he is to succeed. (In Eckstein 1964: 81)

Stage 2 The second phase of the movement begins when the insurgents engage in widespread armed activities. The guerrilla forces expand rapidly in size and firepower. Their demands on the people for men, supplies, information, and support also increase. Aaron contends that during this stage, terror tactics reach their greatest intensity and scope. A spectacular terrorist action may be mounted to promote attention and bolster morale. The abduction of Argentine racing driver Juan Fangio by the Cuban underground is an example of such actions (Aaron, 1974: AS-1–6).

In stage 2, terrorism is effective only when it is used for a purpose. It must be used in conjunction with propaganda, covert political tactics, military action, and possibly foreign aid and actions. According to Thornton, this stage of expansion marks a transition from purely agitational terror to a combination of agitation and enforcement terror in occupied territories (as cited in Eckstein, 1964: 94). It is now that insurgent terrorism can often deal most effectively with counterinsurgency—hopefully causing the regime to overreact. If the government, for example, responds by using detention, torture, or murder of innocent citizens, it runs the risk of alienating its own people. Caught between the terrorism of the insurgents and the counterterror of the government, the people suffer greatly. They may not know which side to turn to for protection.

Stage 3 In the third phase of the movement, terror as a basic weapon is largely replaced by large conventional military forces. As Thornton points out, agitational terror ceases but coercive and enforcement terror continue even after the incumbents have been defeated. In some cases, enforcement terror may reach its highest levels even after victory. The case of Cambodia is particularly illustrative.[38] Following their victory the Communist forces engaged in a reign of terror against former Cambodian elites, and the Khmer Rouge forced the evacuation of most of the cities. The entire population of Cambodia's capital, Phnom Penh, was forced out into the countryside to resettle without food or shelter. Tens of thousands of people are reported to have perished in these resettlement programs and subsequent enforcement policies. Interestingly enough, in Vietnam, where most observers predicted excesses, there was minimum enforcement and no widespread coercive terrorism. In fact, on assuming power, the Communists seem to have made a conscious effort to eliminate regime violence as quickly and thoroughly as possible.

SUMMARY

Our objective has been to discuss terror as a technique of political violence. Terror has been defined as a state of mind induced by the threat or use of violence for political ends. Murders, therefore, are not terror unless the psychological states of fear, anxiety, and/or despair are achieved in the target populations. Other forms of terror, such as kidnapping, hijacking, bombing, and assassination, are also not considered terrorism unless the action makes (either implicit or explicit) political demands, suggests alternative behaviors, and states what will happen if the demands are ignored.

Terrorism can be classified according to its objectives, its tactical considerations, and its stages. Some scholars have distinguished between two types of terror: specific and general. In specific terror the victims are selected, and their reason for dying is clearly identified for the other members of the target population. The expected behavior of the people is made clear through the specific act of terrorism. Selective, discriminate terrorism can be used to disrupt the relationships between the people and their government. Generalized, or indiscriminate, terror is more ambiguous with respect to goals, targets, and expected resulting behavior in the target populations. Victims of such acts appear to have been selected at random. As we have emphasized previously, terrorism often must appear to be indiscriminate in order to achieve certain psychological states in the target. The destruction of crops and livestock in a farm community is an example of generalized terror since the population of the village is given no warning and no opportunity to alter their political support. There are no demands, appropriate alternatives, or probable consequences before the act is carried out. The act appears primarily to have been punishing behavior. The victims may even include potential and real supporters of the terrorist movement. These acts of violence are used infrequently, because general terror tends to cause apathy among some target groups and hostility among others. Indiscriminate terrorism involves a calculated risk.

Terrorism is designed to accomplish one or more of the following objectives: (1) to publicize the existence and political objectives of the terrorist group both within and outside of the state; (2) to build morale within the terrorist organization while at the same time demoralizing the opposition; (3) to disrupt and, where necessary, destroy the framework of the society, thereby psychologically isolating individuals and denying their skills and resources to the incumbents; and (4) to force reprisals by the incumbents in the hope that they will overreact, alienating their own people and disrupting the society.

While we still know very little about the dynamics of terrorist movements, they appear to move through several stages. In the beginning, agitational terror is used by a small group, for disruptive and coercive purposes. As the movement gains support and wins control over certain areas of the country, agitational terror is supplemented with enforcement terror designed to ensure obedience to the movement. As the insurgents are able to mount large-scale military operations, their need for terrorism declines. By the time they win, only selective coercive enforcement occurs. During the consolidation stage of the campaign, terrorism may or may not be widespread, as shown by contrasting experiences in Cambodia and Vietnam.

Patterns of Political Violence: Summary

Political violence is a response to various interrelated social conditions and psychological states. These determinants create discontent—a disposition to engage in aggressive behavior. There are many causes of discontent. It may emerge when people perceive an intolerable gap between their economic expectations and actual conditions. It can also develop when social forces trigger fundamental changes in the society's institutions and values. The resulting strain can generate discontent where there was none, or it can heighten frustration and disorientation that already exist.

By shifting emphasis, it could be argued that another determinant of discontent is relative deprivation—a perceived discrepancy between what people expect and what they know they can get. Relative deprivation results not only in discontent but also in a predisposition to see aggression as a solution. Whether political violence results depends on the intensity of discontent, which can vary from dissatisfaction to deep anger. Prolonged frustration and even mild anger can cause alienation as well. This political estrangement, however, can quickly lead to active withdrawal, radicalization and violence, given a sense of intense futility and anger. The determinants of relative deprivation and alienation are both structural and psychological.

Social discontent can be tempered by a host of forces. Among them are the use of government coercion, traditions against the use of violence, inaccessible terrain, and alternative channels. The use of force generally results in more intense frustration among the people, who then turn against the coercive institutions and elites. In contrast, where the discontented can find alternative institutions to attain their objectives and/or hear their grievances, they are less likely to resort to violence. It is only when people experience intense futility and anger that violence becomes a satisfying mode of behavior. This sense of intense futility and rage may be facilitated by a number of forces: foreign support, a loss of regime legitimacy, and the emergence of protective insurgent organizations. Under certain conditions, intense discontent will turn into aggressive action.

Political violence can take many forms, the most controversial of which is terrorism. Its objectives are in response to the futility and anger of the society. Its tactical considerations, phases, and ultimate success are linked to changes in both the general determinants of discontent and the forces that mediate frustration.

Notes*

1. The format of this chapter is somewhat new. Rather than discussing one manifestation of political violence in detail, as with the Detroit riot in chapter 4, we will examine several types of political violence in different locations.

2. There are two outstanding reviews of the literature on "revolutions" (a term, as we shall see, that is often used in connection with "political violence"). These are: Isaac Kramnick's "Reflections on revolution: Definition and Explanation in Recent Scholarship" and Lawrence Stone's "Theories of Revolution." A more recent but more limited review is Lee Sigelman and Miles Simpson's "A Cross-National Test of the Linkage Between Economic Inequality and Political Violence."

3. To a large extent, what follows may be considered a "review" of reviews on political violence.

4. For an example of both tendencies, see Isaac Kramnick's discussion of the psychological explanation of revolution" (1972: 53–62).

5. Most compare large groups of people rather than estimates based on a particular individual's role in conflict behavior. Davies, Gurr, Feierabend (1969), Sigelman and Simpson all use aggregate data.

6. Harry Eckstein was one of the first to make this distinction between "preconditions" and "precipitants." Eckstein suggested that a "precipitant" is an event which actually starts the violence, while "preconditions" are those circumstances which set the stage for the precipitant (as cited in Feierabend et al., *Anger, Violence, and Politics: Theories and Research*, p. 13). Our discussion focuses primarily on preconditions.

7. For many methodological reasons, cross-national aggregate research has been unable to find evidence for the relationship between economic inequality and political violence. These reasons range from poor indicators of economic inequality to equally poor measurements of political violence. It is perhaps a commentary on the persistence of this hypothesis (or the weakness of cross-national research) that there is still a widespread belief that economic inequality is a good predictor of political violence.

8. We are indebted to Kenneth Southwood for his review of the sociological literature on political violence, entitled "Riot and Revolt: Sociological Theories of Political Violence." It will be referred to in the following discussion.

9. The term "dysfunction" has been used primarily by Chalmers Johnson (1966). He argues that the social system maintains itself in a state of balance through certain functions, such as the processing of demands from the people. The social system survives and adjusts itself through such functions. Sometimes, however, a given function cannot be accommodated by the system. It may then threaten the existence or persistence of the system. When this happens, Johnson says, the result is a "dysfunction."

10. Southwood identifies a third type of change, which he calls "resource change."

---

*Complete citations for the works mentioned here will be found in the Bibliography, pages 133–135.

Since we have already discussed economic determinants of violence, this type of change is omitted here.

11. Johnson's work is particularly difficult to summarize because of his use of special analytical terminology. His technical language has been widely criticized by reviewers.

12. An extremely divisive side effect of normative and value strain is the creation of black-and-white thinking. Each group develops a moral self-image of itself and its actions. As Von der Mehden and others point out, there is the strong belief that God is on "our" side, whatever it happens to be.

13. Eckstein prefers mediational models to purely structural or psychological ones. As he puts it, "patterns of attitudes, while responsive to the settings in which men are placed, seem also to be, to an extent, autonomous of objective conditions, able to survive changes in these conditions or to change without clearly corresponding objective changes" (Eckstein, 1965, as cited in Feierabend, 1972: 19).

14. One should not make too sharp a distinction between psychological and objective states. They should always be thought of as complementing each other.

15. Gurr's theoretical model of civil strife contains several "mediating variables": level of institutionalization within the society, history of violence, and magnitude of countercoercion. These factors are thought to affect the relationship between relative deprivation and aggression. Rather than discuss them now, we will reserve analysis until we can discuss all of the precipitating preconditions of political violence.

16. As Gurr points out, the intensity of frustration and the resulting magnitude of violence depend upon how important the social aspirations are. See his discussion on pp. 59–91 of *Why Men Rebel*.

17. For a complete discussion of these reformulations, see Leonard Berkowitz (ed.), *Advances in Experimental Psychology* and *Aggression: A Social Psychological Analysis*.

18. The answer to Kramnick's question may be this: People turn their discontent on the government rather than on business or the church because they perceive that only the government has the resources, authority, and legitimacy to help them. When the government does not act, the discontented are doubly frustrated. They then turn their anger on the most visible frustrating target—the government, which may not have been the original agent but which can be identified as blocking their attempts at redress.

19. The biggest problem may not be with the thesis itself but with attempts to use it in explaining collective social behavior. There is still a great deal of dispute between scholars such as Gurr and those who contend that there is no evidence to support the transfer from individual to group behavior.

20. David Schwartz has developed a theory of revolutionary behavior that focuses on the interaction between attitudes and behavior during ten stages of development. These stages range from initial political alienation to a phase called "thermidor," where terror is dysfunctional even for the new revolutionary regime. In the discussion that follows, I will examine only stage 1 of Schwartz's theory—initial political alienation and withdrawal. Even here, Schwartz identifies eight separate substages, from allegiance to active political alienation. For a complete presentation of this provocative work, see David C. Schwartz, "A Theory of Revolutionary Behavior."

21. Harry Eckstein was one of the first scholars to systematically examine the forces working against revolutions. Later scholars such as Gurr (1968b, 1969, 1970), expanded on Eckstein's work and examined forces that facilitate as well as inhibit revolutions and other forms of political violence.

22. For an interesting examination of "Establishment Violence," see Fred Von der Mehden's chapter by that title in his *Comparative Political Violence*, pp. 37–52. He contends that all political regimes consider violence to be normal and necessary for ensuring domestic stability by deterring antisocial forces.

23. Gurr and others have shown that political violence tends to vary curvilinearly with coercion or retribution (both anticipated and actual). Violence is most likely when what Gurr calls, without elaborating, a "medium" level of force is used by the government. At this level, coercion by the government runs the risk of backfiring

because of the fear and anger it generates among its victims. For a detailed discussion of the various aspects of coercion in political violence, see Gurr's chapter entitled "The Coercive Balance" in *Why Men Rebel*, pp. 232–273. The relationships are extremely complex. Of necessity, factors such as duration, scope, and intensity of regime retribution, and loyalty of regime forces, have been omitted from this discussion. Later, in the discussion of terror, some of these points will be explored.

24. For a complete discussion of these psychocultural factors as they pertain to civil strife, see chapter 6 ("Perspectives on Violence and Politics: Socialization, Tradition and Legitimacy") of Gurr's *Why Men Rebel*. Two of his hypotheses are germane to our discussion and illustrate the notion of tradition and socialization: (1) The justification of political violence varies strongly with the society's history of political violence. (2) The justification of political violence varies moderately with the emphasis on extreme punishment in socialization (Gurr, 1970: pp. 170 and 165 respectively).

25. For one of the most recent and provocative studies of foreign intervention in the policies of another country, see James N. Rosenau's chapter entitled "Intervention as a Scientific Concept" in his work *The Scientific Study of Foreign Policy*. One of Rosenau's earlier works, *International Aspects of Civil Strife*, consists of a series of stimulating studies on this issue.

26. Several scholars consider the lack of regime legitimacy to be necessary in generating revolutionary potential. Because of its importance, they argue, legitimacy should not be treated as only a mediating factor. Gurr and Schwartz, however, view legitimacy as a mediating factor in regard to relative deprivation and political alienation. However, in later versions of his model, Gurr suggests that legitimacy has "a causal relationship with strife independent either of deprivation or the other intervening variables" (Feierabend et al., 1972: 206).

27. Gurr defines "regime" or "government" primarily in terms of its institutions. We have broadened this definition to include processes and values. These are necessary in discussing Schwartz's notions of alienation here, and the expanded definition does no conceptual damage to Gurr's model.

28. Lack of legitimacy does not have the same effect on all the types of civil strife Gurr has examined. For example, he finds that lack of legitimacy is strongly related to the intensity and scope of strife, but less so to either conspiracy or turmoil, and not at all to internal war (see Feierabend et al., 1972: 206, 208).

29. We wish to thank Major Robert S. Bowes, Department of the Army, U.S. Army Institute for Military Assistance, for providing material on guerrilla terrorism in Indochina. We have relied heavily on selected documents and reports in the following discussion.

33. Thomas Thornton states that terrorism may gain political ends in one of two ways—"either by mobilizing forces and reserves sympathetic to the cause of the insurgents, or by mobilizing forces and reserves that would normally be available to the incumbents" (in Eckstein, 1964: 75).

31. Some scholars, particularly Thornton, argue that the various targets of terror are selected for their symbolic content. Thornton even defines terror as a largely symbolic act and argues that its symbolic nature assures terror a high "rate of return." He states: "If the terrorist comprehends that he is seeking a demonstration effect, he will act upon targets with a maximum symbolic value" (1964: 77).

32. In an interesting survey of part of the literature on terrorism, entitled "Trends on Terror: The Analysis of Political Violence," J. Bowyer Bell observes that "one of the unwritten requirements of writing on terrorism is that abhorrence must be stressed; on the other hand, if revolution be the subject, one can be either in favor or opposed."

33. For a complete and vivid discussion of the Munich Massacre, see Serge Groussand's *The Blood of Israel: The Massacre of Israeli Athletes—The Olympics 1972*.

34. Thornton divides the psychological states (objectives) into positive and negative responses. Since there is only one positive response, enthusiasm, and since we have already discussed the objective of morale building, we will not examine it further here. Instead, we will focus on the negative responses of the people.

35. Richard Clutterbuck's *Protest and the Urban Guerrilla* is an interesting study of the insurgent movement into the cities. Other studies dealing with urban terrorism are V. Anthony Burton's *Urban Terrorism: Theory, Practice and Response* and J. Kohn and J. Litt's *Urban Guerrilla Warfare in Latin America.*

36. For a general survey of international terrorism and the organization's utilization of terror, see the "Hearings Before the Subcommittee on the Near East and South Asia of the Committee on Foreign Affairs, House of Representatives, Ninety-third Congress, Second Session, June 1974" [entitled *International Terrorism*]. A review of this survey is found in J. Bowyer Bell's review essay, cited in note 4. The discussion of stages that follows relies primarily on the work of Thomas Horton and Robert Aaron.

37. Aaron's work is documented in several sources: Office of Media Services, Department of State; Transition, No. 10, April 1967; and United States Army Institute for Military Assistance: PSOYP Officer Training Program, mimeographed documents. It is from this last source that our page citations are drawn.

38. For an excellent general study of the Cambodian conflict, see Sheldon W. Simon's *War and Politics in Cambodia.*

Bibliography

AARON, ROBERT. U.S. Army Institute for Military Assistance, PSOYP Officer Training Program, mimeo documents.

BELL, BOWYER, JR. "Trends on Terror: The Analysis of Political Violence. *World Politics*, 29 (1977), 476–488.

BERKOWITZ, LEONARD (ed.). *Advances in Experimental Psychology*, Vol. 11. New York: Academic Press, 1965.

———. *Aggression: A Social Psychological Analysis*. New York: McGraw-Hill, 1962.

BRINTON, CRANE. *The Anatomy of Revolution*. New York: Norton, 1938. *put. Clevels*

BURTON, ANTHONY V. *Urban Terrorism: Theory, Practice and Response*. New York: Free Press, 1975.

CLUTTERBUCK, RICHARD. *Protest and the Urban Guerrilla*. London: Cassell, 1973.

CROZIER, BRIAN. *A Theory of Conflict*. London: Hamish Hamilton, 1974.

DAVIES, JAMES C. "Toward a Theory of Revolution." *American Sociological Review*, 27 (February 1962), 5–19.

DEUTSCH, KARL W. "External Involvement in Internal War." In Harry Eckstein (ed.). *Internal War: Problems and Approaches*. New York: Free Press, 1964.

ECKSTEIN, HARRY. "On the Etiology of Internal Wars." *History and Theory*, 4 (1965), 133–163.

———, (ed). *Internal War*. New York: Free Press, 1964.

ENDLEMAN, SHALOM (ed.). *Violence in the Streets*. Chicago: Quadrangle, 1968.

FEIERABEND, IVO, ROSALIND FEIERABEND, and TED R. GURR. *Anger, Violence and Politics: Theories and Research*. Englewood Cliffs, N.J.: Prentice-Hall, 1972.

———, ———, and BETTY A. NESVOLD. "Social Change and Political Violence: Cross National Patterns." In Hugh Davis Graham and Ted R. Gurr (eds.), *Violence in America: Historical and Comparative Perspectives*. Washington, D.C.: National Commission on the Causes and Prevention of Violence, 1969.

GALTUNG, JOHAN. "A Structural Theory of Aggression." *Journal of Peace Research*, 11: 2 (1964), 95–119.

GROUSSAND, SERGE. *The Blood of Israel: The Massacre of Israeli Athletes—The Olympics 1972*. New York: Morrow, 1975.

GURR, TED R. *Why Men Rebel*. Princeton, N.J.: Princeton University Press, 1970.

————. "Urban Disorder: Perspectives from the Comparative Study of Civil Strife." *American Behavioral Scientist*, 11 (March–April 1968a), 50–55.

————. "Psychological Factors in Civil Violence." *World Politics*, 20 (January 1968b), 245–278.

————, with CHARLES RUTTENBERG. *The Conditions of Civil Violence: First Tests of a Causal Model.* Princeton N.J.: Center of International Studies, Princeton University, Research Monograph No. 28, 1967.

HUNTINGTON, SAMUEL P. *Political Order in Changing Societies.* New Haven: Yale University Press, 1968.

JOHNSON, CHALMERS. *Revolutionary Change.* Boston: Little, Brown, 1966.

————. *Revolution and the Social System.* Stanford, Conn.: The Hoover Institute on War, Revolution, and Peace, 1964.

KOHN, J., and J. LITT. *Urban Guerrilla Warfare in Latin America.* Boston: MIT Press, 1974.

KRAMNICK, ISAAC. "Reflections on Revolution: Definition and Explanation in Recent Scholarship." *History and Theory.* 11: 1 (1972), 26–63.

LIEF, HAROLD I. "Contemporary Forms of Violence." In Shalom Endlemen (ed.). *Violence in the Streets*, pp. 49–62. Chicago: Quadrangle, 1968.

McNEIL, ELTON B. (ed.). *The Nature of Human Conflict.* Englewood Cliffs, N.J.: Prentice-Hall, 1964.

NIEBURG, H. L. *Political Violence.* New York: St. Martin's, 1969.

ROSENCRANCE, RICHARD N. *Action and Reaction in World Politics.* Boston: Little, Brown, 1963.

ROSENAU, JAMES N. *The Scientific Study of Foreign Policy.* New York: Free Press, 1971.

————. *International Aspects of Civil Strife.* Princeton, N.J.: Princeton University Press, 1964.

RUMMEL, RUDOLPH J. "Dimensions of Conflict Behavior Within and Between Nations." *General Systems Yearbook*, 8 (1963), 1–50.

RUSSETT, BRUCE M. "Inequality and Instability: The Relation of Land Tenure to Politics." *World Politics*, 16 (April 1964), 442–454.

SCHWARTZ, DAVID E. "Political Alienation: The Psychology of Revolution's First Stage." In Ivo K. Feierabend, Rosalind L. Feierabend, and Ted. R. Gurr (eds.). *Anger, Violence and Politics.* Englewood Cliffs, N.J.: Prentice-Hall, 1972.

————. "A Theory of Revolutionary Behavior." In James C. Davies (ed.). *When Men Revolt and Why.* New York: Free Press, 1971.

SEARS, DAVID O., and JOHN B. McCONAHAY. *The Politics of Violence.* Boston: Houghton Mifflin, 1973.

SIGELMAN, LEE, and MILES SIMPSON. "A Cross-National Test of the Linkage Between Economic Inequality and Political Violence." *Journal of Conflict Resolution*, 21 (March 1977), 105–128.

SIMON, SHELDON W. *War and Politics in Cambodia.* Durham, N.C.: Duke University Press, 1974.

SMELSER, NEIL J. *Theory of Collective Behavior.* New York: Free Press, 1962.

SOUTHWOOD, KENNETH. "Riot and Revolt: Sociological Theories of Political

Violence." *Peace Research Reviews,* Canadian Peace Research Institute, 1972.

STONE, LAWRENCE. "Theories of Revolution." *World Politics,* 18: 2 (1966), 159–176.

TANTER, RAYMOND. "Dimensions of Conflict Behavior Within and Between Nations, 1958–1960." *Journal of Conflict Resolution,* 10 (March 1966), 41–64.

THORNTON, THOMAS. "Terror as a Weapon of Political Agitation." In Harry Eckstein (ed.). In *Internal War.* New York: Free Press, 1964.

TILLY, CHARLES. "The Analysis of Counter-Revolution." *History and Theory,* 3 (1963), 39–58.

VON DER MEHDEN, FRED. *Comparative Political Violence.* Englewood Cliffs, N.J.: Prentice-Hall, 1973.

WRIGHT, QUINCY. *A Study of War.* 2nd ed. Chicago: University of Chicago Press, 1965.

6 | PATTERNS OF INTERNATIONAL CONFLICT

This chapter surveys some of the insights we have gained regarding war and peace. There has always been a substantial body of research on this subject. In the last fifteen years, it has grown rapidly in both scope and sophistication. We will rely on this literature to develop a new dimension of conflict. In this chapter, we will describe the patterns of development in relations between countries that lead into conflict. This account, like those of race and revolution, also examines the origins of violence. It seeks to explain why international conflicts often result in armed violence.

Are there discernible patterns in international events that foretell the coming of war? What mediating forces accelerate or retard the movement toward war? How do policy makers view the world? What is the international structure? What are the tensions and stresses of crisis? Why war is so hard to stop once it has begun?

Profile of a War: The October War of 1973[1]

On October 6, 1973, the fourth Arab-Israeli war in twenty-five years shattered the fragile peace of the Middle East. Before it ended, the war would affect the lives of people thousands of miles away. The world would quickly witness a confrontation between its two superpowers, an oil embargo that would seriously affect the Western economies, and a reversal in the regional balance of power.

In the years following the October War, there have been spasmodic military conflicts and threats of renewed large-scale fighting. At the same time, there have been new attempts to resolve conflicts and ensure the peace. What follows is a profile of the October War. In it, we will attempt to identify some of the more important political and military events and decisions that occurred during this brief but violent war.

OPERATION BADR: THE WAR BEGINS

Technically hostilities began at noon on October 6, 1973, when Egyptian artillery units began shelling front-line Israeli forces along the East Bank of the Suez Canal. While the attack did not catch the Israelis totally unprepared, most observers now agree that they were surprised by the scope and coordination of the Egyptian offensive. After two hours of simultaneous artillery and air attacks, Egyptian infantry crossed over and planted their flag on the East Bank. As Egyptian ground forces spread out and secured their beachhead, pontoon bridges were thrown across the canal. The initial infantry assault was then reinforced by armored units and heavy tanks. In less than one and a half hours, the Egyptians had opened eleven bridges across the canal. Thousands of Egyptian troops were now engaged in heavy fighting along Israel's defense perimeter, the Bar Lev Line (Whetten, 1974: 264).

Most military observers now agree that the Egyptians' initial success was due largely to the strategy of defense in depth as they penetrated the Israeli-occupied Sinai. There were two elements of this strategy. First, Egyptian infantry units were protected by hundreds of Soviet-made antitank weapons. As Whetten points out, "In the first three days the Israeli lost 300 to 400 of their 900 tanks earmarked for this sector." Well over 60 percent of these losses were later attributed to antitank weapons. With the Israeli armored counterattacks effectively blunted, Egyptian ground forces could consolidate their front before going on the offensive again. That offensive could have been stopped, however, by the Israeli Air Force had it not been for the second element of the Egyptian strategy—the forward movement of the Egyptian air defense systems.

Before Operation Badr had even begun, Egypt had constructed an air defense system second only to that of the North Vietnamese. It consisted of batteries of SAM-2, SAM-6, and SAM-7 (surface-to-air) missiles. In addition to an estimated 1,200 operational missiles concentrated along the battle front, the Egyptians also had more than 1,000 antiaircraft weapons (Whetten, 1974: 258). As Egyptian troops crossed the Suez Canal, their defense system provided an effective umbrella against Israeli air strikes. The air defense network was so effective, in fact, that an estimated twenty aircraft were shot down over the battle front on October 7 and 8. In spite of their initial battlefield gains, however, Egyptian forces halted their advance by October 9 and began to reinforce their lines.

FIGHTING ON THE GOLAN FRONT

The Egyptian attack on the Sinai was synchronized with a Syrian attack against the Golan Heights. There the Syrians smashed through Israeli lines and established powerful positions within the first hours of the war. The Syrian advance posed some immediate and serious problems for Israel. Following its 1967 war with Syria, Israel had established its fortified boundary position some twenty-five miles east of the crest of the Golan Heights. From the crest of the Heights, the rich kibbutzim of Israel could be viewed below. East of this high ground lay the Syrian plateau, with Syria's capital of Damascus only forty miles to the northeast. Control of the crest was crucial, therefore, to both sides. During the first two days of the war, Syrian forces pushed to within three to five miles of the Golan crest. If they could occupy that crest, they could not only shell the Israeli settlements below, but might effectively repulse any future Israeli counterattacks. For these and other reasons, the Syrian campaign was given first priority by Israel (Whetten, 1974: 243).[2]

Israel mobilized its reserves quickly and committed them immediately to the Syrian front. Throughout October 6 and 7, the Israeli Air Force flew continuous attacks against the advancing Syrian armored columns. Unlike the air war in the Sinai, the Israelis were able to crack the Syrian air defense system. The cost was high, however. Approximately thirty aircraft were lost during the first two days of fighting. By October 8 the Syrian advance had been stopped and Israeli forces moved to counterattack. To blunt the Israeli advance, Syria committed its reserves and called out its air force. Whenever the Israeli counteradvance halted, the Syrians pushed forward. Some of the most intense fighting of the war would rage for the next four days. (October 8–11).

As Syrian forces withdrew and the tide of battle moved to the Israelis, Syria's Arab allies committed their forces. Jordanian, Iraqi, Moroccan, and Kuwaiti forces were thrown into the battle under Syrian command to halt the advance into Syria proper. Sustaining heavy losses, the allied Arab forces fell back to a defense line that (in one place) was only eighteen miles from Damascus. With its forces now on the offensive, the Israeli military objective changed. As Whetten points out, the main purpose of Israel's Syrian offensive now "was to destroy as large a proportion of the Syrian armed forces as possible. As a second objective the Israeli Defense Force sought to reach a dominating position around Damascus" (1974: 252).[3]

By October 13, however, the Israeli advance had been halted by stiffened Syrian resistance. This resistance was the result of an increasing Soviet airlift of weapons replacements. From October 10 to the United Nations ceasefire some thirteen days later, both the Arab and the Israeli military operations would be influenced by the political actions of two nations far removed from the combat zones. Let us turn now to the international dimensions of the war.

THE U.S. PERSPECTIVE "WE WERE SURE THERE WOULDN'T BE A WAR."[4]

According to most accounts, the United States was completely surprised by the Arab attack. Certainly there were enough signals that war was imminent. The Central Intelligence Agency had noted on September 24 that both Egypt and Syria were conducting large-scale military maneuvers opposite Israeli positions along the Suez Canal and the Golan Heights. This troop activity continued past September 29 and was brought to the attention of high-ranking American officials. On October 2, Syria called up its full troop reserves, and Egyptian forces moved into offensive positions along the West Bank of the Suez Canal. During October 2, 3, and 4, U.S. Secretary of State Henry Kissinger met with ranking Arab and Israeli diplomats. According to one report, Kissinger received no hint from the Arabs that an attack was imminent (Kalb and Kalb, 1974: 457). Even when the families of Russian military advisers were removed from Cairo and Damascus on the nights of October 4 and 5, the United States persisted in its view that while war was always possible, it was unlikely at the present time. At 8 A.M. (Washington time) Kissinger was informed that "Egyptian and Syrian forces have commenced military action against Israel" (Kalb and Kalb, 1974: 461). By all reports, Kissinger was surprised, angry, and disappointed.

The obvious question is, How could the United States have misperceived all this intelligence information? There are always a number of perceptual choices in interpreting information. What determines which choice will be made? One explanation focuses on the decision makers' beliefs. Let us apply this explanation to Kissinger's perception that war was not imminent.[5]

The information about the Arab mobilization and the Russian dependents' evacuation are stimuli that can be interpreted in several legitimate ways. From one point of view, the information indicated an impending war. From another, it was a case of Arab posturing—threatening behavior, to be sure, but nothing more. According to Joseph DeRivera, the interpretation eventually selected may be determined by a person's other beliefs, particularly those that are somehow related to the issue in question (1968: 20). Let us examine these beliefs.

Kissinger probably held four beliefs that were commonly accepted in Washington at this time: (1) Israel rather than the Arab states was more likely to go to war first; (2) "the Arabs were too disunited, their political leadership too undistinguished to be able to coordinate an effective assault against Israel"; (3) Egypt and Syria were dependent on Russian aid and equipment (and neither would act unless it was cleared by Moscow); and (4) the Soviet Union had no intention of allowing a conflict to break out in this volatile area and risk a direct confrontation with the United States.[6] If Kissinger had perceived the intelligence information as signaling an imminent Arab attack, this would have conflicted with the four beliefs which indicated that the Arabs would not go to war. The perception that actually occurred (no war was imminent) was the one that required the least reorganization of the policy makers' other beliefs (1968: 22).[7]

After the war had broken out, many of these earlier beliefs changed. As a result, America's objectives changed as well. According to Whetten, U.S. diplomacy had two main objectives: (1) to end the hostilities as quickly as possible and (2) to do so in a manner that would promote a lasting peace in the region (1976: 29).[8] The first objective would be initially thwarted; the second has never been accomplished. This mixture of success and failure can be attributed to many complex factors. One of the most important was the objectives and perspectives of the Soviet Union during the October War.

SOVIET OBJECTIVES AND PERSPECTIVES

Soviet foreign policy in the Middle East appears to have three objectives: (1) avoiding a direct confrontation with the United States, (2) curtailing American influence in the region, and (3) increasing Soviet security and regional influence (McLaurin et al., 1977: 21). All of these objectives are equally important, and success in one area often creates problems in another. R. D. McLaurin has argued that Soviet Middle East policy is designed primarily to avoid superpower conflict. Yet, as Robin Edmonds and others have pointed out, Soviet attempts to increase its influence and curtail American regional power have often generated the forces that put both countries and their client states on a collision course (1975: 138–149).

The Soviet Union's attempts to reconcile these conflicting objectives are too complex to go into here. In the period immediately prior to the October War, and even during the war's early days, the Soviet strategy was apparently based on the premise that avoiding confrontation with the United States was still important. However, this goal should not deter the Soviets from taking tactical advantages of situations where they might increase their power and influence (McLaurin et al., 1977: 25). The October War seemed to provide many advantages. The Soviet Union was informed by Egypt that war would begin on October 6 (Kalb and Kalb, 1974: 453).[9] On the surface, at least, such a war was advantageous to the Soviet Union. If successful (and this really was the key), the Arab attack could dislodge Israel, embarrass the United States, increase Soviet military prestige (the Arabs were trained and equipped by the Russians), and still not damage the growing Soviet detente with the United States. In short, the Russians calculated that they could have both detente and war.

Thus the Soviet Union not only encouraged broad Arab support for Egypt and Syria in the early days of the war but also began preparations for resupplying its Arab allies with much needed military equipment. On October 10–11 a massive Soviet airlift of military supplies began. While the airlift was going on, the Soviets proposed an immediate end to fighting with the hope of freezing the battlefield situation while the Arabs were still on the offensive (Edmonds, 1975: 145). Everything seemed to be going as hoped, but could it continue? The United States began to signal that it could not. An early indication came in a speech on October 8 by Secretary of State Kissinger, warning that "Detente cannot survive irresponsibility in any area, including the Middle East" (U.S. Department of State, 1973). A second hint came on October 13, when American military aircraft began to ferry supplies to Israel. A massive American airlift had begun.[10] Now both the United States and the Soviet Union had intervened in the war, not as combatants but as suppliers of their respective allies. Could the war be contained with such indirect involvement by the superpowers? Was this intervention likely to lead to a direct confrontation between them? As intense fighting resumed on both fronts, the chances of containing the war, controlling hostilities, and preventing a nuclear confrontation seemed to lessen each day.

THE FIGHTING RESUMES: WAR AND SUPERPOWER DIPLOMACY

Both the Soviet and American airlifts had a significant effect on the battlefronts. On the Syrian front, the arrival of Soviet artillery aided the Syrians and their allies in halting the Israeli advance toward Damascus. In spite of its failure to meet all of its Syrian objectives, Israel believed that the Golan-Syrian front was stabilized enough to permit a shifting of its forces to the Sinai. On October 14 Egypt launched a major offensive against Israel in the Sinai. The attack was designed to relieve Israeli pressure on the Syrian front and to gain the initiative in the Sinai before Israeli reserves could be deployed in strength. By October 16 it was obvious that the Egyptian campaign was a failure. Egyptian-Israeli tank losses were at a ratio of 4:1. In the air, the Egyptian-Israeli losses were estimated at 8:1. (Whetten, 1974: 267). By October 15 Israel had not only stopped the Egyptian advance but at one point had breached the Egyptian line and crossed the canal. While the Israeli forces operating west of the canal were small in number, their presence in what they called "Africa" (Egypt proper) marked a dramatic turning point in the war (Kalb and Kalb, 1974: 480).

The Israeli West Bank incursion was systematically widened, with major Egyptian losses. On October 16 it was becoming obvious that if the incursion continued, Egypt's East Bank forces would be cut off from reinforcements. The Egyptian position was becoming increasingly vulnerable. Not only were they now fighting a two-front war in the Sinai (i.e., under Israeli attack from both the west and the east), but Israeli forces had penetrated forty miles into Egypt proper, with the Egyptian capital of Cairo only fifty miles to the east. Egyptian losses were high. Between October 16 and 18, Egypt began to lose much of its canal air defense system. As the system weakened, the Israeli Air Force attacked Egyptian ground forces. Between 250 and 300 tanks were lost west of the canal; the Egyptian Air Force lost approximately 15 to 20 planes per day. As the Israeli forces advanced, activity on the diplomatic front was stimulated.

For the Soviets, the continued success of Israel on the battlefield posed some serious problems. In spite of the massive airlift, its Arab allies were being pushed back with heavy losses. Besides the mounting cost in destroyed materials, the Soviets also had to weigh the possibility that the Israelis might achieve a decisive victory. The Soviet Union had suffered a tremendous loss of regional influence and prestige after the 1967 Arab-Israeli war. This loss was attributed, in part, to the poor showing of Soviet equipment and training on the battlefield (Churchill and Churchill, 1967). Once again it appeared that Israel, armed with American weapons, might win.

On October 16 Soviet Prime Minister Alexei Kosygin arrived in Cairo for talks with Egyptian President Anwar Sadat. Almost immediately the Soviets pressed for a cease-fire. The Egyptians, however, had serious reservations about a cease-fire in place; so did the Israelis. A cease-fire in place meant that fighting would stop, with each side holding the territory then in its possession. Egypt obviously did not want Israeli forces west of the canal, and Israel was determined to destroy Egyptian forces east of the canal. However, whereas both belligerents balked at the idea of a cease-fire, there was little that they could do to block it once the Soviet Union and the United States decided that a continued conflict ran a high risk of endangering their mutually advantageous policy of detente and of embroiling them in war (Kalb and Kalb, 1974: 481).[11]

On October 20 Kissinger left for Moscow to negotiate the terms of a cease-fire with the Soviet Union. The two governments agreed to sponsor jointly a resolution in the United Nations Security Council calling for an immediate cease-fire and for the implementation of Security Council Resolution 242 of November 1967. (The details of the superpower negotiations are too complex to go into here.) Following hurried consultations with other members of the Security Council, the council was convened on Monday, October 22, and unanimously adopted Resolution 338. The cease-fire was scheduled to go into effect that day. On October 23 it was obvious that not only was the cease-fire being violated by the belligerents, but Israel was moving toward a decisive victory against Egypt's Third Corps. The Americans realized that the Soviets could not tolerate such a victory. The Soviets were angry and perplexed at the seeming inability of the

United States to halt the Israeli encirclement of the Egyptians. Soviet complaints about the Israeli cease-fire violations took an ominous turn on October 24, when elements of the Soviet military were put on alert. With these moves, the stage was at last set for a superpower confrontation.

THE CEASE-FIRE ALERT: SUPERPOWER CONFRONTATION AND CRISIS

The Security Council convened again on the evening of October 23 to debate another joint American-Soviet cease-fire resolution. The resolution, which passed that day, called for the following: (1) termination of all military activity in the positions that each party then occupied; (2) an immediate implementation of Security Council Resolution 242 (1967) [to resolve outstanding issues resulting from the 1967 Arab-Israeli war]; and (3) the initiation of negotiations to establish a just and desirable peace in the Middle East.

Claiming that Egyptian troops had not honored the October 22 cease-fire, Israel continued to move against Suez City and to cut the remaining supply lines to the Egyptian Third Corps (20,000 men) trapped on the East Bank.

Soviet leaders grew increasingly apprehensive about the continued Israeli advances. Such advances could force the Egyptians to abandon their hard-won positions, resulting in yet another humiliating defeat for Arab military forces. In response to the Israeli violations of the October 22 and 23 cease-fire resolutions, Communist Party General Secretary Leonid Brezhnev sent a diplomatic note to President Richard Nixon. The communication is believed to have stated that, if the United States could not contain further Israeli advances through diplomatic means, the Soviet Union was prepared to act unilaterally, possibly with troops.[12] The note is further thought to have "suggested" that the United States and the Soviet Union might wish jointly to commit troops to the area in order to enforce the previous U.N. cease-fire resolutions.

In the early morning hours of October 24, the United States responded by replacing its military forces on a worldwide (*Condition Three*) alert. The necessity for this *Condition Three* alert has been much debated. Officially the alert was intended to head off the possible airlift of 50,000 Soviet troops to the Middle East. Whatever the reasons for the alert, which lasted for one week, it was heavily criticized both at home and abroad. Particularly vocal in their criticisms were America's NATO allies.

The NATO alliance had already been strained for economic and political reasons. The fourth Arab-Israeli war appears to have intensified these divisions. The Western European states, which are heavily dependent upon Middle Eastern oil, did not wish to become involved, either directly or indirectly, in the conflict. When the United States began to resupply arms to Israel on October 14, Germany, Britain, Italy, and Spain notified the American government that they did not approve of the use of their airfields and ports for such operations. Only Greece and Portugal cooperated fully. In a news conference on the afternoon of October 24, Kissinger sharply criticized the NATO allies for their reluctance to support U.S. efforts. On October 25, the U.N. Security Council issued its third cease-fire directive; this time, both combatants stopped fighting.

THE FIGHTING ENDS

Military representatives from Egypt and Israel met on November 11 to sign the cease-fire agreement. It was their first face-to-face meeting since 1948. The major points of the agreement were as follows: (1) Both sides would discuss the return to the positions they had held on October 22; (2) the port city of Suez, now almost completely held by Israeli forces, would be supplied with food, water, and medicines; (3) the Egyptian forces (primarily the Third Army) on the East Bank of the Suez Canal would be supplied with food, water, and medicines; (4) U.N. peace-keeping forces (primarily troops from Finland) would police the cease-fire zones; and (5) all prisoners of war would be exchanged.

After months of additional negotiations, primarily under the auspices of Henry Kissinger, Egyptian and Israeli forces were finally disengaged and withdrawn from the October fronts. In May 1974 the Syrian-Israeli disengagement agreement was signed, and the region moved to an uncertain future.

There are many possible explanations for the October War. Most of them can be grouped under the heading of foreign policy decisions, actions, and interactions of the states in question. While the war was in some ways unique in world affairs, it also reflected a number of factors, both specific and general, that characterize the history of Arab-Israeli relations and the elements of international conflict.

Explaining War

In the Middle East alone, there have been four major wars in the last three decades. Why do these wars persist? Why do any wars occur? Do wars grow out of impersonal "historical forces," or do they result from the actions and objectives of policy makers? As Bernard Brodie points out, it is hardly believable that we still do not have complete answers to these persistent questions (1973: 276). What we do have are fragmentary answers—bits and pieces of the complex puzzle of why nations engage in violent conflict. These partial answers consist of hypotheses (the majority of them untested), models, and crude theories. What follows is a brief survey and review of some of the more important "theories" of the causes of war. We will focus on only a few of them. The first analyzes the motives that "lead men to involve their states in war, or to place them on the road to war (Pruitt and Snyder,1969: 15).[13] Fuller details of this and other theories can be found in works by Dougherty and Pfaltzgraff (1971), Michael Haas (1974), and Manus Midlarsky (1975).

SUCCESS AND CONFLICT-ORIENTED GOALS

In the last two chapters, we have seen that whenever scholars examine the motives behind political violence, they end by describing the goals to be obtained. The same approach is applicable to the analysis of war. Like riots and revolutions, war can be understood as a political failure to secure certain goals; when this happens war results, (Midlarsky, 1975: 2). War as a form of political violence is goal-oriented.

Pruitt and Snyder distinguished between two types of goals that motivate war. The first is known as "success-oriented" goals. These goals may include political influence, economic wealth, or the acquisition of territory. Many analysts believe that Egypt was motivated in the 1973 war by a desire to secure territories it had lost to Israel in the 1967 war. The other type is known as "conflict-oriented" goals. These goals are satisfied by engaging in conflict per se, whether "victory is achieved or not" (Pruitt and Snyder, 1969: 16). Examples of this would include national integration (e.g., an increase in national morale and a concurrent decrease in internal domestic conflicts during wartime) and maintaining or revitalizing national honor after a military defeat. The Arab states, for example, suffered a humiliating defeat at the hands of the Israelis in 1967. Throughout the late 1960s and up to October 1973, Arab statesmen pledged that this disgrace had to be redressed on the battlefield. A desire by a nation to restore its honor can be a powerful motive in generating war. The October War is a case in point.

ORIGINS OF GOALS

Economic Even if we could identify all of the goals of war, we would still need to know how these goals develop. A number of "theories" have emerged that purport to explain the origins of these goals. Most of them, however, emphasize only a single set of factors while ignoring other equally important forces. Many of the "economic theories of imperialism and war" suffer from this defect. The works of British economist J. A. Hobson, the philosophical writings of Karl Marx, and the statements of V. I. Lenin, for example, all equate the economic basis of war with imperialism. This economic interpretation fails because it attempts to "build a universal law of history upon the limited experience of a few isolated cases" (Morgenthau, 1966: 42). In other words, the theory can easily be refuted by citing negative instances, many of which are discussed in Raymond Aron's *The Century of Total War* (1955). Aron holds that the fierce competition for colonies among the major European states *declined* just before the outbreak of World War I (Aron, 1955: 59; as cited in Pruitt and Snyder, 1969: 19). According to Marxist theory, this imperialist competition should have increased prior to the war.

The Quest and Balancing of Power Another single-factor theory regarding the origins of goals deals with power. "Power" is one of the most used and abused terms in the study of the sources of war. Many scholars believe that war (and in some cases, all international relations) results from a "struggle for power." Known as *political realists*,[14] these scholars include Reinhold Niebuhr, Hans J. Morgenthau, George F. Kennan, and Henry A. Kissinger. Using their works, let us briefly identify some of the principles they use to explain war.

Central in the writings of Niebuhr is the notion that individual aggressiveness is eventually manifested in the actions of nations. Man has a "will to live" which inevitably leads to a "will to power." National power is a projection of this individual" will to power." Unlike the individual, however, the nation has fewer moral restraints as it strives to enhance its position. As a result, greater violence is likely to occur in national struggles for power (Thompson, 1960: 23–25; as cited in Dougherty and Pfaltzgraff, 1971: 69), Morgenthau, Kennan, and Kissinger also accept this power motive of behavior. Morgenthau states that statesmen "think and act in terms of interest defined as power (1967: 5). Both Kennan and Kissinger contend that statesmen do or should deal with power-motivated realities that can lead to war.

A second important principle of the power explanation is that the quest of national interest (defined as power) is basically unstable. In an international system where states vie for power, and given the tendency for every state to try to encroach on every other, each nation must protect itself. National survival is the ultimate national interest. If any other nation is thought to be threatening this interest, war can and often does result. Henry Kissinger's writings about contemporary and historical state systems make a related point. He contends that as states vie to ensure their own absolute security, they inevitably create absolute insecurity for every other state in the regional or international order (1957). Thus the natural quest for security by one nation can generate insecurity among its neighbors. Paradoxically, then, the goal of peace (through absolute security) can actually cause war. Israel's quest for its own security may have caused its neighbors to ponder their own relative insecurity.

A third and final principle deals with the notion of the "balance of power." In order to guard against the tendency of nations to seek their own interest, balances of power are established. A balance of power is a tacit agreement among nations about the permissible aims and methods of foreign policy. Kissinger refers to the resulting international order based on such agreements as a stable and "legitimate" order (1964). A balance of power, however, does not preclude war. In fact, Morgenthau argues, one of the primary reasons certain nations have gone to war is to preserve the balance of power. Bernard Brodie states that "the history of British diplomacy and warfare stands out for its conspicuous commitment over some three centuries to the balance-of-power idea, but Britain was surely not alone in that respect" (1973: 334–335). Kissinger concludes that once agreement is reached on the operating principles of the world order, states should not let these principles be compromised "even for the sake of peace."

Most of the criticisms of the realist school deal with disagreements on specific policy proposals, controversies over the meaning of "power" and "national interests," and opposition to the use of historical analogies to explain international relations today. In spite of these criticisms—and they are substantial—the emphasis on national interest as the principal motivation for war has proved useful. As Dougherty and Pfaltzgraff point out, "the problems to which realist thought has addressed itself—of the interaction and behavior of humans beings as decision-makers, the nature of power, the foreign policy goals, the techniques for managing power, the impact of environment upon political behavior . . . —are central to the study of international politics" (1971: 101). Their problems are also central to the study of the causes of war.

Subjective Preconditions of War

A number of scholars have spoken of the strange persistence of war throughout the ages. There may be something in human psychology, they say, that either necessitates war or at any rate subtly encourages it. To put it another way, without certain subjective or psychological preconditions, war would be both impossible and inexplicable.

We have already seen that economic goals and a struggle for power cannot be linked directly to acts of war. If this is so, how can we account for their effects on interstate conflict? Our analysis of domestic violence suggests an answer. Instead of thinking of a direct relationship between goals and violence, we should think of the relationship as being mediated by certain psychological factors. Pruitt and Snyder suggest that for goals to lead to war, they must be seen by national decision makers as incompatible with the goals of another state. This notion of *perceived incompatibility* (1969: 22) is the central theme of this text. That is, various objective considerations interact with certain attitudes, values, beliefs, and perceptions to generate a potential for violence. In interstate relations, this may mean war.

In studying the subjective causes of war, the primary concern is to identify the perceptions and beliefs that produce a "war state of mind." Let us now examine some of these beliefs and perceptions.

PERCEPTIONS OF HOSTILITY

One of the most fascinating studies linking perceptions of hostility to war has been done by Dina A. Zinnes. After examining the content of diplomatic messages exchanged between the heads of state prior to the outbreak of World War I, Zinnes argued that a state behaves the way it does (i.e., issues threats and declares war) because of the perceptions and actions of its key decision makers. Hostile behavior (such as war) occurs when decision makers attempt to injure or threaten another state. Two variables are central to Zinnes's study. The first is a state's expression of hostility toward another state; the second is a state's perception that it is the target of another state's hostility (Zinnes, in Singer, 1968: 86). This second variable is termed a *perception of hostility*. As Zinnes points out, whether hostility actually exists is irrelevant. As long as the state feels that it is the target of hostility, it will act accordingly.

Four basic hypotheses are used to explain the relationship between expressions of hostility and perceptions. These are: (1) If country X perceives itself to be the object of hostility, then it will express hostility. (2) If country X perceives that it is the object of Y's hostility, then X will express hostility toward Y. (3) If X expresses hostility toward Y, then Y will perceive that it is the object of X's hostility. (4) If X expresses hostility to Y, then Y will express hostility toward X (Zinnes, in Singer, 1968: 87–88).[15] Taken together, these statements suggest that perceived hostilities often turn into hostile responses toward another state. These responses may contribute to a decision to employ violence against that state.

PERCEPTIONS OF THREAT

Another subjective state that is thought to contribute to the potential for war is *threat perception*. Although difficult to define, "threat" means an expression or intention to inflict injury or punishment on another. Threat is accompanied by certain psychological states, including fear, distrust, and hostility. In fact, perceptions of threat and perceptions of hostility are usually so interrelated that some analysts simply refer to them as a state of tension. Analysis has focused on the effects of threat perception in arms races and international crises.

Since we will be discussing both of these topics later in the chapter, we will now turn to those cases where threat perception is more directly related to war. Two situations come immediately to mind: "preventive wars" and "defensive preparations" to prevent war. Let us look at each in turn.

History provides many examples where one nation says that it has attacked, knowing that another nation was preparing to attack it. The purpose of the war is to strike the first blow. This is known as a "preventive attack." It is based on the assumption that since war is inevitable, it is better to strike first and minimize losses. Preventive attacks usually occur because the decision makers of one country are so threatened by another state's actions that they feel they have no other option. Whereas it is often difficult to determine whether a preventive attack has occurred (because most nations claim that their opponent was readying an attack), some cases do exist. In 1967 Israel launched a preemptive air strike against its Arab opponents based on the assumption that Egypt and Syria were about to go to war against Israel. Here, perceptions of threat actually provided the stimulus to attack.[16]

Where a perception of threat is less serious, countries will often initiate what Pruitt and Snyder call "defensive preparations." They may build up their armed forces, acquire specific weapons systems, take the diplomatic offensive, and secure politico-military alliances (1969: 73). The purpose of such preparation is to let a potential adversary know that the country is ready to deter an attack. In some cases, preparations do deter war. In others, however, the reverse happens. Because defensive preparations usually take place in a tense environment, nations may perceive each other's defensive preparation as a prelude to war. This has often been the case in the Middle East. Defensive preparations themselves can increase the probability of war if the resulting perceptions of threat become strong enough. The actual mechanisms of preparedness races will be discussed later, when we analyze Robert North's "conflict spiral" thesis. For now, let us consider how threat perception is determined.

THE SINGER CONSTRUCT

In "Threat Perceptions and National Decision Makers," J. David Singer (1958) suggests that the factors leading to threat perception are as vital as the link between these perceptions and war. Singer contends that each nation's threat perception of the other depends on both estimated capability and estimated intent. He states this relationship in quasi-mathematical form: Threat Perception = Estimated Capability × Estimated Intent. The most threatening situation occurs when a country has both the military capability to damage an opponent and has expressed strong hostility toward that opponent. Conversely, whenever capability or intent disappear, threat perception diminishes (1958: 105). In 1967 Israel perceived Egypt as posing a significant threat because Egypt had both the military capability and the estimated hostile intent to inflict serious damage on Israel. However, one might argue that in 1973 Israel misperceived Egypt's military capability (in light of its poor showing in the 1967 war). As a result, Israel did not perceive Egyptian actions prior to the October War as posing a serious threat.[17]

One important factor that Singer omits from his calculation is the predisposition of nations to perceive threat. Estimates of intention and trustworthiness, previous experiences, perceptions about current behavior, and predictions about future behavior are all involved in the tendency to see threatening behavior in others (even where these threats may not logically be present). Ross Stagner points out that tension and anxiety often induce *polarization*—an exaggeration of threat which might be unobserved or appear slight under "normal" circumstances (Stagner, in McNeil, 1965: 56). Dean Pruitt (in Kelman, 1965) adds another dimension when he contends that the behavior and intentions of many nations are *ambiguous*. In this case, it is difficult to gain sufficient evidence on which to base a perception of threat. Stagner points out, however, that some individuals cannot tolerate ambiguity. These people tend to "read in" some meaning to the evidence even where cues are absent. Such individuals are more likely to see threats in highly ambiguous situations (Stagner, in McNeil, 1965: 57). Whatever the source of this tendency, Pruitt's hypothesis seems correct: "The stronger the predisposition to perceive threat, the more likely it is that threat will be perceived."

IMAGES OF SELF AND OTHERS

So far, we have looked at some of the perceptions that may predispose a nation to go to war. Apart from these perceptions, however, there are some basic images of the self and others that may predispose a nation to use violence. Ralph K. White contends (1961) that hostile nations often have "mirror images" of each other. For example, Americans see the Soviet leaders as bad. To the Russians, the United States is a threat but their own country is peace-loving; to the American, these relations are reversed.

The mirror image, according to White, has two components. The first is the similarity of the psychological processes, particularly that of selective perception, between cultures that are otherwise different. White contends that the ethnocentric black-and-white picture that emerges applies to all cultures. We have already seen in chapters 3 and 4 the impact that ethnocentrism can have on perceptions, attitudes, and behavior. The second element of the mirror image is the positive view of one's own nation and the negative view of the opponent. The "self" is perceived as virile and moral, while the "other" is viewed as diabolical (1970: 319–320). These elements of the mirror image may go a long way in explaining the perceptions that predispose nations to use military force. White's thesis may also explain why wars are so difficult to resolve once they are underway—opponents may have such rigid perceptions of themselves and each other that there is almost no basis for compromise and negotiation. Let us apply White's notions to the views that Arabs and Israelis had of themselves and each other in the early 1970s.

Perceptions of the Enemy: Mirror Images

The objectives of a nation's foreign policy are affected by many factors. One set of factors is perception of the opponent or enemy. It is often difficult to discuss these determinants. For one thing, the discussion must be broad enough to encompass an individual's belief and value system. Second, many of these beliefs, values, and resulting images change both substantively and qualitatively, depending upon time or circumstance.

In light of these problems, no description can hope to be complete. We will focus here on the images and attitudes of decision makers about their opponents and how these might influence foreign policy. We believe these factors to be crucial, since the way individuals view situations, events, or issues often affects their behavior.

Egypt's and Israel's objectives, actions, and responses to situations are determined partly by their perceptions of reality. Psychologists tell us that people act and react according to their images of the world; the state of that world does not matter so much as what each believes that state to be. In Hadley Cantril's words, we live in different "reality worlds." In their different reality worlds, Egyptians and Israelis often assume that what seems real, good or bad, friendly or hostile to them is the same for the other as well. But, of course, this is not the case. Egyptians and Israelis perceive reality differently. Each nation evaluates the goals and actions of the other differently, and each assigns different meanings to them. We can scarcely begin to understand each country's behavior until we know how their reality worlds differ. One way to delineate these worlds is to examine what each says about itself and the other.

IMAGE OF THE ENEMY

Egyptian media and the policy makers who control them have focused on the "illegitimate," "imperialistic," and "illegal" character of Israeli "aggression," which has violated all principles of international law, Arab sovereignty and territorial integrity, and the rights of the Palestinian people. Egyptian Foreign Minister Mohammed El-Zayyat:

> Israel is an expansionist regime bent on annexing all Arab areas. Israel has never tried to gain acceptance of its presence in the area, only to impose itself through arms and conquest. The idea that you can speak only from the mouth of a gun has always been Israel's idea.

As this statement suggests, Egypt perceives Israel as "evil." The aggressiveness of Israel reflects the general evil of war and the specific evil of one country's imposing its rule on another by force. This aggression and expansionism violate two basic human values: hatred of war and love of freedom and integrity.

This image does not necessarily apply to all Israelis. In fact, Jews are not blamed for Israel's aggression. As El-Zayyat expressed it: "We have nothing against the Israelis as Semites or Jews. What we have against the rulers of Israel is their aggressive and colonialist policy." Here, as in many other statements, Arab decision makers differentiate between the people and the leaders of Israel. This distinction is what Ralph White calls the "black top" image of the enemy. White contends that this image serves a number of psychological purposes: it relieves one side of the painful thought that they may be going against the majority wishes of the other; it replaces such thoughts with a self-image of actually helping these people against their leaders, who have involved them in an unjust cause; and it raises the hope that once the leaders have been taught a lesson, the conflict will be over. In its most important form, Egypt's image of Israel is based on the conviction that Israel has committed self-evident aggression and that Egypt and the Arabs are blameless.

Israel's image of the Arabs is the mirror image of this contention. Israel believes that Egypt and the other Arab states are committed to "total confrontation," with the expressed purpose of annihilating Israel and its people. In the words of Israel's Foreign Minister Abba Eban:

> I tell you, a massacre more hideous than Auschwitz would have been a real prospect [had the Arab armies been successful in the 1973 war] and Israel's survival would be in doubt. . . . [W]hen the Arabs speak to their *own* people, their leaders say frankly that if they got us back to the 1967 lines [Israel's border before the June 1967 war], this would be the first stage, to be followed by the decisive blow to the head and heart.

As this and other statements suggest, Israelis view the Arabs as intensely evil. On four separate occasions the Arabs have either initiated or precipitated war against Israel. They have supported "criminal," "inhumane," and "barbaric" terrorist attacks on unarmed civilians. They are "guilty" of aggression and genocidal policies that are abhorrent to the values of civilized people and the principles of international law. Furthermore, Arab aggression violates Israel's rights of territorial sovereignty and integrity.

SELF-IMAGE: COURAGE AND JUSTICE

Individuals respond not only to other objects and people but to their own thoughts and feelings. In so doing, they develop thoughts and opinions about the self as a central and valued object. Important wants and actions emerge, centering on the enhancement and defense of the *self-image*. This self-image becomes a nucleus around which diverse goals and actions become organized. How, then, do Arabs and Israelis see themselves? What are the self-images that influence or affect their objectives and actions?

Basically Arab and Israeli self-images can be ordered along two dimensions: *strong versus weak* and *right versus wrong*. The most accurate descriptions are "courage" and "justice" or perhaps "virile" and "righteous." While these self-images have changed with time and circumstance, they appear to be broadly similar.

Strength and Courage The emotional importance of Arab and Israeli images of strength and power is clear. These images are central in official statements. One's own militant policy is described as determined and unflinching. A theme of courageous action is predominant; each country sees itself as having the fortitude to stand by its actions, in a mood that is grim and at times belligerent. There is a fierce pride in strength and determination. Take, for example, an address by President Anwar Sadat of Egypt, made after the first eleven days of the October War:

In the name of God, brothers and sisters: I do not think you expect me to stand in front of you so that we may boast together about what we have realized in eleven days—the most dangerous, magnificent and glorious days in our history. The day will come when we shall recount what each of us has done and how each one bore his trust, how the heroes of this people and this nation went out in a dark period carrying the torches of light and pointing out the road between despair and hope. . . .

The Egyptian armed forces performed a miracle, by any military standard. I would not be exaggerating if I say that military historians will long pause to examine and study the operation carried out on Oct. 6. The risk was enormous and the sacrifices were grave. But the results of the first six-hour battle of our war were magnificent. Our wounded nation has restored its honor and the political map of the Middle East has been changed.

Even following military defeats, this self-image is strong. Immediately after the Israeli victory in the June 1967 war, Radio Damascus proclaimed that "our forces are standing firm . . . everyone of us is ready for his coffin for the sake of our destiny." Similarly, in Cairo Egyptians proclaimed, "We swear by God and our sacred principles that despite conspiracies [which lead to our defeat] we shall turn setback into victory. Death to them, victory to us." For almost seven years following the 1967 war, Egyptians stressed their "humiliation" and "disgrace." Closely related to this negative self-image was the feeling that others regarded the Arabs in general, and Egypt in particular, as being less determined and less powerful than Israel. This negative self-image, and a feeling of having lost prestige, are interrelated. As Egyptian Foreign Minister El-Zayyat put it, "The Israeli attitude has been to assume that . . . we were meek and weak. They pictured Egyptians as people who would never fight." One can speculate that this preoccupation with courage and strength, and the fear of losing power and prestige, has been a powerful motive behind Egyptian objectives and actions.

Similarly in Israeli statements, we find the terms "fight," "struggle," and "valor." Following Israel's victory in 1967, General Moshe Dayan stated, "The sands of the desert and the rocks of Galilee are drenched with [our] blood. Victory is ours. Return your swords to your scabbards but keep them ever ready." In more prosaic terms, General Itzhak Rabin stated, "Everyone fought like lions. . . . We have made mincemeat of their air forces. We are now making mincemeat of everything on the ground." Israel, like Egypt, views itself as steadfast, determined, and self-reliant. Their pride in their own courage reinforces their image of Israel as a tough, victorious fighter ready to go to war against great odds to secure its rights.

Justice and Honor Most Arabs and Israelis see many "good" reasons for being at war with each other: to resist aggression (Arab aggression against Israel, Israeli aggression against Arabs), to protect both peace and freedom; to teach "Arab fanatics" and "Zionist aggressors" that war does not pay; to preserve or restore independence; and to fulfill commitments (to the Palestinians, to the Jews). Their public statements imply that each nation sees its own motives as wholly good and honorable, reflecting the highest ideals of all peoples. It is perhaps ironic that both sides regard themselves as wholly good in terms of the same value system: peacefulness, respect for territorial integrity, loyalty, truthfulness, and patriotism. For example, see the following statements on peace, the first one Egyptian and the second, Israeli:

> We are fighting for the sake of peace, the only peace that is worth the name: that is, peace based on justice. (President Anwar Sadat, October 1973)

> We shall not attack any state as long as it does not wage war on us. (Abba Eban, June 1967)

Also see the following statements on respect for territorial integrity, the first one Egyptian and the second, Israeli:

Our intentions are not to occupy Israeli territory or to drive Israel into the sea. . . . What we are asking for is very simple: that our territorial integrity . . . be respected. (Mohammed El-Zayyat. October 1973)

[Israel's arms are] to frustrate the attempt of the Arab armies to capture our land, to break their encirclement and to break the seige of aggression that has been established around us. (Abba Eban, June 1967)

These statements imply that each country views morality as limited and one-sided. That is, if Egypt's objectives and actions are "right" or "morally correct," then those of Israel must be totally "wrong." The reverse belief is held by Israel: their actions and objectives are totally "correct."

Where do such images of self and others often lead? On the level of public discourse, in debates before the United Nations, or in propaganda attacks against each other, Egypt and Israel call each other "aggressor," accuse each other of various crimes, assert their own peacefulness and valor, and vow to drive out the enemy no matter what the cost or consequences. In short, each side tends to engage in black-and-white thinking. On the psychological level, this often leads to military overconfidence (for Egypt in 1948, 1956, and 1967; for Israel in 1973) and an inability to understand the other's point of view. This lack of empathy, or what Edward Azar calls the Arab-Israeli inability to live up to the "facts of life" that Arabs and Israelis will, eventually, have to negotiate with each other, generates a hostility that separates Egypt's and Israel's reality worlds. Hostile words and actions on one side, reinforced by images and untempered by empathy, evoke further suspicion and hostility on the other side. When the first side responds in kind, a vicious spiral of blind involvement begins. The final result, in the words of psychologist Jerome Frank, is that these psychological forces "promote escalation of the conflict, and each step up the ladder in turn intensifies them, until destruction of the enemy becomes the overriding goal, and compromise becomes impossible."

SOME EFFECTS OF BLACK-AND-WHITE THINKING

Having examined some of the manifestations of black-and-white thinking in the Middle East, we can speculate on some of the possible effects of such thinking. Ralph White suggests three effects: selective inattention, lack of empathy, and military overconfidence.

White argues that when nations are hostile to each other, they tend to gloss over the white or gray elements of the enemy's image and focus on the black. There is no room for images that do not "fit." When a dissonant image occurs, it is soft-pedaled or pushed out of the mind temporarily (1970: 299). This selective inattention to details has two aspects: (i.e., the policy maker's belief that he has only a short time in which to make his decision and thus cannot afford to be "confused" by a conflicting image of his opponent) and narrow space perspective (i.e., the policy maker's belief that he has only a few alternatives available to him in reaching a decision).

Another danger of black-and-white thinking is that it ensures a lack of empathy. As White points out, "empathy normally has the disturbing effect of requiring us to see double—to hold in suspension two interpretations of the same facts, the other fellow's and one's own. Complexity and uncertainty are introduced. The human mind, seeking simplicity and certainty, rebels. And empathy is choked off" (1970: 284). Once empathy is gone, a nation loses the ability to see the other's point of view. The effect on the predisposition to use force is obvious.

The third element of White's thesis is that black-and-white thinking leads to military overconfidence. This is closely related to the absence of empathy. Nations often do not see that their potential opponents, like themselves, might "be living up to an indomitable self-image, fearful of showing fear, and therefore irrationally ready to fight" (1970: 16). Laurence Whetten has pointed out that Israel suffered from such military overconfidence before the outbreak of the October War. Military overconfidence also leads a country to downplay the possibility that the allies of the enemy might intervene. Israel's willingness to break the cease-fire agreement on October 23 may have stemmed, in part, from its perception that the Soviet Union would not support the Arabs. Only intense U.S. pressure and the chance of a superpower confrontation caused them to reverse their actions.

SUMMARY

Many motivational and perceptual forces may predispose nations to go to war. The sources—both objective and subjective—of these forces are also crucial. Among those that we have examined are estimated capability, estimated intent, tension, anxiety, ambiguity, and images of the self and others. Our discussion of the theories of war is incomplete, however; we have only identified some of the elements. What is left is to discuss how these elements are interrelated, and how they change in specific patterns. In other words, what stages do nations go through as they move to war?

Analysis of Foreign Policy Decision Making

In exploring the relationships between factors, models and theories are used. A theory, as we have seen, is a way of organizing our knowledge about a phenomenon in order to try to explain it. By examining various theories regarding foreign policy, we move closer to our goal: to explain the dynamics of war. However, a word of caution is in order.

First, we have few proven or accepted theories of foreign policy. Unlike the natural sciences, the "science" of foreign policy analysis is very young. For this reason, the "theories" and models we will discuss offer only partial and approximate explanations. These theories and models do not account for all the properties of the real world. Furthermore, the theories may have certain artificial properties that are not duplicated in the real world. With these limitations in mind, let us analyze the foreign policy process.

UNIT OF ANALYSIS: THE DECISION MAKER

In analyzing foreign policy, we must first identify our *unit of analysis:* Who or what are the primary actors in foreign policy? Is it the state—e.g., Egypt or Israel? Is it institutional groups, such as the Egyptian military establishment or the Israeli Knesset (parliament)? Or is it key decision makers, such as Anwar Sadat or Golda Meir? Upon which unit—state, groups, or individuals—should we focus? None of these units is analytically superior to the others. One unit is better for some purposes, other units for yet other purposes. Unfortunately, since space does not permit us to discuss all three, we will concentrate on the decision maker(s).

Who is a key decision maker? Basically this is an individual who, by virtue of his or her position, has the power to make and implement decisions—such as foreign policy—which are binding on all citizens. Such decision makers might include heads of state—presidents and prime ministers, secretaries and ministers of state or defense, and even lower-level functionaries, such as advisors and ministry officials. The number of key foreign policy decision makers varies with the country and the situation.

Why choose foreign policy decision makers as our primary unit of analysis? First of all, the concept of "decision maker" is crucial in many conceptualizations of foreign policy and war. In discussing some of the images of conflict, we analyzed the images of decision makers and suggested that these influence a nation's conflict behavior. Clearly, foreign policy involves people. It follows, therefore, that if individuals play such an important role in foreign policy, they should be our basic unit of analysis.

A second reason for choosing foreign policy decision makers is that by focusing on individuals, we can still consider larger units, such as institutions, or other determinants, such as the environment. The key foreign policy decision makers do not operate in a vacuum; they work within a complex of organizational and societal factors. Furthermore, decision makers work within the *total perceived* environment, which *may* include all of the elements that we have previously mentioned. In short, the unit of the decision maker is precise enough for us to know what we are studying while broad enough to include some of the more important environmental elements in our analysis.

DECISION MAKERS: BELIEFS AND ACTIONS

How do decision makers arrive at their images and perceptions? To answer this question, we must look at the psychological attributes of decision makers. One of the more important early works in this area is Kenneth Boulding's *The Image*. Boulding contends that images are formulated on the basis of the individual's past experiences. What the decision maker believes to be fact is really only subjective knowledge. This subjective knowledge, in turn, is the result of changing values based on past experiences.

Ole Holsti and the researchers at Stanford University, in studying crises, have advanced a similar idea: It is clear that the "real" world for the president, prime minister, the foreign secretary—and for most of their counterparts in friendly and hostile nations—is the perceptual world (Holsti et al., in Singer, 1968: 127).

The images that decision makers hold are the result, at least partially, of values and beliefs developed through past experiences. How do these images originate? Ole Holsti, a former member of the Stanford group, has examined the interrelationships among belief systems, images of events and situations, and resulting foreign policy actions. He contends that the relationship between images of other countries and foreign policy decisions is as follows:

> Decision-makers act upon their definiton of the situation and their images of states. . . . These images are in turn dependent upon the decision-maker's belief system, and these may or may not be accurate representations of "reality." Thus . . . international conflict frequently is not between states, but rather between distorted images of states. (Holsti, in Coplin and Kegley, 1971: 42)

Holsti further argues that besides organizing personal perceptions into a guide for action, the belief system structures policy goals and preferences. These relationships among beliefs, images, perceptions, policy objectives, and action are diagrammed in Figure 6.1.

Like Boulding, Holsti argues that there are no "facts" for a decision maker; instead, there is a constant barrage of informational stimuli. Whether he or she receives the message, how it is interpreted, what other messages it is linked to, and how it is finally reported as a perception depends upon images. The belief system will indirectly affect the final decision by generating the "facts" upon which perceptions of reality are based. As Figure 6.1 also shows, the belief system may directly affect decisions by serving as a "value guide" for policy objectives and their implementation. That is, information is

Figure 6.1 THE DUAL RELATIONSHIP BETWEEN BELIEF SYSTEM AND DECISION MAKING

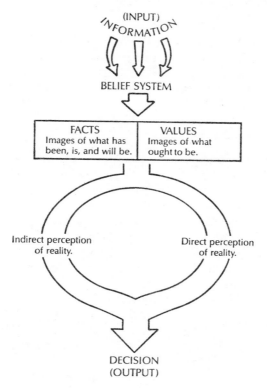

SOURCE: Ole R. Holsti, "The Belief System and National Images: A Case Study," *The Journal of Conflict Resolution* VI, 3 (1962). Reprinted with the permission of the University of Michigan and the author.

scanned and linked to existing values. These values prescribe the "proper" decision to make, given the existing information. Holsti's work on belief systems is a more detailed elaboration of the "perception of the situation" cells in the mediated stimulus-response model (see pp. 160–162) used by the Stanford group in their analysis of crisis situations.

Other scholars have analyzed the possible relationship between image and personality. If perceptions are based on images, and images on beliefs and values, how do individuals develop and maintain their values and beliefs? This research, unfortunately, has not advanced very far. At best, we have only a list of potentially relevant personality variables. These include: willingness to assume high risks, tolerance of ambiguity, intelligence, creativity, self-esteem, submissiveness, need for power, willingness to use force, psychological flexibility or rigidity, and cognitive complexity. Most of these personality factors have not been linked, as yet, with foreign policy decisions and actions.

The Prewar Period: Factors and Patterns

What are the patterns of change in motivation, perception, decision making, and action that mark the movement toward war? To examine this issue, we have chosen one model which incorporates most of the important concepts and notions previously discussed. To illustrate this model, the works of Ole R. Holsti, Robert C. North, and Richard A. Brody will be used.

CRISIS DECISION MAKING

A key element of foreign policy analysis is the notion of situations. A "situation" is a set of events or conditions arising in either the foreign or domestic environment that confronts a country's decision makers. Situational analysis assumes that the actions of decision makers depend on the situations they confront. Charles Hermann has developed eight categories of decision-making situations: innovative, circumstantial, reflexive, deliberative, routinized, administrative, inertia, and crisis (in Rosenau, 1969). Hermann has focused mainly on the crisis situation.

"Crisis" has been variously described as "intensive inputs to the international system," as "involving significant actual or potential international conflict," as a "situation of unanticipated threat to important goals and values where the time for decision is restricted,"[18] or as "a set of rapidly unfolding events which raises the impact of destabilizing forces . . . substantially above 'normal' . . . and increases the likelihood of violence." The use of crisis is similar to the stimulus-response models of psychology; crisis acts as a stimulus, and the decision maker's reaction is the response.

Some of the most interesting work on crisis decision making has been undertaken by researchers in the Stanford University Studies in International Conflict and Integration (see Holsti et al., in Singer, 1968: 123–158). Their work focuses on the relationships among crisis situations, the decision makers' perception of these events, and their resultant actions. The researchers argue that since we are looking at decision makers, their perceptions are important. Thus, decision makers' *perception* of these events stands between (mediates) the crisis situation and the resultant actions. Examining the 1914 crisis that preceded World War I, these researchers have employed what they called the *two-step mediated stimulus-response* model.

This model is presented in Figure 6.2. We will use Egypt and Israel as specific referents.

The diagram identifies the following elements of the interaction model. A physical event or verbal act occurs in either the external or domestic environment of a country. This event is called a *stimulus* (S).

Figure 6.2 MEDIATED STIMULUS-RESPONSE MODEL

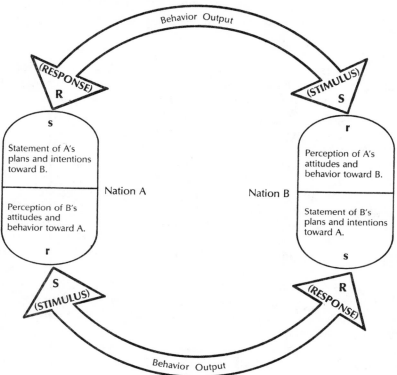

SOURCE: Modified from J. David Singer (ed.), *Quantitative International Politics* (New York: Free Press, 1968), p. 133. Copyright 1968. Reprinted with the permission of Macmillan Publishing Co., Inc.

This stimulus may or may not be perceived by the decision makers, and the same stimulus may be perceived and evaluated differently by various decision makers. For example, on May 21, 1967, Israel called up its military reserves and deployed troops along the borders with Syria and Jordan. Although its intention may have been only to counter previous Egyptian mobilization, this action served as a stimulus (S) to Egypt, which announced the next day that it intended to reinstitute the blockade against Israeli shipping in the Strait of Tiran.

In the model, the *perception* (r) of the stimulus (S) refers to the way the situation is defined by the decision makers. For example, we have seen how Egyptian and Israeli decision makers perceived each other's actions as hostile and threatening. These perceptions were based on their attitudes, values, and cognitions. These perceptions, in turn, influence the objectives, policies, and decisions of a country. The actual policies or decisions are shown in the model as *statements of plans and intentions* (s). For example, Egyptian President Anwar Sadat, in defining the 1972–1973 stalemate in Egyptian-Israeli relations, formulated three policy objectives against Israel: to forge Arab unity, to isolate Israel diplomatically, and to develop Arab oil as a political weapon. These tactics reflected Egypt's plans and intentions toward Israel.

Influenced by their perceptions of the other's attitudes and behavior, and by their strategies and intentions, both countries' decision makers act. A *response* (R) is an action by the decision makers. For example, President Sadat traveled to the African states to secure diplomatic support (R), signed an alliance with King Faisal of Saudi Arabia (R), and got the oil-exporting nations to agree to an oil boycott of Israel (R).

Each of these Egyptian actions (R) served as stimuli (S) to Israeli foreign policy decision makers. They, in turn, defined the situation (r) generated by Egyptian actions, analyzed their objectives toward Egypt (s), and reacted (R) by approaching the United States for additional arms and solidifying their hold on the occupied territories.

In crisis situations, decision makers seem to reveal consistent patterns of perceiving hostility, experiencing rising tensions, expressing hostility, and escalating their hostile actions until violence occurs. One possible explanation of foreign policy actions begins to emerge: If a country (say, Egypt) correctly or incorrectly perceives itself threatened by another country (say, Israel), there is a high probability that the initial country (Egypt) will respond with threats of hostile action. As the second country (Israel) begins to perceive this hostility directed to itself, it, too, will probably behave in a hostile and defensive manner. This threatening behavior (by Israel) will confirm for the initial state (Egypt) that its perceptions were correct, and it (Egypt) will be inclined to increase its hostile actions. A spiral, increasingly hostile, threatening, and injurious forms; the resulting escalation may lead to violence. Let us examine some of the more important elements of this interactionist model in more detail.

THE ELEMENT OF STRESS

In discussing perceptions, we noted how anxiety and stress (particularly in crisis situations) affect decision makers' views of their environment. Ole Holsti contends that stress is also significant in terms of foreign policy. In order to examine these effects, Holsti composed a list of traits that are considered essential to effective decision making. They include the ability to: "(1) identify major alternative courses of action, (2) estimate the probable cost and gains of each alternative course, (3) resist premature cognitive closure (the tendency to ignore conflicting perceptions, images, and beliefs), (4) distinguish between the possible and the probable, (5) assess the situation from the perspective of other parties, (6) discriminate between the relevant and irrelevant information, (7) tolerate ambiguity, (8) resist premature action, (9) make adjustments to meet real changes in the situation" (1972: 10).

Holsti argues that stress generally affects individual performance. Citing a number of experiments in psychology,[19] he points out that high stress can cause individuals to: increase their rate of error; regress to stereotypic perceptions; become rigid in their problem solving; reduce the ability to discriminate the dangerous from the trivial; and diminish their focus of attention (1972: 13). Taken together, these effects of high stress wipe out the ability to see the essential aspects of the situation and rigidify behavior. As Holsti points out, foreign policy decisions require the very attributes and skills that are most susceptible to stress.

Another factor affected by stress is communication. According to Holsti, effective decision making depends largely on the ability to discriminate between relevant and trivial information: "the adequacy of communication both in the physical sense of open channels of communication and in the sense of 'pragmatics'—the correspondence between the sender's intent and the recipient's decoding—has been a major concern in studies of decision making" (1972:18). Various studies have shown that under high stress, individuals increase their selective perceptions of information, fail to discern the relevant from the irrelevant, and limit their search for new information (see Hermann, 1972).

EFFECTS OF CRISIS AND STRESS: POLICY OPTIONS

Karl Deutsch contends that governments frequently decide to go to war when they believe they have no other alternative (1957: 200). According to Holsti, crisis and the resulting stress make such a perception more likely. As he puts it: (1) "In a crisis situation decision-makers will tend to perceive the range of their own alternatives to be more restricted than those of their adversaries"; (2) "As stress increases, decision-makers will tend to perceive the range of alternatives open to themselves as becoming narrower" (1972: 145). Data from the 1914 prewar crisis support both of these hypotheses. Does this mean that whenever this sense of helplessness and resignation sets in, war will occur? Bruce Russett argues not. He contends that there are really two phases of a crisis: the *point of surprise*, when policy makers realize that war is a possibility, and the *point of no escape*, when they must make a definite decision about action that reduces the number of future alternatives and thus makes war a certainty.

Pruitt and Snyder, in discussing Russett's work, point out that "the likelihood of war depends on the amount of time elapsing between the two points. The more time that elapses . . . the less likeli-hood there is that they will close off all alternatives but those that lead to war at the point of no escape" (1969: 56). Holsti's data seem to support Russett's contentions. In the Cuban missile crisis of 1962, the United States and the Soviet Union were able to avert war because their decision makers were able to "buy" time to generate enough alternatives so as to avoid Russett's point of no escape (Holsti, 1972: 169–197).

THE CONFLICT SPIRAL THESIS: SUMMARY

Our examination of the mediated stimulus-response model, crisis, and perceptions of threat and hostility makes it clear that war, or any other foreign policy behavior, is often seen as the result of interac-tions between two or more nations. Particularly in the case of war, the pattern of events consists of a spiral of mutually reinforcing ten-sions, stress, hostility, and threats between two antagonists (North et al., 1964: 1–14). This pattern of events, which North has labelled the "conflict spiral," can be summarized as follows:

1. State A, either correctly or incorrectly, perceives goal incompatibility between itself and another state (B). The more highly valued the goal, the greater the perceived threat coming from State B. Black-and-white thinking may play a significant role in magnifying the perceptions of threat.
2. If State A perceives threat and hostility coming from State B, it will express threats and engage in hostile actions. Should the perceived threat be sufficiently high, State A may even launch a preemptive attack on State B. If this does not occur, then
3. As State B begins to perceive this hostility directed toward itself from A, it is probable that B, too, will respond with hostile actions. A "prepar-edness race" may even begin in State B.
4. B's defensive preparations will appear threatening to State A, and may even convince A that its initial perceptions were correct. A's lack of empathy for B, its selective inattention, and its military overconfidence will cause it to intensify its hostile actions toward B. It, too, may join the preparedness race.
5. As hostilities between the two countries become increasingly threaten-ing and/or damaging, a crisis results.
6. Under the intense stress of the resulting crisis, various psychological, decisional, and communicational events occur that propel actions to the point of no escape, where the threat to goals is so great that the only alternative is to go to war.

Obviously not all wars begin in the manner just described. There are other contributing factors and patterns. Our attention has been directed at a very small, selective set of forces that both illustrate and elaborate on the basic elements of violent conflict that have been presented throughout this text. The reader, no doubt, will have recognized some of the same elements in war that appeared in the discussion of riots and revolutions. We will now examine some situations where conflict exists but where violence is not used. This is the "strategy of conflict"—the use of bargaining and negotiation in conflict situations.

Notes*

1. There are many good studies of the political, military and economic dimensions of the October War. Three stand out: Laurence L. Whetten's *The Canal War: Four Power Conflict in the Middle East;* Walter Laqueur's *Confrontations: The Middle East War and World Politics;* and R. D. McLaurin et al., *Foreign Policy Making in the Middle East.*

2. As Walter Laqueur and Martin Gilbert have subsequently pointed out, the Golan Heights did not contain the necessary space for either troop maneuverability or a strategy of trading territory for time. Laurence L. Whetten, who has closely examined the military aspects of the war, cites additional reasons for the Israeli strategy of concentrating its forces on pp. 243–245 of *The Canal War.*

3. Whetten estimates that by October 13, Israel had destroyed approximately 55 percent of Syria's tank force and 30 percent of its air force.

4. Because U.S. policies in the Middle East have been reviewed and discussed frequently, we shall address only the immediate perceptions and behavior of the United States during the October War.

5. Here we are talking about what governs a perception rather than a decision.

6. These and other beliefs are discussed in some detail in Marvin and Bernard Kalb's *Kissinger,* pp. 450–459. Another useful summary of the American beliefs at the time is Laurence L. Whetten's *The Arab-Israeli Dispute: Great Power Behavior.* Further discussion of Kissinger's beliefs will be found in chapter 8 of this text.

7. Interestingly, DeRivera also points out that when foreign policy misperceptions occur, there is a tendency to blame them on errors in information and not on errors in interpretation. Later, during the 1975 congressional hearing on the activities of the Central Intelligence Agency, the agency was charged with failing to provide adequate information that the October War was imminent. Blame was once again placed on lack of information rather than interpretation.

8. The strategy that the United States actually followed to secure these objectives has been the subject of much speculation and debate. See, for example, Kalb and Kalb's interpretation in their book *Kissinger,* pp. 450–499, and Matti Golan's *The Secret Conversations of Henry Kissinger.* There are two central questions: (1) Did the United States use Israeli dependence on American arms to influence Israeli political and military actions? Did the United States and the Soviet Union strike a bargain to pressure their respective clients to end hostilities?

9. Whether the Soviet Union knew the exact details and time of attack is debatable. Some analysts like Laurence Whetten, contend that the Soviets knew only that an Arab attack was imminent, but neither the specific time nor details of the military operation.

10. Space does not permit us to discuss the bureaucratic complexities and conflicting domestic forces that eventually led to the U.S. decision to resupply Israel. This decision was greatly complicated by bureaucratic forces inside the United States. These

*Complete citations for the works mentioned here will be found in the Bibliography, pages 167–169.

included the alleged conflict between Secretary of State Kissinger and Secretary of Defense Schlesinger; economic forces outside the country, such as the threatened Arab oil embargo; and the general U.S. political climate caused by Watergate.

11. Both superpowers had tremendous political leverage over their client states because of their dependence on superpower weapons and supplies. For a complete discussion of this "patron-client" relationship, see *Current History*, February 1975. As Israel, Egypt, and Syria became more and more dependent on the airlift to continue the fighting, the superpowers increased their influence.

12. According to Kalb and Kalb, approximately seven Soviet combat divisions (approximately 50,000 troops) had been placed on alert. In addition to strengthening the Soviet Mediterranean Fleet, the Soviet Union had dispatched twelve cargo planes to Cairo. As Kalb and Kalb speculated (p. 488), "analysts wondered if they might be carrying some of those airborne troops. An airborne command post had been established in Southern Russia. And, finally, special military orders had been intercepted, suggesting the Russians might be preparing to intervene in the Middle East."

13. Although there are a number of articulate spokesmen for this school of thought, we have relied heavily on the edited readings of Dean G. Pruitt and Richard C. Snyder. Their work, *Theory and Research on the Causes of War*, is still one of the best collections of writings in this area. We have supplemented and updated this work with appropriate examples from more recent research. In utilizing their approach, we are accepting the individual decision maker as our primary unit of analysis in explaining state behavior.

14. For a perceptive and articulate review of the political realism school of thought in international relations, see Cecil V. Crabb's *Policy Makers and Critics*, pp. 165–213.

15. Using data from the pre-World War I period, Zinnes was able to support hypotheses 1 and 2 and found mixed results for hypotheses 3 and 4.

16. For a complete discussion of the decisions and actions that resulted in Israel's preemptive attack, see Walter Laqueur's *The Road to War, 1967*.

17. One of the most stimulating books on perceptions of intentions is Robert Jervis's *Perception and Misperception in International Politics*. Jervis examines not only intention but also the process of perception.

18. This third definition is the one that we will use in our discussion.

19. There is a rich experimental literature on the effects of stress on various forms of behavior. Among those we found useful are Richard Lazarus, *Psychological Stress and the Coping Process* and his article "Stress."

Bibliography

ALLISON, GRAHAM. *The Essence of Decision*. Boston: Little, Brown, 1971.

————, and MORTON H. HALPERIN. "Bureaucratic Politics: A Paradigm and Some Policy Implications." *World Politics*, 24 (Spring 1972), 40–79.

ARON, RAYMOND. *The Century of Total War*. Boston: Beacon Press, 1955.

BOULDING,KENNETH. *The Image*. Ann Arbor: University of Michigan Press, 1956.

BRODIE, BERNARD. *War and Politics*. New York: Macmillan, 1973.

CHURCHILL, R. S., and W. S. CHURCHILL, *The Six Day War*. Boston: Houghton Mifflin, 1967.

COPLIN, WILLIAM D. and CHARLES KEGLEY. *Multimethod Introduction to International Politics*. Chicago: Markham, 1971.

CRABB, CECIL V. *Policy Makers and Critics*. New York: Praeger, 1976.

DeRIVERA, JOSEPH H. *The Psychological Dimensions of Foreign Policy*. Columbus, Ohio: Charles E. Merrill, 1968.

DEUTSCH, KARL W. "Mass Communication and the Loss of Freedom in National Decision Making." *Journal of Conflict Resolution*, 1:2 (1957), 200–211.

DOUGHERTY, JAMES E. and ROBERT L. PFALTZGRAFF. *Contending Theories of International Relations*. Philadelphia: Lippincott, 1971.

EDMONDS, ROBIN. *Soviet Foreign Policy 1962–1973: The Paradox of Super Power*. London: Oxford University Press, 1975.

FISHER, ROGER. *International Conflict for Beginners*. New York: Harper, 1969.

FRANK, JEROME D. *Sanity and Survival: Psychological Aspects of War and Peace*. New York: Vintage, 1968.

GILBERT, MARTIN. *Atlas of the Arab-Israeli Conflict*. New York: Macmillan, 1974.

GOLAN, MATTI. *The Secret Conversations of Henry Kissinger*. New York: Quadrangle Books, 1976.

HAAS, MICHAEL. *International Conflict*. Indianapolis: Bobbs-Merrill, 1974.

HERMANN, CHARLES F. (ed.). *International Crises: Insights for Behavioral Research*. New York: Free Press, 1972.

————. "International Crisis as a Situational Variable." In James N. Rosenau (ed.). *International Relations and Foreign Policy*. New York: Free Press, 1969.

HOLSTI, OLE R. *Crisis Escalation War*. Montreal: McGill-Queen's University Press, 1972.

————, ROBERT C. NORTH, and RICHARD BRODY. "Perception and Action in the 1914 Crisis." In J. David Singer. *Quantitative International Politics*. New York: Free Press, 1968.

JERVIS, ROBERT. *Perception and Misperception in International Politics*, Princeton, New Jersey: Princeton University Press, 1976.

KALB, BERNARD, and MARVIN KALB. *Kissinger*. Boston: Little, Brown, 1974.

KENNAN, GEORGE F. *Realities of American Foreign Policy*. New York: Norton, 1966.

KISSINGER, HENRY A. *A World Restored*. New York: Grosset and Dunlap, 1964.

———. *Nuclear Weapons and Foreign Policy*. New York: Harper & Brothers for the Council on Foreign Relations, 1957.

LAQUEUR, WALTER. *Confrontations: The Middle East War and World Politics*. London: Wildwood Press, 1974.

———. *The Road to War, 1967*. London: Camelot Press, 1969.

LAZARUS, RICHARD. "Stress." *International Encyclopedia of the Social Sciences*, 15 (1968).

———. *Psychological Stress and the Coping Process*. New York: McGraw-Hill, 1966.

McLAURIN, R. D., et al. *Foreign Policy Decision Making in the Middle East*. New York: Praeger, 1977.

McNEIL, ELTON B. (ed.). *The Nature of Human Conflict*. Englewood Cliffs, N.J.: Prentice-Hall, 1965.

MIDLARSKY, MANUS J. *On War: Political Violence in the International System*. New York: Free Press, 1975.

MORGENTHAU, HANS J. *Politics Among Nations*. New York: Knopf, 1967.

NIEBUHR, REINHOLD. *Christian Realism and Political Problems*. New York: Scribners, 1953.

———. *Christianity and Power Politics*. New York: Scribners, 1940.

NORTH, ROBERT C., et al. "Some Empirical Data on the Conflict Spiral." Peace Research Society (International) Papers, 1 (1964), 1–14.

PLANO, JACK C. and ROY OLTON. *The International Relations Dictionary*. New York: Holt, 1969.

PRUITT, DEAN G., and RICHARD C. SNYDER. *Theory and Research on the Causes of War*. Englewood Cliffs, N.J.: Prentice-Hall, 1969.

———. "Definition of the Situation as a Determinant of International Behavior." In H. C. Kelman (ed.). *International Behavior*. New York: Holt, 1965.

ROSENAU, JAMES N. (ed.). *International Relations and Foreign Policy*. New York: Free Press, 1969.

RUSSETT, BRUCE M. "Cause, Surprise and No Escape." *The Journal of Politics*, 24:1 (1964), 3–22.

SINGER, J. DAVID. *Quantitative International Politics*. New York: Free Press, 1968.

———. "Threat Perception and the Armament-Tension Dilemma." *Journal of Conflict Resolution*, 2 (1958), 90–105.

STAGNER, ROSS. "The Psychology of Human Conflict." In Elton B. McNeil (ed.). *The Nature of Human Conflict*. Englewood Cliffs, N.J.: Prentice-Hall, 1965.

THOMPSON, KENNETH W. *Political Realism and the Crisis of World Politics.* Princeton, N.J.: Princeton University Press, 1960.

WHETTEN, LAURENCE L. *The Arab-Israeli Dispute: Great Power Behavior.* London: The International Institute for Strategic Studies, 1976.

———. *The Canal War: Four Power Conflict in the Middle East.* Cambridge, Mass.: MIT Press, 1974.

WHITE, RALPH K. *Nobody Wanted War.* Garden City, N.Y.: Doubleday, 1970.

———. "Mirror Images in the East-West Conflict." Presented at American Psychological Association Convention, Sept. 4, 1961.

ZINNES, DINA A. "The Expression and Perception of Hostility in Prewar Crisis: 1914." In J. David Singer (ed.). *Quantitative International Politics.* New York: Free Press, 1968.

7 | CONFLICT RESOLUTION: A STRATEGY OF BARGAINING

Almost any conflict situation can be seen as an attempt by one actor to influence another actor either to act or to not act. That is, individuals, groups, and nations want others to change their minds with regard to something they have done or are threatening to do. Whether that something is a riot, a revolution, or a war does not matter. There is some decision "they" can make which will avoid "our" resorting to violence. Naturally, we may not get everything we want, but we can perceive conflict resolution as getting "them" to make a choice.

What we have been discussing are *bargaining situations.* These, according to Thomas C. Schelling, are "situations in which the ability of one participant to gain his ends is dependent to an important degree on the choices or decisions that the other participant will make" (1963: 5). Schelling's work on bargaining, or what he calls a *theory of interdependent decision making*, points to an important aspect of the study of human conflict: conflict is not only the opposition of hostile and violent forces but rather a "more complex and delicate phenomenon in which antagonism *and cooperation* subtly interact in the adversary relationship" (cited in Dougherty and Pfaltzgraff, 1971: 364; emphasis added).

In this chapter, we will examine this other aspect of conflict by analyzing the bargaining process. After looking at some of the characteristics of bargaining situations, we will discuss the more important elements. The social, physical, issue, and individual components of bargaining will be introduced. Finally, we will explore the various interrelationships among these components, particularly in situations where threats and promises are made.

Characteristics of Bargaining Situations[1]

Bargaining is the process whereby two or more parties seek to agree on what each shall give and take or perform and receive in a transaction between them (Rubin and Brown, 1975: 1–2): This definition assumes that while conflict is taken for granted, there are also common interests between adversaries. Further, the agreement which is struck between them is based on rational value-maximizing behavior, and each adversary's "best" choice of action depends on what the other party is expected to do (Schelling, 1963: 15). Let us explore these assumptions in detail.

INTERACTION

Bargaining is first and foremost an interactive process that requires two or more participants. Whether this interaction takes place between individuals, groups, or nations is not important here.[2] What is important is the notion of interaction. A central feature of bargaining is that conflict issues arise where other actors have the power to make decisions. These actors are generally beyond our control. If we wish to have these conflicts peacefully resolved, decisions and actions by others are required. Conflict resolution is therefore an interactive process. If there is some agreement we want, then our task is to influence the decisions and actions of others. It is only through their behavior that resolution can come about. Schelling focuses on the interactive nature of bargaining with his concept of the "strategy of conflict." He states that " 'strategic behavior' is concerned with influencing another's choice by working on his expectation of how one's own behavior is related to his" (1963: 15).

CONFLICT OF INTERESTS

The bargaining relationship is based on a conflict of interest regarding some goal, motive, event, or issue. Conflict, like bargaining, is an interaction process. It assumes that at least two or more actors or participants (to use Schelling's term) are involved. One element of conflict, however, may not be so obvious. Whereas bargaining takes conflict for granted, it also assumes that "pure" conflict—that is, a situation in which the interests of two antagonists are completely opposed—is not present.[3] As Schelling and others have pointed out, if conflict is to be waged to the finish, and if there is no basis of mutual accommodation, then there is nothing left to bargain. Only pure conflict can result.

If, on the other hand, conflict is not present in "pure" form, but rather allows for mutual accommodation, then the basis of bargaining exists.[4] Even in situations where violence occurs, bargaining may also take place—if for no other reason than to minimize the resulting damage (Schelling, 1963: 5).

SEQUENCES AND COMMUNICATION

Rubin and Brown contend that bargaining is a sequential activity (1975: 14). In a typical bargaining sequence a presentation of demands by one or the other party is followed by concessions, and then by counterproposals. This notion of sequential behavior is important, primarily because it focuses on communication in the bargaining process. When this process begins, each participant may know only what his own interests are. Furthermore, each participant probably knows only what his own preferred outcome is, though each probably has some ideas as to what the other wants. Citing the research of Kelly and Thibault, Rubin and Brown argue that in order to bargain effectively, each party must know the other's wishes (1975: 14). This information can be provided only by the other party. In short, communication must take place.

Schelling identifies two types of bargaining communications: "tacit" and "explicit." In tacit bargaining, communications between participants are either incomplete or indirect. For some reason, one or both parties either cannot or will not communicate with the other. How do parties communicate in such cases? Schelling contends that one way that bargaining preferences can be transmitted is by the *coordination* of actions that reflect each party's preferences. (1963: 54). Before Anwar Sadat's historic trip to Israel in 1977, Egypt and Israel engaged in tacit bargaining. Where face-to-face communications exist, coordination is also important; here the parties coordinate their expectations about what each ultimately wants, rather than having to first draw inferences from behavior. As Rubin and Brown suggest, no matter what type of communication is involved, each party is dependent on the other for information in structuring its own preferences and bargaining strategy (1975: 14, citing the work of Kelly and Thibault, 1969).

The Effectiveness Approach

Since the bargaining process is so complex, it can be approached in many ways. One popular approach is to specify the goals that parties are trying to achieve, and then ask how effective their efforts were (Marshall, 1971; Nierenberg, 1971; Walton, 1965). The central questions of the effectiveness approach are: Did bargaining work? Did it allow the participants to resolve their differences? Were there excessive costs and damages to each?

Rubin and Brown have elaborated upon these questions. (1975: 32).[5] As a number of authors have pointed out, bargaining effectiveness is not easy to evaluate. What makes the evaluation so complex is the number of factors involved. For example, one must explore the criteria for making mutually profitable adjustments to goals, expectations, and behavior (Schelling, 1963: 21). In addition, two sets of factors might affect bargaining effectiveness: the institutional (or social) components of bargaining and the individual characteristics of the negotiators.[6] Let us examine each of these crucial sets of factors in detail.

STRUCTURAL VARIABLES IN BARGAINING

The structural dimensions of bargaining are those institutional and procedural factors that influence our predispositions, expectations, and behavior. Suppose we wondered what caused an actor to make the first offer: what caused him to find making a commitment easy or difficult? Schelling suggests that one possible factor is whether a bargaining agent is present. In 1973 through 1974, both the Arabs and the Israelis were able to bargain and to make commitments to each other because of the presence of a bargaining agent: U.S. Secretary of State Henry Kissinger. Why could the Arabs and Israelis make such commitments? One reason might have been that the agent (i.e., the United States) had an incentive of its own to see that the commitments of both parties were honored. Where such an agent also has power over one or both parties, each party's commitments, once made, are difficult, if not impossible, to change (Schelling, 1963: 29). The presence of a bargaining agent is one structural variable affecting bargaining.

AVAILABILITY AND FUNCTIONS OF THIRD PARTIES[7]

Throughout history, and particularly in international affairs, nations have played the role of the third party. This role includes acting as conciliator, mediator, arbitrator, and fact finder. In formal bargaining situations, the role of the third party is legally defined (e.g., in labor arbitrations), or it is specified in advance by both antagonists. Since the roles that a third party can play are spelled out in detail elsewhere, we will not elaborate upon them here (see, for example, Bishop, 1931; Balch, 1962). What is important to remember is that neither antagonist is bound to abide by the third party's actions and suggestions. As Rubin and Brown point out, the effectiveness of third-party intervention rests not so much on legality as on the personal characteristics of the third party, his reputation and skills, and his influence on the bargaining situation (1975: 55).

We believe that the roles of third parties are much more interesting in informal bargaining situations. Here, the third party can play a number of challenging roles, such as transmitting messages between adversaries who cannot or will not communicate directly. Since a third party may be viewed with suspicion by both sides—can antagonists, for example, be certain that the third party does not favor one or the other?—one of the hardest tasks is to establish his or her neutrality.

The mere availability or presence of a third party may facilitate an agreement.[8] For example, the third party may be able to suggest possible concessions which neither side would propose for fear of appearing weak. There are some other important functions that a third party can perform. Let us examine these briefly.

Two studies on the functions of third parties are R. E. Walton's *Interpersonal Peacemaking: Confrontations and Third-Party Consultation* (1969) and Charles Kerr's article entitled "Industrial Conflict and Its Resolution" (1954). Since both of these studies are discussed elsewhere,[9] we will list the functions they identify. These include reducing irrationality; exploring alternative solutions; providing opportunities for graceful retreat or face saving, regulating the costs of conflict; regulating public interference; identifying and promoting the use of additional "hidden" resources; establishing and reinforcing norms and rules of procedure; influencing the negotiations by selecting bargaining sites; formulating and manipulating agenda; and setting time constraints.

Another study that analyzes the role of a third party in a specific international dispute is Amos Perlmutter's study of the 1973–1974 Middle East negotiations (1975). Perlmutter contends that third parties often act as "crisis managers," attempting to affect the course, structure, and outcomes of negotiations through the use of diplomacy. Another function is to establish intimacy and empathy with each adversary. Perlmutter contends that Kissinger was able to work so effectively with the Arabs and Israelis because he convinced both sides that he understood their aspirations, goals, and fears (1975: 319–320). Thus he was able to function as advocate, surrogate arbitrator, and confidant. Kissinger's relatively successful Middle East negotiations of 1973 through 1974 and President Jimmy Carter's success at the Camp David summit in 1978 suggest the importance of examining those factors that determine third-party effectiveness.[10]

MANAGING THE INTERACTION SETTING

It is obvious that bargaining takes place in a physical context. Delegates come together at specific locations, arrive at particular rooms, enter and are seated in prearranged places. They follow an agenda that has been painstakingly deliberated. Most people know that all of this occurs, but they often do not realize that these elements are usually linked to the issues in conflict. Let us look at a few of these physical elements and their effect on bargaining situations.

Two have been singled out for analysis—the location of and physical arrangements at the negotiating site, and communications channels.

The Physical Setting[11] The bargaining site may affect the psychological climate of the negotiations. "Psychological climate" usually refers to the elements of power and status. For example, "a bargainer who views himself as having higher status than his opponent may seek control over the bargaining site in order to arrange it in a manner that both affirms his superiority and is likely to induce deference from the other" (Rubin and Brown, 1975: 82).

In considering international negotiations, Fred C. Iklé has shown some of the interrelationships that may exist among physical elements, status, and bargaining effectiveness (1964). He contends that nations must avoid disputes about status because such disputes can hamper the negotiations. U.S.-French relations became quite cool, for example, after Charles De Gaulle refused to meet Lyndon B. Johnson during the funeral for President John F. Kennedy except on French soil (fortunately, the French Embassy in Washington, D.C., served this purpose).

Many nations may refuse invitations to bargain in the opponent's country because they feel themselves to be at a psychological disadvantage. There are, of course, a number of options that can defuse this sensitive issue. Traditionally, nations have chosen a neutral bargaining site. This neutrality refers not only to the host country's politics or position on the issue but also to the psychological attitude of the opponents. The Strategic Arms Limitation Talks, for example, rotated between two neutral sites, Helsinki, Finland, and Vienna, Austria. All later SALT talks have been held in Geneva, Switzerland. Often more imaginative ways can be found to neutralize the psychological advantages of negotiating "at home." Henry Kissinger's creative and skillful use of "shuttle diplomacy" between Cairo, Jerusalem, and Damascus allowed all the parties the benefits of negotiating in their respective national capitals. Kissinger simply became the surrogate opponent, the "guest" in whichever country he happened to be.

Communications Channels We have seen that interdependence is part of the structure of bargaining. Some kind of collaboration or mutual accommodation is necessary for bargaining to be effective. Bargaining is really a form of coordinated problem solving. Thus its ultimate success depends on the transmission of intentions or plans. This emphasizes the need for communication, for it is only by communicating that these intentions or perception of intentions can be transmitted, received, and acted upon. The effectiveness of any bargaining situation, therefore, depends largely on an exchange and interpretation of information. Since communication has already been discussed (particularly in chapters 1 and 6, and earlier in this chapter), let us review some of its dimensions.

During conflict situations, particularly crises, communication between opponents tends to decrease. Holsti has shown that during the pre-World War I crisis, communications between opponents decreased while communications between allies increased. Ironically, communications between opponents decrease at the very moment when information is needed to reduce perceptions of threat and hostility and coordinate actions to prevent war. The former is especially important. If perceptions of threat and hostility reach a "critical mass," no amount of communication will help. In fact, if one nation decides that its interest lies in launching a preemptive attack, it will deliberately break off communications to maximize the effect of its aggression. Morton Deutsch further suggests that in a crisis, the information coming from an opponent is perceived as being unreliable. Thus there is no incentive for the other party either to utilize it or to seek additional information (1969).

However, not all bargaining occurs in a crisis environment. How do communications affect the process in more "normal" conflict situations? Schelling has shown that in this case, communication between opponents can be either verbal or inferential—that is, drawn from behavior. Which form is more effective? Rubin and Brown conclude that "other things being equal, bargaining effectiveness may be sustained at a satisfactory level if the parties cannot see one another; but if verbal (spoken) communications is eliminated or interfered with, effectiveness is likely to suffer" (1975: 99). Schelling, on the other hand, stresses the effectiveness of behavioral communications, particularly when verbal communication either cannot exist or is seen as less convincing than action (1963: 53–80). All these findings clearly suggest the indirect influence of physical and psychological factors. These situational factors can affect a host of motivations and perceptions, which, in turn, can limit or expand the influence of communication. Various studies suggest that situational factors, such as exchanging information under stress, hostility, or suspicion, may influence not only the parties' perceptions of the message but also the manner in which they chose to communicate and their receptivity to the message.

ISSUE VARIABLES

There are hundreds of issues over which actors can bargain. Iklé classifies these issues into five types: extension, normalization, redistribution, innovation, and side effect issues (1964: 26). The issues over which nations bargain affect not only the subject of negotiations but the negotiating process as well. For example, let us examine the normalization agreements between the United States and the People's

Republic of China. These two nations recently have sought to reestablish diplomatic relations. The actual negotiations toward this end have been influenced by such situational factors as the continuation of U.S. relations with Taiwan, Chinese hostilities toward the Soviet Union, and lobbying within the United States against the recognition of the Communist regime in Peking. Iklé further contends that nations often negotiate over "side effects" that are not directly related to the primary outcome of the bargaining situation. These side effects may include such things as maintaining contact between antagonists, substituting negotiation for violent action, gathering information, deception, and propaganda (1964: 43–58). We will return to these side effects in a minute. For now, let us explore the idea that the bargaining relationship involves a number of issues. Often the objective is to produce side effects as much as it is to solve the conflict issue.

Rubin and Brown distinguish between issues involving a "tangible" resource or concern, and "intangible" factors, such as honor, reputation, or status. They agree, however, that the intangible issues may become as important in bargaining as the tangible ones. Research by Ralph White on the Vietnam conflict and negotiations provides ample supporting evidence of both Iklé's and Rubin's arguments.

Why are intangible issues introduced into bargaining situations? The answer depends on whether one chooses to explore psychological or political factors. From the psychological perspective, the need to "save face," to generate a public image, and to enhance self-esteem are caused by a desire to appear strong, either to the opponent or to other audiences. This need to project a "virile self-image" (to use one of White's terms) is usually accomplished through propaganda. As Iklé points out, some governments value bargaining for its propaganda side effect because they wish to enhance their prestige. This may have motivated, in part, the Soviet Union's frequent demands for summit meetings with the United States in the late 1950s (1964: 53). Such needs for prestige appear to be based on the assumption that one must look strong or prestigious to be in a favorable bargaining situation.

In the political realm, there are other reasons why intangibles or side effects are introduced into bargaining situations. As we have seen, it is important for lines of communication among antagonists to remain open. In some cases, this can be done by bargaining over "hopeless" issues. Iklé identifies two reasons for remaining in contact. First, the continuation of talks provide a forum for the exchange of views. Such an exchange can, in turn, influence both parties' motivations and perceptions. Second, maintaining communication could be useful for the future, should emergency talks and crisis bargaining be necessary (1964: 44).

PSYCHOLOGICAL VARIABLES

Bargaining and negotiations are carried out by individuals representing their respective groups or nations. These negotiations are influenced by their own loyalties, motivations, and perceptions. They, like the parties they represent, respond with anger, hostility, goodwill, and cooperation. Since we have already examined various psychological states, we will limit our discussion to a few of the variables that influence bargaining effectiveness. [12]

Risk Taking   Risk taking is the willingness to expose oneself to hazard or peril. Holsti has argued that in some instances of stress, individuals are more willing to make decisions or act in ways that expose them and others to possible injury or danger. In other cases of stress, however, persons become more cautious, primarily because they realize that greater certainty is needed before acting (1972: 21). Further, whereas stress does change individual perceptions, it does not necessarily induce higher risk taking (1972: 22).

It was long believed that while individual policy makers might be willing to take greater risks, their actions would be controlled and moderated by bureaucratic or group policy making. Several studies have now challenged this thesis. One of the more interesting is Irving Janis's analysis of "groupthink." Janis argues that collective judgments arising out of group discussions often involve riskier courses of action than the individual members would be prepared to take (1972: 6). How does one explain this? Citing the research in group psychology, Janis argues that the explanation lies in the effect that cohesive ingroups have on the beliefs and attitudes of their members. In such cohesive groups, members strike for unanimity at the expense of realistic appraisals of their and others' actions. This deterioration of mental efficiency, reality testing, and moral judgment is known as "groupthink."

How does groupthink cause individuals to shift to riskier behavior? For one thing, groupthink often creates an illusion of invulnerability in the group. The notion is "if our leader and everyone else in our group decides that it is okay, the plan is bound to succeed. Even if it is quite risky, luck will be on our side" (Janis, 1972: 36). This sense of unlimited confidence parallels the perception of military overconfidence developed by Ralph White and discussed in the previous chapter.

Other elements in groupthink can interact with this sense of invulnerability and encourage risk taking. These include personality traits of the group members, suppression of personal doubts about the risky course of action, and the presence of dominating members who suppress deviating points of view. The total effect is to create excessive optimism and encourage extreme risk taking (Janis, 1972: 197).[13]

How does such heightened risk taking influence bargaining behavior? Limited research (e.g., Dolbear and Lane, 1969) suggests that high risk takers begin bargaining with a predisposition to neither cooperate nor compete with the opponent. High risk takers seek to maximize their own gains. They are not interested in mutual accommodation. They do not care about or react to variations in the opponent's behavior. Such bargainers like to structure the bargaining situation so that it will produce a zero-sum outcome. Since they are not interested in mutual gain, they tend to make fewer concessions. Furthermore, they are likely to manipulate the flow of information to the opponent, hoping that this will restrict the opponent's bargaining behavior and result in a maximum payoff for themselves.

Reputation and Self-Concept[14] The manner in which bargainers interact with opponents, and the conditions under which they make threats and promises, have an important effect on their bargaining position in the future. In most bargaining situations, participants are trying not only to influence the current bargaining process, but also to increase their future effectiveness. Bargainers are often concerned with their reputations. Furthermore, a negotiator's reputation is "shaped by the way in which he has reached agreements in the past and it affects his power to influence agreements in the future" (Iklé 1964: 76). Often negotiators become unwilling to make concessions, perhaps fearing that such concessions might damage their reputation. Such individuals may also become overly cautious in preparing their bargaining strategy. In both cases, a concern for reputation can affect the negotiation process and its outcomes.

How does one explain this concern for reputation? An important variable may be self-concept—"the set of feelings and beliefs a person has about how he looks in his own eyes and the *eyes of others*" (Rubin and Brown, 1975: 178; emphasis added). Generally speaking, individuals with a positive self-concept are believed to be less concerned about how they look to others than those with a negative self-concept. A number of factors are thought to influence self-esteem. For example, it has been shown that highly cohesive groups provide a source of security for their members which serves to reduce anxiety and to heighten self-esteem. When members depend on the group to bolster their self-image, they tend to support the judgment and actions of that group no matter what their own misgivings. With respect to bargaining, it is thought that "individuals with a negative self concept tend to bargain more competitively than those with a positive view of themselves" (Rubin and Brown, 1975: 178). Why this relationship exists is not clear. Faucheux and Moscovici argue that highly competitive bargaining may reflect high anxiety. Persons with low self-esteem tend to overcompensate by becoming more aggressive and competitive in bargaining situations (1968).

Attitudes: The Dulles Case Of the many psychological variables that affect bargaining, one of the most important is attitudes. We have seen that attitudes strongly influence an individual's psychological predisposition. It has been found that cooperatively oriented bargainers (i.e., those with positive self-concepts and trust in others) behave more cooperatively than those who are competitively oriented (Rubin and Brown, 1975: 184). Furthermore, competitors behave competitively regardless of the other's behavior, while co-operators work hand-in-hand in the presence of cooperation and compete when confronted with competition (Kelly and Stahelski, 1970). These findings suggest that attitudes about others tend to resist change even in the light of conflicting evidence.[15] This can have a significant impact on bargaining situations. Let us examine a case in point.

In the early 1950s the U.S. government under the administration of Dwight D. Eisenhower was publicly committed to try to find an accommodation with the Soviet Union—in particular, to obtain an agreement on the control of nuclear weapons (DeRivera, 1968: 24). By 1954, following certain changes in Soviet policy, the atmosphere seemed appropriate for reaching an arms control agreement. One man would be of critical importance to such negotiations. He was John Foster Dulles, the American secretary of state.

Dulles's attitudes and beliefs showed him to be deeply suspicious of the Soviet Union. He did not believe that the Soviets could be trusted. To him, "Soviet Communism starts with an atheistic, God-less premise. Everything else flows from that premise" (Holsti, 1962). Because of his overwhelmingly negative attitudes toward the Soviet Union, Dulles gave arms control a low priority: "whenever there was a decision between arms control and alliance strength, he [Dulles] chose to support alliance strength. This policy, of course, eventually defeated the arms control talks" (DeRivera, 1968: 25).

Holsti contends that Dulles's actions were based on his negative attitudes toward the Soviet Union. To use Ralph White's term, Dulles saw the Soviet Union as the "diabolical enemy." What would happen to Dulles's attitudes in the face of contradictory evidence? Would his attitudes and behavior change if the Soviets communicated a willingness to engage in meaningful bargaining on arms control? Holsti's data provides dramatic support for Kelly and Stahelski's hypothesis that regardless of the other's behavior, competitors who hold strongly negative attitudes about their opponent will behave competitively, no matter what the evidence. Holsti found that whether Dulles perceived Soviet policy as hostile or relatively friendly did not affect his attitudes toward them at all. Furthermore, he continued to act negatively toward them, always trying to maximize the U.S. position.

SUMMARY

As we have seen, bargaining is a complex phenomenon. It is an interaction process that requires at least two parties before it can begin. Furthermore, bargaining is based on a conflict of interests on one or more issues. Like conflict and the use of violence, it is based on motivation. While there are numerous outcomes, bargaining usually involves a sequence: presentation of proposals and the evaluation of them by an opponent, followed by a new cycle in the process.

Whether each party is effective in bargaining depends on a host of factors. We have grouped these factors into two general categories: those that are socially determined and those that are individually or psychologically determined. There is a close interaction between these two sets of variables, so that, practically speaking, they must be considered together in discussing an actual bargaining situation. The psychological states of stress and anxiety, as well as a predisposition to be competitive or cooperative, interact with an array of structural properties to affect the bargainers' choice of perceptions and actions, thus influencing their bargaining effectiveness. Bargaining is a process of interdependent decision making. It is an attempt at coordinated problem solving that depends on the transmission and perception of intentions and actions. Let us now turn to the methods of bargaining—in particular, the use of threats and promises.

The Use of Threats and Promises

Thomas Schelling has argued that interdependent decision making is concerned primarily with constraining an adversary. This can be done by threats and promises. A threat, as defined earlier, is an expression of intent to do or say something that may harm the interests of another. A promise is an expressed intention that may be helpful or beneficial to the other. Both forms can be effective, depending upon how they affect each bargainer's perception of the other's preferences and intentions (Fisher, 1969: 28).

THREATS

The efficacy of threat in a bargaining situation depends upon its credibility. Will the other party believe that one is likely to carry it out? As we have already seen, perceptions of threat and credibility are affected by whether the threatening party has the capability, intent, and predisposition to act.

How effective, then, is an influence attempt based on threat? It is effective to the extent that it actually causes the other party to change his mind and thus his previous course of action.[16] Roger Fisher contends that threats are a poor weapon. The opponent may have anticipated the costs of rejecting a threat when he decided to act as he did. The costs implied in the threat are therefore not sufficient to deter his actions. To now threaten increased costs may be ineffective because the opponent may have already taken these new costs into account. Fisher puts it this way: threats of sanctions exert influence only if they communicate something about the future. "They are intended to convey a convincing message that unless the decision we desire is made, the situation will get worse" (1969: 31). If the costs that are being threatened are no worse than those the opponent has expected, the opponent has no reason to change his behavior.

There are many ways in which a bargainer can enhance the efficacy of his threat. One way is to make a commitment to carry it out. This is potentially dangerous, because one is committed in advance to an act that one would prefer not to carry out (Schelling 1963: 36). As Schelling points out, therefore, care must be used in defining the threat and estimating its potential costs.

Threat involves further dangers and costs. For one thing, the option to bluff or to implement the threat is not as open as bargainers may believe. If, for example, the bargainer makes a commitment to carrying out the threat (for example, staking his reputation as collateral), he may find himself forced to carry it out even when new circumstances make this unnecessary (Fisher, 1969: 43). To counter such a danger, Schelling points out, the use of threat can be a matter of degree; threats can be used in stages. There are problems here, too; it is often difficult to know when the threat will be deemed intolerable. Thus if the party making the threat cannot define this "critical point," the threat may lose its effectiveness (1963: 42). Finally, the use of threat, as we have seen in chapter 6, tends to make the opponent more hostile. Once his perception of threat crosses a particular threshold, he may destroy the bargaining relationship and either immediately resort to violence or precipitate events that may lead to violence.

PROMISES

Opponents, as we have seen, consider the consequences of their decisions. Using a crude form of cost-benefit analysis, actors compare the expected results of making a certain decision with the expected results of not making it. As J. David Singer and others have argued, one way to influence others is to try to alter their perceptions of some of these expected results (1963, as cited in Rosenau, 1969). Fisher contends that in international relations "the effective pressure upon a government to decide one way or the other depends upon the difference between the perceived net 'pay-off' of making the decision weighed against the perceived net 'pay-off' of not doing so" (1969: 100). A promise is another way of exerting such influence. Basically a promise or offer seeks to enhance the attractiveness of the choice that one wants another to make.

Promise, like threat, also involves making a commitment. Yet, Schelling suggests, it is often quite difficult to make a convincing, binding promise. Why is this the case? Probably one reason is that the fulfillment of the promise is not always observable. For example, if we promise to vote for a candidate in a secret election, there is no way of knowing how we actually voted. (1963: 44). This suggests that promises must not only be credible, they must also have sufficient commitment as a backup. How can an offer be made more credible? Obviously, the other actor wants a reasonable guarantee that the promised benefits will materialize (Fisher, 1969: 116). Schelling suggests one possible strategy: "if a number of preparatory bargains can be struck on a small scale, each may be willing to risk a small investment to create a tradition of trust. The purpose is to let each party demonstrate that he appreciates the need for trust and that he knows the other does too" (1960: 45). In other words, parties can build up a reserve of credibility by making and keeping promises on minor issues. Then when a major issue emerges and a major offer is made, both sides know that each is aware of the long-term value of maintaining good faith (1963: 45). Fisher lists some additional strategies. These include: making the offer more specific, creating a detailed plan for implementing it, maintaining a reputation for honoring commitments, extending the benefits sooner, and limiting the time for accepting the offer (1969: 112–127).

Thus the utility of threats and promises depends on many factors. One of the most important is the course of the bargaining itself. As Rubin and Brown point out, when the issue is relatively small, both threats and promises may be used effectively to coordinate mutual expectations and intentions. Where the issue is large, threats and promises may lead to violence.

Conflicts of interest can often be settled effectively by bargaining. Certain conditions must be present, however, before this can occur. Even when violence is taking place, bargaining can help to limit its destructiveness. But, again, certain elements must be present. Our purpose has been to explore some of these elements and to discuss their interrelationships. In the next chapter we will analyze a specific situation that illustrates a number of these dimensions of bargaining.

Notes*

1. There are a number of excellent reviews of the literature on bargaining. The most extensive is Jeffrey Z. Rubin and Bert R. Brown's *The Social Psychology of Bargaining and Negotiation*. This review covers more than 500 studies of bargaining between 1960 and 1974. Because of its thoroughness, we have used it extensively in developing this chapter.

2. Later in this chapter and in chapter 8, which deals with international negotiations, we will see some subtle and important differences among interpersonal, intergroup, and international bargaining processes. For now, these differences will be ignored.

3. Another term for "pure conflict" that emerges from the literature on game theory is a "zero-sum game." In a zero-sum game between A and B, what A wins, B loses. Each game ends with one player having a score of plus one and the other minus one, with the value of "one" depending upon the stakes of the game. Among the examples of real-life situations that contain elements of zero-sum games, Dougherty and Pfaltzgraff cite elections and most military operations (1971: 349).

4. The game term for such "limited" conflict is "non-zero-sum." The difference here is that what one gains, another need not lose. In other words, the gains and losses need not add up to zero; there is room for cooperation.

5. Among the most frequent questions about bargaining effectiveness found in the literature, according to Rubin and Brown, are: (1) Was the agreement reached on all or only some of the issues involved? (2) How long did it take before agreement was reached? (3) How were the available outcomes distributed among the parties? (4) How many of each party's initial goals were ultimately obtained? (5) How satisfied were the parties with the outcomes? There are scores of other questions, but the reader will find these helpful analyzing specific bargaining situations.

6. These are the same two sets of factors used to explain social behavior. They reflect our primary thesis: political behavior results from the interaction between psychological predispositions and social institutions and structures.

7. There is a wealth of materials on the role of third parties in bargaining situations. The field of labor negotiations is particularly helpful. Among the texts that we have consulted in preparing this section are *Collective Bargaining Contracts: Techniques of Negotiations and Administration;* John T. Dunlop, *Collective Bargaining: Principles and Cases;* and Eileen B. Hoffman, *Resolving Labor-Management Disputes: A Nine-Country Comparison.*

8. Whereas Rubin and Brown cite a number of studies to illustrate this thesis, we found the article "Style of Third-Party Intervention, Face Saving and Bargaining Behavior," by D. F. Johnson and W. L. Fullar, to be particularly useful.

9. Both works are cited in Rubin and Brown, pp. 60–61.

10. Karl Kressel (1971) has found general agreement among prominent labor mediators that the first and most important task of the third party is to gain the trust and confidence of all direct participants in the bargaining situation. Perlmutter suggests that this is what Kissinger did, and it accounts for his effectiveness. Rubin and Brown elaborate on the Kressel findings and hypothesize that "all other things being equal, the greater the trust and confidence in a third party, the more effective his interventions are likely to be" (p. 62).

11. Various countries develop particular and intense feelings about such factors as site. See, for example, Charles T. Joy, *How Communists Negotiate.*

12. Much of the literature on the psychology of bargaining effectiveness deals with personality variables. Since, for the most part, we have ignored personality variables

*Complete citations for the works mentioned here will be found in the Bibliography, pages 186–187.

in this text, we will focus on the individual's beliefs and values and how these create predispositions that influence bargaining behavior.

13. Janis cites several instances of groupthink and resulting risk-taking behavior. Possibly his most effective arguments deal with the abortive Bay of Pigs invasion; see pp. 14–49 of *Victims of Groupthink*.

14. At this point, the reader may want to review the discussion of "self-image" in chapter 2.

15. We have avoided discussing the various theories of attitude change. While some may view this as a serious omission, we contend that to fully understand these theories, a more thorough background is required in social psychology than we have room to provide. For outside reading, we recommend Chester A. Insko's *Theories of Attitude Change*.

16. Or continue on a course of action when, in fact, there was some indication that a new course was imminent.

Bibliography

BALCH, THOMAS. *International Courts of Arbitration*. Philadelphia: Allen, Lane and Scott, 1962.

BISHOP, CRAWFORD M. *International Arbitration Procedure*. Washington: J. Byrne, 1931.

CARLSTON, KENNETH S. *The Process of International Arbitration*. New York: Columbia University Press, 1946.

DeRIVERA, JOSEPH H. *The Psychological Dimensions of Foreign Policy*. Columbus, Ohio: Charles E. Merrill, 1968.

DEUTSCH, MORTON. "Conflicts: Productive and Destructive." *Journal of Social Issues*, 25 (1969), 7–41.

DOLBEAR, F. T., and L. B. LANE et al. "Collusion in the Prisoner's Dilemma: Number of Strategies." *Journal of Conflict Resolution*, 13 (1969), 252–261.

DOUGHERTY, JAMES E. and ROBERT L. PFALTZGRAFF, JR. *Contending Theories of International Relations*. Philadelphia: Lippincott, 1971.

DUNLOP, JOHN T. *Collective Bargaining: Principles and Cases*. Chicago: R. D. Irvin, 1942.

FAUCHEUX, C., and S. MOSCOVICI. "Self-esteem and Exploitative Behavior in a Game Against Chance and Nature." *Journal of Personality and Social Psychology*, 8 (1968), 83–88.

FISHER, ROGER. *International Conflict for Beginners*. New York: Harper, 1969.

HOFFMAN, EILEEN B. *Resolving Labor-Management Disputes: A Nine-Country Comparison*. New York: The Conference Board, 1973.

HOLSTI, OLE R. *Crisis Escalation and War*. Montreal: McGill-Queen's University Press, 1972.

————. "The Belief System and National Images: A Case Study." *Journal of Conflict Resolution*, 6 (1962), 244–252.

IKLÉ, FRED C. *How Nations Negotiate*. New York: Praeger, 1964.

INSKO, CHESTER A. *Theories of Attitude Change*. New York: Appleton, 1967.

JANIS, IRVING L. *Victims of Groupthink*. Boston: Houghton Mifflin, 1972.

JOHNSON, D. F., and W. L. FULLAR. "Style of Third-Party Intervention, Face Saving and Bargaining Behavior." *Journal of Experimental Social Psychology*, 8 (1972), 319–330.

JOY, CHARLES T. *How Communists Negotiate*. New York: Macmillan, 1955.

KELLY, H. H., and A. J. STAHELSKI. "Errors in Perception of Intentions in Mixed Motive Game." *Journal of Experimental Social Psychology*, 16 (1970), 411–438.

KERR, CHARLES. "Industrial Conflict and Its Resolution." *American Journal of Sociology*, 60 (1954), 230–245.

KRESSEL, KARL. *Labor Mediation: An Exploratory Survey* (cited in Jeffrey Z. Rubin and Bert R. Brown. *The Social Psychology of Bargaining and Negotiation*. New York: Academic Press, 1975). Unpublished manuscript, Columbia University, 1971.

LINDSEY, G., and E. ARONSON (eds.). *Handbook of Social Psychology*, vol. IV. (2nd ed.) Reading, Mass.: Addison-Wesley, 1969.

MARSHALL, HOWARD DRAKE. *Collective Bargaining*. New York: Random House, 1971.

NIERENBERG, GERALD L. *Creative Business Negotiating: Skills and Successful Strategies*. New York: Hawthorn Books, 1971.

PERLMUTTER, AMOS. "Crisis Management: Kissinger's Middle East Negotiations." *International Studies Quarterly*, 19:3 (1975), 316–343.

ROSENAU, JAMES N. (ed.). *International Politics and Foreign Policy*. New York: Free Press, 1969.

RUBIN, JEFFREY , and BERT R. BROWN. *The Social Psychology of Bargaining and Negotiation*. New York: Academic Press, 1975.

SCHELLING, THOMAS C. *The Strategy of Conflict*. New York: Galaxy Books, 1963.

SINGER, J. DAVID. "Inter-Nation Influence: A Formal Model. *American Political Science Review*, 57 (1963), 420–430.

WALTON, RICHARD E. *Interpersonal Peacemaking: Confrontations and Third-Party Consultation*. Reading, Mass.: Addison-Wesley, 1969.

————. *A Behavioral Theory of Labor Negotiations: An Analysis of a Social Interaction System*. New York: McGraw-Hill, 1965.

8 | INTERNATIONAL NEGOTIATIONS: THE ROLE OF INDIVIDUAL PERCEPTIONS AND ENVIRONMENTAL FACTORS

Parties that seek to achieve objectives or defend interests must communicate with other actors whom they wish to deter, alter, or reinforce. Diplomacy is defined as the management of the relations between independent states by the process of negotiation (Nicholson, 1970: 41). The term "negotiation" is often used to describe this bargaining and communicating between nations. In reality, "bargaining" and "negotiation" are synonymous. Both require two or more actors, some form of interaction, and the resolution of conflict. Although the terms are often used interchangeably, "negotiation" is often more formal. In addition, "negotiation" is used to describe interactions among more complex social units, such as nations, while "bargaining" is reserved for interactions between individuals. It is to the concept of "negotiations" that we now turn.

International negotiations have taken place throughout history. None has been more important for the future of the world, however, than the recent diplomatic efforts by the United States and the Soviet Union to limit strategic nuclear weapons. Because of its inherent importance, and because it illustrates so many of the basic concepts and theories of bargaining, we have selected the Strategic Arms Limitation Talks (SALT) prior to the actual SALT I agreement in 1972 as our case study. While our primary goal is to show some of the major dimensions of negotiation, we shall also seek to explain why certain bargaining moves were made and how these influenced bargaining effectiveness.

The psychological and structural factors that influenced U.S. bargaining behavior will be closely examined, particularly the beliefs and behavior of Henry A. Kissinger.[1] Our goal is to explain how certain of

Kissinger's beliefs about the nature of the international system affected his perceptions and behavior in the SALT negotiations. However, we must remember that situational factors are also important. In the following discussion, a number of them will be identified. Let us now turn to a brief history of the SALT I negotiations.

A Profile of SALT: Environmental Factors

Some analysts have called it one of the most important achievements in American foreign policy. A few refer to it as the most crucial agreement of this century. Between November 1969 and May 1972, the United States and the Soviet Union negotiated the first agreements to place limits and restraints on some of their most important armaments. Talks are still going on to reconfirm and extend these agreements. What follows is a profile of the events that have made up these negotiations. We will identify the origins of these talks, the factors that influenced them, and some of the important outcomes and existing problems.

ORIGINS OF SALT[2]

It is difficult to identify the origins of SALT I. From one perspective, it includes all the efforts to control nuclear weapons since 1945. From another, it consists of more recent events that set these particular negotiations into motion. Using the latter viewpoint, we will trace the origins of SALT I to the mid-1960s.

In November 1966, President Lyndon Johnson met with his top Defense Department aides to discuss recent Soviet military policy. In particular, the United States was concerned with intelligence data indicating that the Soviet Union had begun to deploy an antiballistic missile system (ABM) around Moscow.[3] The United States had worked on an ABM system of its own for years, but it had been plagued by spiraling costs and questionable effectiveness. President Johnson believed that the system's usefulness was too limited to justify its cost. Public and congressional pressure, however, continued for U.S. deployment of an ABM system.[4] At the November meeting it was still considered too early to make a final decision on deployment (Roberts in Willrich and Rhinelander, 1974: 20).

Following the meeting, the United States began an exchange of communications with Soviet leaders on strategic weapons deployment. The specific content is not known, but the purpose was probably an informal strategic arms control dialogue. The Soviet Union refused to set a date to begin formal talks. There was some concern in Moscow about the wisdom of entering into formal negotiations with the United States on arms control. Some believed that the Soviet

Union should acquire strategic parity first (Edmonds, 1975: 79). We have seen in the previous chapter how actors hesitate to begin negotiations if they perceive themselves to be at a disadvantage. Such may have been behind the Soviet Union's initial refusal to begin talks in 1966–1967. Unless both parties could meet as equals (i.e., with approximately the same number of weapons), no formal talks could begin.

THE CHANGING ENVIRONMENT: THE PRE-SALT I PERIOD

While these preliminary communications were going on, a number of important events were occurring that affected the desire of each side to negotiate. These included improved intelligence systems in both countries, the U.S. decision to deploy its ABM system, the Soviet invasion of Czechoslovakia, and the Soviet Union's achieving nuclear parity. Let us review each of these developments.

By 1968, both the United States and the Soviet Union had perfected their spy satellites so that each had relatively independent sources of information about the other's weapons deployment (Roberts, in Willrich and Rhinelander, 1974: 21). One of the major stumbling blocks in previous arms control negotiations had been their inability to police the terms of an agreement. Because each nation's security rested on compliance, each had to be certain that neither was guilty of violations. The Soviet Union had traditionally rejected "on-site inspection." With the development of the satellites, however, each side had a relatively foolproof method of counting the strategic weapons systems of the other. In other words, if there were an agreement, such proof could ensure the compliance of both sides.

In September 1967, the United States announced that it was going ahead with the deployment of its ABM system. The announcement stated, however, that it would build a "thin" ABM system whose primary objective was to defend against a projected Chinese ICBM capability and "accidental" Soviet launches. Secretary of Defense Robert McNamara hastened to point out that the system was not directed against the Soviet Union, whose missile capability was recognized as such that no ABM system could effectively deal with it.[5] McNamara meant to communicate to the Soviet Union that the United States was not attempting to escalate the strategic arms race. In bargaining terminology, it was a clear signal to the Soviets that we perceived the mutual interdependence of each other's strategic deployments.

A third important development during this period was the Soviet achievement of nuclear parity with the United States in late 1968. As Edmonds points out, while the United States remained well ahead of the Soviet Union in terms of submarine-launched ballistic missiles

(SLBM) and strategic bombers, the Soviet Union now had an equal number of land-based ICBMs. By the end of 1968 the Soviet Union had 1,200 land-based ICBMs, the United States' 1,054 (Edmonds, 1975: 79). Thus the serious reservations in the Soviet leadership (particularly among the military) about beginning negotiations until parity was reached had been overcome.[6]

By the summer of 1968, both countries were beginning to make the preliminary decisions to initiate formal talks. In fact, on July 1, 1968, President Johnson announced at the signing of the Non-Proliferation Treaty that agreement had been reached with the Soviet Union to begin discussions on "limiting and reducing both strategic nuclear weapons delivery systems and defenses against ballistic missiles" (ACDA, 1975: 126). Roberts contends that Moscow and Washington had agreed privately to a visit by the American President in Moscow during September. At this meeting, the SALT negotiations would begin (Roberts, in Willrich and Rhinelander, 1974: 22). The climate now seemed conducive to negotiations when on August 20, 1968, the Soviet Union invaded Czechoslovakia to suppress the liberal communist regime of Alexander Dubĉek. This action immediately disrupted the movement toward formal negotiation. The United States questioned publicly "why the Soviet Union had decided to use force to resolve its differences with Czechoslovakia?" Did this indicate a new aggressiveness in Soviet policy? Did it have any significance for SALT? The United States now had to reevaluate Soviet intentions and motives. Until this took place, the United States was unwilling to engage in meaningful talks. The immediate effect was to cancel Johnson's visit. A more long-term effect was a delay in beginning the SALT negotiations while the United States sought to interpret the Soviet invasion of Czechoslovakia.

BARGAINING ON PRELIMINARIES

On January 20, 1969, the day President Richard M. Nixon assumed office, the Soviet Union communicated that it was "ready to 'start a serious exchange of views' on limiting the nuclear arsenals of the two superpowers. 'When the representatives of the Nixon Administration are ready to sit down, we are ready' " (Kalb and Kalb, 1974: 100). The suddenness of the Soviet announcement supposedly caught Washington off guard. After three years of jockeying for position, suddenly the Soviets announce their willingness to begin formal talks. Why they now moved with such dispatch is not known. Kalb and Kalb, however, suggest that since late 1968, the Soviet Union had awaited a conciliatory signal from the United States following its condemnation of their·invasion of Czechoslovakia. Furthermore, the new Nixon administration posed certain "unknowns" for the Soviet leadership; President Nixon, for example, was noted for his anticommunist sentiments. The Soviets had to ask themselves whether he was still the "cold warrior," and if he was, could he be dealt with? President Nixon's first signal to the Soviet Union was one of both conciliation and hope. As he put it, "after a period of confrontation, we are entering an era of negotiations."

In spite of the conciliatory signals from both sides, few plans were being made to discuss preliminary negotiations. One of the primary reasons rested with the United States. Neither President Nixon nor his special advisor for national security affairs, Henry A. Kissinger, wanted to begin direct talks with the Russians until the United States had the opportunity to reformulate basic American policy. In particular, the new administration viewed SALT not as an isolated issue but as part of a much broader negotiation strategy, known as "linkage," to be used in dealing with the Soviet Union. We will return to linkage later; for now, it can be defined as a view of the international order whereby one country's interest (particularly if that country is a "great power") is connected to the interests of another country. Conflict or cooperation in one interest area would affect conflict or cooperation on all other areas as well. As President Nixon stated in a news conference:

> What I want to do is to see to it that we have strategic arms talks in a way and at a time that will promote, if possible, progress on outstanding political problems *at the same time*—for example, on the problem of the Middle East and on other outstanding problems in which the United States and the Soviet Union, acting together, can serve the cause of peace. (Kalb and Kalb, 1974: 104–105; emphasis added by them)

Whereas the United States wanted to negotiate the limitation of nuclear weapons, it wished to do so as part of a comprehensive foreign policy stategy. The Soviets, on the other hand, wanted to treat weapons limitations as a separate issue, free from other political considerations. As a result of this conflict in defining the issue, the initial momentum for beginning the negotiations was slowed. During this time the United States, under Kissinger's guidance, began to formulate its future negotiation strategy. It was not until November 17, 1969, that the Strategic Arms Limitation Talks would begin in Helsinki, Finland,—a neutral site that both parties had agreed to previously. It was also agreed that the first session would consist of an exchange of views, an examination of the issues that might be discussed, and an agreement on procedures (ACDA, 1975: 126).

These procedural matters are interesting in light of our discussion on the physical elements of bargaining. Both parties agreed that future talks would rotate between Helsinki and Vienna. Both countries appeared aware of the pressures that might affect the negotiations should the talks be held in either Moscow or Washington. In Vienna or Helsinki, the negotiators would meet on a rotating basis in facilities provided by their hosts as well as in their respective embassies. Both parties also agreed that the talks would be held in private "to encourage a free and frank exchange." Once again, acutely aware of the effect that external pressures could have on the bargaining process, the two countries were determined to eliminate outside influence. At the same time, however, they were aware of the propaganda value of the talks. Each country agreed, therefore, to make periodic public announcements outlining (in the most general terms) the progress to date.[7]

AN ASIDE ON WEAPONS

Any discussion of SALT is incomplete without knowing the number, type, and capability of the weapon sytems involved. By 1970, the strategic arsenals of the United States and the Soviet Union were awesome. Each nation could destroy the other many times over. In terms of actual number of missiles and strategic bombers, there was an imbalance. Soviet ICBM production had not only caught up with the United States but had surpassed it. The Soviet inventory by 1972 was more than 1,500 land-based ICBMs, and according to American sources the Soviet Union was producing approximately 200 new missiles annually. The United States had not added to its inventory since 1967, when its inventory reached 1,054 ICBMs.[8]

However, whereas the number of American ICBMs remained the same, their reliability and accuracy had improved (ACDA, 1975: 127). Another refinement was the introduction of the Multiple Independently Targeted Reentry Vehicle (MIRV). The MIRV permits a single missile to carry a number of warheads that can be programed to its separate targets. By substituting a MIRV warhead for a single one, the United States had vastly increased the number of warheads that it could direct against an opponent. The Soviet Union had not perfected a MIRV capability at that time. It had developed missiles, however, with such huge single-warhead capacity that they posed a potential threat to U.S. missiles protected in underground launch silos (ACDA, 1975: 127).

In the area of submarine-launched ballistic missiles, the Soviet Union was quickly approaching parity. Such missiles, launched from beneath the oceans from nuclear submarines, were crucial to each nation's ability to survive an initial attack by the other and respond with a devastating second strike. Because of their relative invulnerability, the Polaris missile-firing submarine and its Soviet counterpart were vital to each country's strategic posture.

The final system under negotiation was the antiballistic missile.

Both countries had moved beyond the research and development stage, with the Soviets deploying a system around Moscow and the United States beginning deployment at two missile complexes in an effort to protect its retaliatory forces (ACDA, 1975: 127). These awesome weapons systems were the subject of the SALT negotiations.

MOVING TOWARD A DEADLOCK

The talks that began in Helsinki in 1969 would go on for over two and a half years. According to most informed sources, the bargaining focused on two general issues: defining the boundaries of the future agreement (e.g., what constituted a strategic nuclear weapon) and negotiating on the major issues (e.g., the limitations on various weapons systems). During the negotiations, a number of external events transpired that were potentially disruptive. One of them was the U.S. escalation of the fighting in Vietnam. It is perhaps a commentary on both sides' commitment that such events were not permitted to disrupt the cooperative mood of the talks. Nevertheless, some substantial differences still separated the two countries. The negotiations that sought to resolve these differences were long and complex.[9] One major difference was each side's perception of offensive and defensive weapons systems. The American position was that the two systems were interrelated. The United States argued that to limit the ABM system (which the Soviets were anxious to do) without restricting the growth of offensive weapons such as SLBMs (which the Soviets were not yet willing to do) was unacceptable.[10] In spite of a May 20, 1971, announcement that progress was being made on an ABM agreement, the negotiations were in fact becoming hopelessly deadlocked as each country's position on these issues hardened. It is at this point that a second level of negotiations became important. These negotiations, often referred to as "back-channel" negotiations, involved bargaining at the highest levels of the two governments.

KISSINGER AND BACK-CHANNEL COMMUNICATIONS[11]

John Newhouse argues that in conducting sensitive negotiations, governments often utilize both "front-channel" and "back-channel" communications. Front-channel communications are the (usually) classified exchanges between a government and its negotiating delegation. A back-channel communication refers to the private contacts between an official of one government and that of another. Usually such contacts are so private that only the heads of state know of them. Such a back-channel system was set up in 1971 by the United States and the Soviet Union. Some of the most effective and noteworthy negotiations in the later stages of SALT were conducted this way (Newhouse, 1973: 203).

The principal American actor in these back-channel negotiations was Henry Kissinger, a proponent of this style of personal and secret diplomacy. Kissinger believed that this type of negotiation was particularly useful in overcoming deadlocks, and most analysts now agree that he used it effectively during the often stalled SALT I negotiations (e.g., Newhouse, 1973: 204–205). Whenever the larger negotiating team seemed unable to resolve issues, Kissinger turned to face-to-face negotiations with either the Kremlin leaders or the Soviet ambassador to the United States. Interestingly enough, neither of the delegations knew of these personal high-level efforts. Almost as if by magic, deadlocks were resolved and compromises extended without either delegation knowing why their government's positions had changed.

By the time of the Nixon-Brezhnev summit meeting in May 1972, a number of the problems were approaching resolution. All the key issues of an ABM agreement had been agreed upon. The remaining problems dealing with a limitation on offensive weapons were resolved through direct negotiations between President Nixon and Secretary General Brezhnev.[12] Since the exact terms of these agreements are detailed elsewhere, we will not discuss them here. In the main, the agreement signed in Moscow indicated that both countries were now aware of each other's mutual interests and advantages. It also incorporated the central premises of bargaining. As Kissinger stated in his testimony before the U.S. Senate Committee on Finance on March 7, 1974:

> We are ideological adversaries and we will in all likelihood remain so for the foreseeable future. We are political and military competitors and neither can be indifferent to the advances by the other in either of these fields. . . . Although we compete, the conflict will not admit resolution by victory in the classicial sense. . . . The SALT agreement does not stand alone, isolated and incongruous in the relationship of hostility . . . it stands, rather, linked organically, to a chain of agreements and to a broad understanding about international conduct appropriate to the dangers of the nuclear age.

American Negotiating Behavior: The Cognitive Approach

A number of approaches could be used to explain American negotiating behavior during SALT. One could, for example, analyze the external and domestic factors that affected the negotiating environment. What effects, for example, did the Vietnam War, the Czechoslovakian invasion, and electoral politics have on American motivations, perceptions, and negotiating behavior? Another approach might focus on the structural and bureaucratic aspects of American policy making. Since decisions are supposedly the result of a bureaucracy's standard operating procedures, one might analyze these negotiating procedures. Still another approach that has been used with partial success is the cognitive approach. Here the focus is on psychological phenomena. Behavior is seen as resulting from the beliefs and perceptions of the decision makers (or, in our case, the negotiators).

The cognitive approach to the study of foreign policy decision making has declined. Yet, as Ole Holsti has pointed out, in a number of cases, this approach can be useful (1975), especially given one or more of the following conditions: an innovative decision-making situation, long-range policy planning situations; decisions required under highly complex, ambiguous, or unanticipated circumstances; and decisions are made by top-ranking bureaucrats (as cited in Walker, 1977: 130). All of these conditions existed during the SALT I negotiations. There is some evidence to suggest, for example, that the Soviet's immediate acceptance of President Nixon's January 20, 1969, call for negotiations did create an innovative decisional situation for the United States. We know, furthermore, that the United States stalled in opening the talks until it could plan a long-range policy position. As the negotiations progressed a number of highly complex, ambiguous, and unanticipated issues emerged. Often, for example, when deadlocks occurred over the nature and interrelationship of offensive and defensive weapons, decisions had to be made. Finally, back-channel communications and negotiations were carried out at the highest levels of government.

The above conditions, taken together, present the SALT I negotiations from a highly individual perspective. In fact, the individual becomes primary in the negotiating process. Since SALT I is a situation where individuals were important and where their decisions did affect the bargaining process, a cognitive analysis of individual psychological predispositions would be useful. The most obvious American actor to select for such an analysis is Henry Kissinger. Throughout, we have seen his importance not only in formulating the American bargaining position but also in the actual negotiating process. For this reason, we will now turn to the interrelationships between Kissinger's beliefs and U.S. negotiating behavior.

KISSINGER'S BELIEFS ABOUT SECURITY

Kissinger's paramount concern for safety is found throughout his works, but it is particularly evident in his examination of two international systems. In the "revolutionary" system, Kissinger characterizes international political life as "violent," "chaotic," "confrontational," "prone to war," "unorderly," "tense," "insecure," "antagonistic," and "dangerous." Life in a "legitimate" system, on the other hand, is described as "orderly," "stable," "competitive," "secure," "prone to reconciliation," "peaceful," and "just." While Kissinger does not believe that competition, aggression, or even violence will not occur in a legitimate order, he does appear to believe that the threat to safety is minimal, and that even if violence is used, it will eventually result in, or restore, safety and security. Aggression is viewed by Kissinger as a corrective process within the legitimate social order. It is primarily self-defensive and/or adjustive in nature, and it ultimately ensures the goal of safety.

Kissinger's emphasis on safety suggests that he believes that the SALT I negotiations were crucial in ensuring international security. Did Kissinger believe there could ever be absolute security within any international order? In the "revolutionary" order, for example, he observes a tendency to seek absolute solutions in foreign policy; that is, there is a quest for absolute safety which ultimately leads to complete insecurity. Writing about the Congress of Vienna, Kissinger stated that "the foundation of a stable order is the relative security—and therefore the relative insecurity—of its members" (1956c: 264). For Kissinger the legitimate order defines its security through an equilibrium—a harmony or balance of conflicting claims for safety. Such an equilibrium had to characterize the SALT I treaties. As Kissinger states, "The security of a domestic order resides in the preponderant power of authority, that of an international order in the balance of forces and in its expression, the equilibrium" (1956c: 265). In his negotiations with the Soviets, Kissinger sought to strike a balance between Soviet quantitative weapons superiority and U.S. qualitative superiority. Without such a weapons equilibrium, he believed that there could be no ultimate security for either nation.

KISSINGER'S PREFERENCE FOR HARMONY

Analysis of Kissinger's statements indicates that harmony, too, is crucial in his beliefs about bargaining. Both cognitively and functionally, his beliefs about harmony are linked to the belief about safety as well as to beliefs about stability. Kissinger uses a number of terms which are synonymous with his notion of "harmony"; these include "commensurability," "proportionality," "equilibrium," and "confluence."

Three primary elements make up Kissinger's perception of harmony: dependency, mutual accomodation, and restraint. Kissinger believes, as do a number of conflict theorists, that the central issues of international politics are beyond unilateral control. When a nation thinks it alone has the power to resolve a conflict or provide for its own security, Kissinger contends that instability results. Thomas Schelling, whose statements in *The Strategy of Conflict* are similar to Kissinger's early writings, puts it this way: " . . . conflict situations are essentially bargaining situations. They are situations in which the ability of one participant to gain his ends is *dependent* [my emphasis] to an important degree on the choices or decisions that other participants will make" (1963: 5). Kissinger believed that there is mutual dependency as well as opposition in U.S. and Soviet weapons policies. He contended that both sides had to be aware of this dependency if mutually damaging wars and a costly arms race were to be avoided. One important task of the SALT I negotiations was to identify these mutual dependencies so that both nations might adequately evaluate the consequences of their actions. Once the purpose of negotiation is so seen, the task of diplomatic bargaining is guided by one central principle: The best course of action for any nation depends upon what it expects another nation to do, and strategy involves influencing the other nation's choices by working on its expectation of one's own behavior. I think Kissinger would accept Schelling's term for such a conception—"the theory of interdependent decision" (1963: 16). At the core of any such theory is the belief that mutual dependencies exist and are acted upon. Kissinger's statements about harmony indicate that independent action in diplomatic negotiation leads to disequilibrium in the international order, which generates instability and ultimately threatens international security.

Kissinger also contends that if nations are aware of mutual dependency, they will find it easier to arrive at mutual accommodations in their negotiations. In the terminology of game theory, international conflicts need not be viewed as "constant-sum games." Only in the revolutionary system is more-for-one inexorably linked with less-for-the-other. As Kissinger contends, the task of diplomatic negotiation is to point out that some outcomes are either worse or better than others for *both* conflicting parties. Throughout his writings, Kissinger seems to prefer the mutual accommodation of disputes. One of his primary criticisms of "massive retaliation," for example, was that this doctrine indicated no awareness of the advantage of interdependency. This lack of awareness generated a "paralysis of policy" in the United States during the 1950s, thus freeing the Soviet Union from the need for accommodation (Kissinger, 1956b). During his back-channel negotiations with the Soviets, Kissinger is reported to have stressed the need for mutual accommodation in nuclear weapons policy.

The third aspect of Kissinger's emphasis on harmony is his preference for restraint. As illustrated in his writings about the Congress of Vienna, Kissinger contends that no nation can achieve security without it. His notion of restraint follows logically from his beliefs about interdependency and the quest for mutual accommodation. In the revolutionary system, he contends, there is no restraint because both of these beliefs are absent. Once accommodation becomes a goal, some restraint on conflict is inevitable. Without restraint there can be no harmony, and without harmony there can be no stability and consequently no security.

Our previous discussion of Kissinger's preference for harmony drew certain parallels between his beliefs and those of other bargaining theorists, particularly Thomas Schelling. Kissinger's beliefs about dependency, mutual accommodation, and restraint each have counterparts in Schelling's "strategy of conflict," discussed in chapter 7. Schelling contends that strategy is "not concerned with the efficient application of force but with the exploitation of potential force" (1963: 5). See how closely Schelling's concept of strategy parallels Kissinger's concept of the interdependence of force and diplomacy in the following statement: "Force and diplomacy are not discrete realms; on the contrary, the ultimate pressures during negotiation have always been the possibility that recourse might be had to force" (Kissinger, 1956b: 352). Without the ability to exploit potential force, a nation limits its diplomacy. It also reduces its ability to ensure concessions in negotiations with other states, and, as such, it disrupts the basis for mutual accommodation and restraint. As Kissinger says of the doctrine of massive retaliation and its slogan "There is no alternative to peace": "To the extent that the slogan . . . is taken seriously by the Soviets as a statement of American intentions it will remove a powerful brake on Soviet probing actions and any incentive for the Soviet Union to make concessions" (Kissinger, 1956b: 352). According to Kissinger, the exploitation of potential force is an element of harmony and may be necessary for successful negotiations.

Kissinger's Instrumental Beliefs

Instrumental beliefs are preferred modes of conduct in achieving social and personal goals. The following analysis identifies some of the means that Kissinger perceived as useful in achieving these goals. For example, we have argued that two of Kissinger's preferred objectives were security and harmony. Now we shall examine why he favors knowledge and "flexibility" as the means of realizing both of these goals.

THE UTILITY OF KNOWLEDGE

It is hardly a revelation that Henry Kissinger values knowledge. However, the central importance of knowledge as one of his instrumental beliefs merits some discussion. Several studies have noted Kissinger's frequent admonition that nations and statesmen must proceed cautiously in their international actions. Without a comprehensive grasp of the factors and relationships of the international order, without an awareness of the problems that emerge from this order, and without a delineation and definition of the principal issues in statecraft, Kissinger contends that negotiations run the risk of magnifying the uncertainty and potential instability that already exist (Walker, 1975).

The most frequent terms that Kissinger uses when discussing knowledge are "concept," "conception," "framework," and "conceptual framework." They comprise elements of what Kissinger means by the term "knowledge." His preference for knowledge stems directly from his perception of its utility in guiding action and realizing preferred goals, particularly the goals of safety, security, and harmony. A closer examination of his statements indicates that Kissinger sees the following benefits in having a conceptual image of the international order. First of all, Kissinger argues that conceptualization aids the analyst in "imposing a pattern on events or . . . impart[ing] a sense of direction to his action" (Kissinger, 1959b: 31). Both of these traits are valued, particularly in an environment that Kissinger sees as being chaotic and threatening.

Second, by imposing a pattern on events and by thus defining the issues, conceptual frameworks help to reduce the uncertainty of statemanship (Kissinger, 1959b, 1957, 1956a). Kissinger contends that uncertainty is a quality that can never be entirely eliminated. Nevertheless, he believes that a framework can reduce this uncertainty. The importance that Kissinger places on "conception" is indicated by the fact that throughout his writings he transforms specific issues (such as the doctrine of massive retaliation, the defense of Western Europe, and "summitry") into the conceptual issues within these topics. Throughout his writings (and later in his public statements), Kissinger displays an enduring preference for the comprehensiveness that he sees in a conceptual framework. Effective policymaking does not depend solely on each individual decision or action but more importantly on "their relationships to each other" (Kissinger, 1959b: 31). Whenever problems are viewed as isolated cases, and whenever the attention of the policy maker is limited to the immediate solution of specific problems, Kissinger believes that there is the tendency to stress particular and isolated factors while losing sight of their ultimate relationship to the whole (Kissinger, 1959b: 31). Kissinger was convinced that the SALT I negotiations had to be conceptually linked to other outstanding issues that separated the United States and the Soviet Union.

THE FUNCTIONS OF FLEXIBILITY

If Kissinger's preference for conceptualization is instrumentally related to the values of safety and security, then his preference for flexibility is linked to his value of harmony. By analyzing his statements about flexibility, we can identify the attributes that Kissinger values. Flexibility provides: increased maneuverability (in policy making and implementation), a check on dogmatism, and sensitivity to the fluidity and relativity of the international environment. Together these attributes are supposed to enable countries to adjust their actions and thus ultimately to arrive at a reconciliation of their differences.

Throughout Kissinger's writings, whether he is discussing a revolutionary system, massive retaliation, or policy making in the United States, he exhibits a marked distaste for rigidity. However, he approves of resolve. A nation must have a clear understanding of its primary objectives—it must know what it wants (Kissinger, 1955b: 419). Negotiations often presuppose prior agreement on fundamentals, which can then be adjusted but not created. The key notion is that bargaining can adjust disputes. If this cannot occur, then there can be no mutual accommodation, and the conflict becomes a zero-sum situation. "By leaving no alternative between total nuclear war and an uneasy armistice, it prevents attempts to ameliorate the situation progressively. . . . " (Kissinger, 1955b: 425). The goal of negotiation is to maintain "fluidity in the diplomatic situation." Kissinger warns that once rigidity sets in, there can be no harmony, no stability, and ultimately, no safety.

Within the realm of negotiation, flexibility is important in creating multiple contingencies. Kissinger's early proposals for the limited use of tactical nuclear weapons and his "little war thesis," (a "little war" is one which stops short of massive nuclear retaliation) are examples of his attempts to generate various alternatives for American policy. His thinking about the utility of freedom of action can be found throughout the literature on international politics. Karl Deutsch, writing in 1957, makes a similar argument. He states that if neither party wants war, war will be averted if the policy makers can keep enough freedom of action always to have an acceptable alternative to war (Deutsch, 1957: 200).

By having a number of acceptable alternatives (i.e., manifesting flexibility in negotiations), the diplomat can come up with variations on the same theme. Variation and maneuverability both show a "feeling for nuance"—an awareness of the subtle interrelationships that characterize statesmanship (Kissinger, 1956a: 40). Subtlety, as we shall see, is another of Kissinger's instrumental values.

SELF-ASSURANCE AND PERSONAL DIPLOMACY

Kissinger believes that knowledge gives the individual a sense of self-assurance, self-confidence, and the inner security necessary for formulating "profound policy." This is the single most important attribute of personal skills. The quality of self-assurance is highly prized by Kissinger. One sees this in his writings about key figures in nineteenth-century European politics, and (more indirectly) in his criticisms of contemporary policy making in the United States. As he states:

> The situation is compounded by the personal humility that is one of the most attractive American traits. Most Americans are convinced that no one is ever entirely "right," or, as the saying goes, that if there is disagreement each party is probably a little in error. . . . But the corollary of the tentativeness of most views is an incurable inward insecurity. Even very eminent people are reluctant to stand alone. (Kissinger, 1959c: 31)

Among the results which he attributes to a lack of self-assurance are: a reduced capacity for innovation, an inability to react spontaneously to a fluid environment, a timidity in conceptualization, and an inability to take and use risks in problem solving. As one might expect, there is a close link between Kissinger's beliefs about the usefulness of conceptualization, the value of harmony, and personal confidence. As he puts it: "effective policy depends not only on the skill of individual moves but even more importantly on their relationship to each other. It requires a sense of proportion; a sense of style provides it with inner disciplines" (Kissinger, 1959: 31). In this statement we see a mingled belief in harmony and proportion, a preference for conceptualization that stresses the interrelationship of facets of the environment, and a preference for the intangible quality of discipline or self-confidence.

Throughout his writings, Kissinger restates his hope that statesmen can transcend the experience of their societies—that they can act upon their intuitions or their subjective evaluation of issues. As Kissinger states in describing the nature of statesmanship:

> Statesmen must act as if their intuition were already experience, as if their aspiration were truth. The statesman is therefore like one of the heroes of a classical tragedy who has had an intuition of the future, but who cannot transmit it directly to his fellowman and who cannot validate its "truth." (Kissinger, 1956a: 53)

If the statesman possesses the self-assurance of knowledge and intelligence, he can break away from conventional wisdom, be innovative and creative in his actions, and effectively meet the challenges posed by the ever-changing environment. Without self-confidence, the individual will be pulled into the stagnation that Kissinger believes characterizes the status quo (Kissinger, 1956a: 54). Kissinger's preference for boldness, innovation, creativity, and imagination (the cognitive elements of creative self-expression) are also related to this belief in the ultimate benefit of knowledge. Security, or its manifestation, courage—like personal safety and national security—is an important motivation in Kissinger's thinking. He believes that "knowledge" provides this motivation and thus directly contributes to the realization of goals.

THE UTILITY OF RISK: AN INCONSISTENCY?

We have seen how much Kissinger values safety and security. Thus we might logically conclude that he would abhor risk taking. Risks, by their very nature, generate uncertainty, and Kissinger seeks to reduce uncertainty through use of the conceptual framework. Another commonly held notion is that risk taking involves a threat to cherished goals and objectives. A preference for risk taking, as we normally think of it, should be incongruent with a number of Kissinger's beliefs. And yet, we find in his writings belief in the value of risk and risk taking. One of the values of self-assurance is that it permits risk taking. Webster's New Collegiate Dictionary defines risk as follows: "To entertain chance; to act on the basis of conjecture without knowing all the facts; daring, uncertainty—without certitude." These attributes of risk are inconsistent with a preference for safety and security. And yet, Kissinger highly values both security and risk taking.

Kissinger feels that risk taking is instrumental in generating flexibility, which subsequently enhances harmony and stability. Those who view the future only in the light of their fears and past experience are blinded to possible opportunities. Without a willingness to take risks, a nation will ultimately face a "paralysis of its policy" and a loss of achievement: " . . . while our history may leave us not well enough prepared to deal with tragedy, it can teach us that great achievement does not result from a quest for safety" (Kissinger, 1956a: 56). Kissinger also believes that without risk taking, we lose an opportunity for creativity and innovation: "A statesman who limits his policy to the experience of his people will doom himself to sterility. . . . " (Kissinger, 1956c: 54). Likewise, in criticizing policy making by committee, he contends that the system "stresses avoidance of risk rather than boldness of conception" (Kissinger, 1959c: 31). "Energetic," "bold," "creative," and "profound" policy rests on a willingness to accept risk. Without it, a nation cannot hope to cope with a revolutionary power in a rapidly changing international order: "Our society requires above all to overcome its current lassitude to risk itself on new approaches" (Kissinger, 1959c: 35).

Kissinger's arguments about risk taking suggest that he would subscribe to the following chain of ideas: Without risk taking there will be stagnation; such stagnation would result in a reduction of alternatives; where options are limited, inflexibility in action and response sets in; without flexibility there can be no pressure or motivation for harmony (particularly for accommodation or restraint); such disharmony inevitably leads to instability or heightens existing instability; without stability and a sense of proportion there can ultimately be no safety and security. If Kissinger's beliefs and preferences do resemble these, then his thinking about risk and security is somewhat similar to his ideas of force and security. That is, just as force and aggression may ultimately contribute to security, so too may risk taking. A preference for both may seem just as inconsistent as a preference for risk taking and security. Yet Kissinger seems to believe both force and risk taking to be valuable because they ultimately, though indirectly, lead to the realization of several of his goals.

SUMMARY

In identifying some of Henry Kissinger's beliefs, and tracing their influences on his general thinking and actions, we have also learned something about his world view. Many writers have recently commented on the apparent pessimism reflected in Kissinger's writings and public statements. Kissinger *is* a pessimist. One reason is that he sees the world and its problems as posing an almost insurmountable obstacle to the realization of his goals. Kissinger values security; yet the world he sees is filled with conflict and aggression. Kissinger values stability and harmony; yet the world he sees is filled with tension, anxiety, and a lack of accommodation. Kissinger has faith in the long-range utility of personal knowledge, creativity, and boldness; yet he confronts a society that does not always value these qualities. Kissinger believes in his conception of international politics; yet he is increasingly confronted with alternative and opposing conceptualizations.

Kissinger's statements reflect his attempt to deal with these obstacles—to locate himself in both time and situation. In some cases, he has sought to redefine his environment—to view it in such a way that his goals and motivations might be realized, even given the circumstances that he confronts. He has also sought to contain, modify, or reverse contrary policies and forces. And he has often tried to educate others so that they might share his image of the world and its problems.

If there is pessimism in Kissinger's statements, there is optimism as well. Kissinger believes that knowledge, intelligence, determination, flexibility, and creativity eventually can lead to solutions. He affirms a belief that humanity has some control over the environment. Indeed, it is in the challenge of the obstacles that our hope lies. Only in adversity does the individual command certain intangibles of value and purpose—self-assurance, confidence, creativity, vision, and a sense of timing. The influence of Kissinger's perceptions on his behavior cannot be overstated.

SALT: The Link Between Beliefs and Behavior

DEALING WITH THE SOVIET UNION

Kissinger once regarded the Soviet Union as the world's leading revolutionary power. By the time he became secretary of state, however, his views had changed. Based on the mutual desire to avoid nuclear war, Kissinger believed a network of interests and a relaxation of tensions could evolve between the United States and the Soviet Union. Whereas Kissinger once thought that negotiation was purely symbolic in a revolutionary period and that force was the means to prevent the revolutionary power from achieving its unlimited objectives, by the late 1960s he had changed his beliefs. The Vietnam War had shown him that the United States might be less than willing to utilize even limited war in the future to secure international stability. Negotiations, therefore, had to take the place of force in resolving conflicts. But arms limitation agreements would depend on the ability to affect Soviet foreign policy and its perceptions of American motives and behavior.

In explaining the SALT I agreement to congressional leaders in June 1974, Kissinger stated that "we were guided not so much by the tactical solution . . . but by an understanding philosophy and a specific perception of international reality" (1974: 139). A central element of this reality was that the world aspiration for peace depended on the ability of the two superpowers to forge an agreement between themselves.

Kissinger was not so naïve as to believe that the Soviets had changed. He had written in 1957 that "whenever peace—conceived of as the avoidance of war—has been the primary objective of a power . . . the international system has been at the mercy of the most ruthless member of the international community. Whenever the international order has acknowledged that certain principles could not be compromised even for the sake of peace, stability based on an equilibrium of forces was at least conceivable" (1957: 1). He recognized that both superpowers would continue to be ideological, political, and military competitors "to meet the threat implicit in the other's strength and aims" (1974: 140). At the same time, conflict could no longer be traditionally resolved with the use of force; each power's survival depended on its ability to coexist. "We have an inescapable obligation to build jointly a structure for peace. Recognition of this reality is the beginning of wisdom for a sane and effective foreign policy today" (1974: 140). Since security requires equilibrium and potentially aggressive states must be restrained, a balance-of-power concept was necessary. But since a balance of power implies a quest for superiority, this is no longer the case in the nuclear age.

SALT DEADLOCK

Kissinger's specific aim in the SALT negotiation was to establish a "rough" weapons equilibrium between the two superpowers. Whereas military superiority was incompatible with deterrence, precise parity was impossible because of differences between the Soviet and American nuclear arsenals. "Sufficiency" thus became the goal. Another goal was to use the arms negotiation as a building block in the creation of a detente with the Soviet Union. However, while both sides came to want a SALT agreement, the negotiations became deadlocked. John Borawski argues that two events broke the deadlock. First, in December 1970, uprisings took place in Gdansk, Poland. Since the Polish riots could have provided a disruptive example for the other Eastern European states, the Soviet Union insisted they be suppressed. An aide of Kissinger's remarked: "After the Polish rioting, Brezhnev realized that his hold on power had suddenly become vulnerable; that he too could lose power, as Gomulka had, unless he drastically overhauled Soviet society—most especially the economy" (Kalb and Kalb 1975: 245). Soon after the incident, Nixon sent Brezhnev a note indicating that the United States was ready to help him modernize the Soviet economy if the Soviets were willing to be more flexible on a number of stalled political issues, such as SALT I. Second, Kissinger's visit to China in July 1971 created great concern within the Kremlin. Suddenly Moscow found the United States courting its ideological opponent in the communist world. To counter the improving relations between the United States and China, Brezhnev realized that a bit more flexibility on the deadlocked SALT negotiation was necessary. As a result of these two occurrences, progress on SALT resumed, no doubt further stimulated by the U.S. foiling of the Soviet attempt to construct a nuclear submarine base in Cuba and the failure of the Syrian invasion of Jordan (both events occurred in September 1970). On May 26, 1972, President Nixon and Secretary Brezhnev concluded a series of agreements at the Moscow summit, including an ABM limitation treaty and an interim agreement limiting ICBM and SLBM systems. Although the latter gave the Soviets a substantial quantitative advantage, Kissinger defended the concessions by noting that these advantages were offset by the U.S. qualitative lead. Without the concession, Kissinger claimed, the Soviets would never have agreed.

PERSONAL DIPLOMACY

Throughout the negotiations, Kissinger remained in a position of authority. He had assembled a panel of first-rate experts, consistent with his belief in the need for knowledge to provide a clear negotiating position, but remained in command to avoid bureaucratic stagnation. Yet he also remained flexible, beginning with a "building-block" approach rather than the previous "all-or-nothing" stance that had characterized arms control talks.

The question of personal summitry also arises. Kissinger once wrote that it was irresponsible to conduct diplomacy on a personal rather than on an institutional level. Although the summit had the power to settle disputes, since their prestige was at stake, any concession would appear to be an "intolerable loss of face" (1961: 189). Kissinger's disdain for the bureaucracy, as well as his belief in authority, overcame his previous views on personal diplomacy. As long as the negotiating program was coherent and purposeful, summitry could be effective. In 1974, as secretary of state, he stated that the summit was useful for "an acceleration of agreements that would probably be made anyway, but which, if they take their bureaucratic course, could be delayed for many months and sometimes years." Thus his need for authority to realize his objectives, and his impatience with the bureaucracy, led Kissinger to choose personal summitry.

Kissinger's impatience with bureaucratic slowness was also related to a time factor. Kissinger knew that there existed a definite time pressure in negotiations because the pace of weapons technology would soon make strategic superiority impossible to define. Unless arms control was maintained, there would soon be such a technological explosion that negotiations would be of negligible value. At the same time, however, he stated: "We are not running a race with ourselves. This is a problem which . . . will be with us for a long time, and it shouldn't be seen in terms of hitting a home run on any one occasion."

Political pressures, however, put extra strain on the negotiation during the last few days of the Moscow summit. Indeed, the SSBN "under construction" issue was solved in late-night strategy sessions between Kissinger and his Soviet counterpart literally hours away from the signing ceremonies. A few days before, agreement had seemed impossible. Both Brezhnev and Nixon needed a SALT accord as tangible proof of a successful detente to gain domestic support. One wonders, however, whether it was agreement for agreement's sake (Borawski, 1976). Kissinger's remarks in 1961 about negotiation must surely be a striking irony in retrospect: "It is trivial to pretend that problems of the complexity of those which have rent the world for a decade and a half can be solved in a few days by harassed men meeting in the full light of publicity" (1961: 185).

Notes*

1. The author wishes to acknowledge the collaboration of John H. Borawski in preparing this chapter, particularly the sections dealing with Kissinger's belief system and its effect on his SALT I behavior.

2. There are a number of excellent discussions of the SALT I talks. We have relied heavily on Mason Willrich and John B. Rhinelander (eds.), *SALT: The Moscow Agreements and Beyond*; John Newhouse, *The Cold Dawn: The Story of SALT*; and *Arms Control and Disarmament Agreements* (ACDA).

3. The purpose of an ABM is to neutralize or destroy the warhead of an incoming intercontinental ballistic missile (ICBM).

4. For an interesting discussion on the ABM controversy, see Abram Chayes and Jerome B. Wiesner (eds.), *ABM: An Evaluation of the Decision to Deploy An Antiballistic Missile System*.

5. For an account of the decisions that led up to Secretary McNamara's announcement, see Morton H. Halperin, *Bureaucratic Politics and Foreign Policy*.

6. Another reason for changing Soviet attitudes on beginning the talks was alluded to by Soviet Foreign Minister Andrei Gromyko. He suggested that the Soviet Union was becoming increasingly concerned with the spiraling costs of weapons that appeared to produce less rather than more security for either side. (See Roberts, 1974: 24).

7. Chalmers Roberts points out that after seven negotiating sessions, nothing was officially made public other than meaningless communiques (Roberts, 1974: 25).

8. See J. P. Ruina's "U. S. and Soviet Strategic Arsenals" (in Willrich and Rhinelander, 1974: 34–65).

9. For a detailed discussion of these negotiations see, for example, pp. 166–207 of John Newhouse's *The Cold Dawn*.

10. It is interesting to note that both sides wished to limit the system that the other either did not possess or had in sufficient number. Thus the Soviets wanted to halt the deployment of the American ABM (they had an operational system, the United States did not), while the United States sought to curb Soviet ICBM deployment. Neither side had any apparent interest in MIRV negotiations.

11. Although Kissinger is introduced in the later stages of our discussion of SALT, his role was not limited to this period. In fact, he was deeply involved in the U.S. efforts from the very start (i.e., Nixon's January 20, 1969, message), and played a guiding role in the formulation and implementation of all aspects of the American negotiating policy.

12. Besides the ABM agreement and an Interim Offensive Agreement (which was limited to five years' duration and has subsequently expired), subsidiary agreements were made on improving "hot-line" communications between Moscow and Washington, and a second agreement was made to curtail the possibilities of accidental nuclear war.

*Complete citations for the works mentioned here will be found in the Bibliography, pages 209–211.

Bibliography

Arms Control and Disarmament Agreements (ACDA). Washington, D.C.: United States Arms Control and Disarmament Agency, 1975.

AXELROD, ROBERT O. "Schema Theory: An Information Processing Model of Perception and Cognition," *American Political Science Review*, 67 (1973), 1248–1266.

————. "Psycho-Algebra: A Mathematical Theory of Cognition and Choice with an Application to the British Eastern Committee in 1918." *Peace Research Society Papers*, 18 (1972), 113–131.

BELL, DAVID. *Power, Influence, Authority*. New York: Oxford University Press, 1974.

BELOFF, NORA. "Professor Bismarck Goes to Washington," *Atlantic Monthly*, December 1969, 77–89.

BORAWSKI, JOHN. *Henry Kissinger's Conceptual Framework*. Unpublished manuscript. Duke University, 1976.

CHAYES, ABRAM, and JEROME WIESNER, (eds.). *ABM: An Evaluation of the Decision to Deploy An Anti-ballistic Missile System*, New York: Signet, 1969.

DEUTSCH, KARL. "Mass Communications and the Loss of Freedom in National Decision-Making: A Possible Research Approach to Interstate Conflicts." *Journal of Conflict Resolution*, 1 (1957).

EDMONDS, ROBIN. *Soviet Foreign Policy: 1962–1973: The Paradox of Super Power*. London: Oxford University Press, 1975.

FISHBEIN, MARTIN. "An Investigation of the Relationships Between Beliefs About an Object and the Attitude Toward that Object." *Journal of Human Relations*, 16 (1963), 233–240.

GEORGE, ALEXANDER. "The 'Operational-Code': A Neglected Approach to the Study of Political Leaders and Decision-Making." *International Studies Quarterly* 13 (1969), 190–222.

GRAUBARD, STEPHEN. *Kissinger: Portrait of a Mind*. New York: Norton, 1973.

HALPERIN, MORTON H. *Bureaucratic Politics and Foreign Policy*. Washington, D.C.: The Brookings Institution, 1974.

HOLSTI, OLE R. "The 'Operational Code' Approach to the Study of Political Leaders: John Foster Dulles' Philosophical and Instrumental Beliefs." *Canadian Journal of Political Science*, 3 (1970), 123–157.

HOUSE OF REPRESENTATIVES, THE COMMITTEE ON FOREIGN AFFAIRS, "Testimony of the Secretary of State." U.S. Government Printing Office, Washington, D.C., 1974.

KALB, MARVIN, and BERNARD KALB. *Kissinger*. Boston: Little, Brown, 1974.

KISSINGER, HENRY A. *The Necessity for Choice.* Harper, 1961.

———. "The Search for Stability." *Foreign Affairs,* July 1959a, pp. 535–560.

———. "Strategy and Organization." *Foreign Affairs,* April 1959b, pp. 379–394.

———. "The Policymaker and the Intellectual." *The Reporter,* March 1959c, pp. 30–35.

———. *Nuclear Weapons and Foreign Policy.* New York: Harper, 1957.

———. "Reflections on American Diplomacy." *Foreign Affairs,* October 1956a, pp. 35–56.

———. "Force and Diplomacy in the Nuclear Age." *Foreign Affairs,* April 1956b, pp. 348–366.

———. "The Congress of Vienna: A Reappraisal." *World Politics,* January 1956c, pp. 264–280.

———. "The Limitations of Diplomacy." *New Republic,* May 1955a, pp. 7–9.

———. "Military Policy and Defense of the 'Grey Areas.' " *Foreign Affairs,* April 1955b, pp. 416–448.

———. "American Policy and Preventive War." *Yale Review,* 44 (March 1955c), 60–75.

KRAFT, JOSEPH. "In Search of Kissinger." *Harper's,* January 1971, pp. 54–61.

LANDAU, DAVID. *Kissinger: The Uses of Power.* Boston: Houghton Mifflin, 1972.

NEWHOUSE, JOHN. *The Cold Dawn: The Story of SALT.* New York: Holt, 1973.

NICHOLSON, HAROLD. *Diplomacy.* 3rd ed. London: Oxford University Press, 1970.

ROBERTS, CHALMERS M. "The Road to Moscow." In Mason Willrich and John B. Rhinelander. *SALT: The Moscow Agreements and Beyond.* New York: The Free Press, 1974, pp. 3–33.

ROKEACH, MILTON. *Beliefs, Attitudes and Values.* San Francisco: Jossey-Bass, 1972.

RUSSETT, BRUCE. "Cause, Surprise, and No Escape." *The Journal of Politics,* 24:1 (1962), 3–22.

SCHELLING, THOMAS C. *The Strategy of Conflict.* New York: Oxford University Press, 1963.

STONE, I. F. "The Flowering of Henry Kissinger." *New York Review of Books,* November 2, 1972, pp. 19–24.

TWERASER, KURT. "Senator Fulbright's Operational Code as Warrant for His Foreign Policy Advocacy, 1943–1967: Toward Increasing the Explanatory Power of Decisional Premises." Paper prepared for the annual meeting of the American Political Science Association, New Orleans, September 1973.

U.S. Arms Control and Disarmament Agency. *Arms Control and Disarmament Agreements: Texts and History of Negotiations.* Washington, D.C.: ACDA, 1975.

WALKER, STEPHEN G. "The Interface Between Beliefs and Behavior." *Journal of Conflict Resolution,* 21:1, (1977), 129–173.

———. "Cognitive Maps and International Realities: Henry A. Kissinger's

Operational Code." Paper prepared for the annual meeting of the American Political Science Association, San Francisco, September 1975.

WHITE, RALPH K. *Value Analysis: The Nature and Use of the Method.* Ann Arbor, Mich.: Society for the Psychological Study of Social Issues, 1951.

————. "Hitler, Roosevelt, and the Nature of War Propaganda." *Journal of Abnormal Social Psychology,* 44 (1949), 157–174.

————. "Case Report: Black Boy: A Value Analysis." *Journal of Abnormal Social Psychology,* 42, (1947), 440–461.

WILLRICH, MASON, and JOHN B. RHINELANDER. *SALT: The Moscow Agreements and Beyond.* New York: Free Press, 1974.

9 | CONCLUSIONS

Our discussion of the causes, processes, and effects of human conflict has been so diversified that perspective may be difficult to maintain. In this concluding chapter, therefore, we will attempt to bring the picture back into focus. After reviewing the most important concepts, we will show how perception adds to our understanding of human conflict. Finally, we will identify several measures which individuals (either personally or as policy makers) may wish to consider as they deal with others and a changing social world.

The Importance of Images

One of the central propositions of our analysis is that an actor's behavior depends upon his or her image of the environment. Such images are sometimes referred to as knowledge. We have avoided this term because it implies validity or truth. The young urban black in Detroit, the revolutionary in a developing state, the foreign-policy decision maker—each believes that his or her view of social reality is correct. It is, therefore, what each person *thinks* the world is like that may influence behavior. What, then, determines these images?

Basically, images are built up from past experiences. This accumulation of images is usually called learning. It consists of sets of building blocks—beliefs, attitudes, and motivations. For example, when we speak of an actor's perceptions of a social issue or event, we are referring to a complex and interrelated set of these mental building blocks.

We live in an ever-changing social environment. Economic, ideological, political, and social conditions and institutions are in a constant state of flux. As these conditions are altered, new information about the social world is generated. This information is communicated to the individual in the form of messages. When these messages are received, a number of things can happen to earlier images. For one thing, the images may remain unaffected. As we have seen, our beliefs, attitudes, and values, once formed, are resistant to change. Thus our first impulse is either to reject any message that conflicts with our images or to fit the information into preexisting beliefs. People usually underestimate the impact of established beliefs and predispositions. We are therefore slower to change our minds than we think we are. As a result, individuals are likely to overestimate their sensitivity to changes in their environment and the ability of their images to adjust to these changes.

Does this mean that the image of oneself, of others, and of the social world cannot change? Of course not. Just as individuals can adapt to changing circumstances and needs, so can they modify the images of their environment. Some elements of our images, however, are more susceptible to change than others. Beliefs seem less resistant to change than attitudes, and attitudes are more easily changed than values. In each instance of change, however, both the degree and the substance of the change are determined by such individual and contextual factors as self-concept and group membership.

As people interact with their social environment, they inevitably interact with one another. Our behavior is based upon our interactions with other persons and events. Conflict is a form of interactive behavior. Each actor in a conflict relationship perceives the factors that join them. Each, for example, formulates images of their respective beliefs, attitudes, values, and intentions. Each actor also engages in adaptive behavior as a consequence of his or her perceptions. Conflict is one form of adaptive behavior. The analysis of conflict is deepened by the perceptual dimension. We can now ask how the traditional dimensions of conflict, such as economic, political, and social factors, come into play as individuals adapt their behavior.

The Importance of Context

Whether adaptive behavior is conflictual, and whether it manifests itself in violence, depends upon a host of personal and situational factors. The assertion that conflicts begin in the human mind is an intuitively satisfying explanation. And yet, the examination of motives, emotions, perceptions, and values is only part of the task of understanding conflict. Of equal importance is the environment in which actors interact and to which they must adapt. And environmental conditions can interact with psychological predispositions in such a way as to induce conflict and violence.

Throughout this book, we have identified the effects of group and cultural factors on conflict. Of particular interest here are the effects of competition and cooperation on the willingness to use violence or nonviolence to obtain one's objectives. In examining race riots, revolutions, wars, and negotiations, we found that competition stresses the differences between actors while masking their similarities. As actors become more aware of what separates them rather than of what joins them, attitudes of suspicion and hostility emerge. Such suspicions and images of threat further widen the social distance between them. As social distance increases, communications are either broken or the quality of the information passing along existing links is reduced. When the social distance increases between racial groups, between the government and the people, or between one nation and another, black-and-white thinking results.

In cooperation, actors tend to emphasize their similarities rather than their differences. This is not to say that differences are forgotten or that identities and interests are destroyed. Rather, as we saw in our examination of the SALT agreements, common interests are identified and differences are played down. In cooperative situations, ethnocentrism is unlikely; therefore, it is difficult for black-and-white thinking to emerge. Whereas it is difficult to generalize beyond the three cases which we have examined, it does appear that in the absence of black-and-white thinking, cooperation can occur and the possibility of violence can be diminished. In addition, cooperation tends to be self-perpetuating. One of the reasons nations negotiate with one another (even if their differences are never completely resolved) is to create an environment where attitudes toward each other can become more positive, and where communication channels can be maintained.

Motives, Goals, Patterns, and Processes

We have focused on the motives or goals that lead actors to conflict with one another, and the perceptions and images that influence these goals. We have also examined a number of objectives that actors believe can be gained through violence. These include such specific goals as the redress of grievances by black ghetto residents and more general success-oriented goals of revolutionary groups and nations, such as acquiring political power, economic status, and social legitimacy. Similarly we have examined a number of perceptions and images that underlie and interact with these goals. These include perceptions of goal incompatibility, relative deprivation and frustration, alienation, and hostility. Regardless of the level of analysis and the conflict issues studied, our central concern has been the interaction between motivations and perceptions in conflict. We have also discussed the basis of these motivations and perceptions. The situational and psychological roots of various types of confct and violence are similar.

The patterns of change in the context, motivation, perception, and subsequent behavior that characterize potentially violent situations are crucial. The processes of violence, its stages and sequential interrelationships, have long intrigued scholars. We have described and analyzed the changing patterns in the relations between actors prior to the actual outbreak of violence. The emphasis is on patterns rather than on a single pattern of development. No one pattern can fit all the situations we have described. And yet, one cannot help but be struck by some important similarities in the riots, revolutions, and wars that we have examined. These include: an initial stage of perceived goal incompatibility, resulting in a competitive though interdependent relationship; a rising competitiveness, along with an increase in perceived threat, hostility, frustration, anxiety, and tension among the interdependent actors; intermediate interaction marked by increasingly aggressive behavior, increased stress, and black-and-white thinking; and a final stage, where a specific event shows violence to be a satisfying response.

By studying violent conflict as a process, we can see it as a culmination of events that often involve an intensification of the objective and subjective factors examined earlier. However, there are a number of mediating factors that can hinder the forces leading to violence. In examining political violence, for example, we saw how regime coercion, alternative institutional support, and cultural traditions can prevent intense discontent from turning into political violence. In race relations as well as in international relations, restraints do exist that reduce the attractiveness of violence. These restraints generally reduce the perceived value of using violence by increasing the perceived cost resulting from violence. There are, however, certain cases where these restraints may not work. In particular, when war is inevitable, questions of cost do not deter the use of violence.

Goal incompatibility that might otherwise lead to violence can sometimes be resolved peacefully through negotiation and bargaining. Certain conditions must be present, however, before this type of resolution can occur. Probably the single most important factor is that the conflict cannot be "pure conflict"—that is, total opposition between the two parties. If a conflict is to be waged to the finish and if there is no basis for mutual accommodation, then there is nothing left to bargain. Only pure conflict of an extremely competitive and violent type can result. However, if mutual accommodation is possible, then the basis of bargaining can exist.

Bargaining was analyzed in much the same way as violence. We identified some of the important antecedents of bargaining, such as the structure of the negotiating environment, the nature and quality of communications, issue variables, and psychological predispositions of the negotiators. The bargaining process was seen as a complex series of interactions between actors. Basically this involves a presentation of demands or proposals by both parties, followed by concessions or threats resulting in an evaluation of these offers, which in turn stimulate a new cycle in the process. The importance of communication is evident. When bargaining begins, each participant may only know what his own interests and preferred outcomes are. To bargain effectively, each must learn about the other's preferences. And since this information can be provided only by the other participant, communications of some sort must take place.

Even when all the necessary preconditions are present, each actor's bargaining power is affected by a number of factors. These include the actor's willingness to take risks and grant concessions, his negotiating reputation, and a host of structural variables, such as location of the negotiating site, public opinion, and the availability of communication channels. Generally speaking, an actor's effectiveness in bargaining is determined by how well he is able to coordinate the choices or decisions that the other participant will make. To illustrate the various dimensions of bargaining and negotiation, we analyzed the Strategic Arms Limitation Talks of 1969–1972. Using a combination of cognitive and structural analysis, we examined the interplay between one negotiator's beliefs and perceptions and his bargaining behavior.

This book is an introduction to the theoretical and empirical literature on the causes, processes, and effects of violent and nonviolent conflict. A diverse picture has emerged. While many propositions, hypotheses, and theories have been presented, no single comprehensive explanation of human conflict was found. Each of the "theories" we have examined aided us in understanding certain aspects of conflict and pointed the way toward future research inquiries.

Utilizing Conflict Research

Many important questions have been raised about the utilization of conflict research. One of the first is, Is conflict research sophisticated enough to be useful for individuals, groups, or decision makers? As we have seen, we know a great deal about many factors which either induce or prevent violence. Some of the findings have produced plausible explanations for certain aspects of certain types of conflict behavior. Many of these findings are based on empirical analysis. And yet, most of the research on human conflict lacks a completeness and comprehensiveness that would make it immediately valuable for policy making. This is not to argue that certain sets of findings are unimportant, or that they do not hold important implications for questions of policy. What we do argue is that there is no complete body of conflict research now available for systematic policy use. Furthermore, conflict research is still in its formative stage. In many cases, we have only identified important sets of variables and delineated some of the more critical relationships among them. Because of its interdisciplinary nature, conflict research still lacks a central analytical focus. Much multidisciplinary research must be done before the field has the unity it needs to move to the next stage. Even in this early period, however, some ideas deserve attention. They will be presented shortly.

A second important question concerning the use of conflict research is, Who best can use these findings? A number of potential users can be identified: national decision makers, the general public, and special interest groups. Since each of these has specific motives, it is difficult to make any general statements about who best could use conflict research. From the conflict analyst's perspective, the national decision makers are the most important and controversial clients. The ends to which decision makers could put conflict research is a matter of intense disagreement and concern. However, the purpose of this book has been to educate and enlighten students of conflict analysis. Thus we are in a somewhat easier position to identify the usefulness of our discussion. Let us therefore turn to some of the implications of our study that might be useful to students of human conflict as they learn more about conflict and adapt their behavior to a changing environment.

Minimizing Perceptual Errors and Increasing Empathy

We have focused on the ways in which perceptions affect conflict behavior. We hope that readers, knowing the pervasive influence of images, may be able to compensate for them in their social interactions with others. Images play a constructive role in our lives; yet we must guard against unwarranted confidence in our perceptions. We must become more sensitive to alternative images of social reality. No readings or discussions, however, will ever provide us with a formula for discovering which images of the world are correct. Because of the complexities and ambiguities of social reality, individuals will always have to draw inferences about the information they receive. These inferences will often prove to be incorrect, and individuals must realize this. As we have seen, people are all too often unaware that there are many different images and interpretations of the same social events. Too often we assimilate information into our preexisting beliefs and refuse to see any alternatives. Unless we are aware of this predisposition, we are likely to exclude alternative perceptions and fall back complacently on our preexisting views. Such overconfidence not only creates a potential for conflict but can also obscure the quest for peace. Unfortunately, individuals are slower to change their images of reality than they suspect. And yet, such changes may be crucial if nonviolent solutions are to be found.

Throughout this text, and particularly in discussing bargaining and negotiation, we have seen that an actor's ability to secure his objectives often depends on how well he can interpret another actor's behavior and adapt his own behavior most favorably. Such interdependent behavior requires that each actor try to see the world the way the other sees it. This is often extremely difficult. Socialization patterns, social norms, group pressures, and personal attitudes and beliefs may all hinder this search for other possible perspectives. Most certainly, as we have seen, they will hinder the development of empathy. This is crucial, for empathy may be one of the most important abilities we can develop. As long as we commit the perceptual error of assuming that the way we see the world is the only possible way, many forms of nonviolent conflict resolution are blocked and several avenues leading to violence are opened. Ralph White has suggested that we must educate ourselves in "tough-minded empathy." We agree. Individuals must develop the capacity to put themselves in their adversaries' position. Neither White nor we suggest that we must sympathize with our opponents. Real conflicts of interest do exist, and cases of pure aggression must be met with resolve. But these are not the limited cases we mean. We refer to the great mass of social interactions which consist of both competition and cooperation. It is here that empathy can mean the difference between potentially violent or nonviolent conflict resolution.

The need for multiple perspectives and empathy is clear. But how might this be accomplished? Unfortunately space does not permit us to discuss how such prescriptions can be translated into social actions and policy. However, certain practical possibilities can be identified, and many of them already exist. One possibility is increased communications between potential adversaries. The simple acts of listening, paying attention, and trying to understand what opponents are saying may be valuable. It is not as easy as it may sound. Because of our preexisting beliefs, attitudes, and perceptions, we seek to confirm our images rather than to modify them. Studies of attitude change, for example, show that even after repeated social interactions, some stereotypes resist change. Nevertheless, images can be expanded and changed under positive circumstances, and it should be our goal to identify and nurture such circumstances. Cooperation toward easily identifiable common goals may be one answer. Cooperative situations, by their very nature, increase the tendency to empathize.

Even when the potential for cooperation is limited, there are still ways to minimize perceptual errors and increase empathy. Decision makers, for example, have seen the utility of having "devil's advocates" in their ranks. There is a growing body of literature on the functions and utilities of such actors in foreign policy decision making. In this area at least, the decision maker has the advantage over the average citizen (if he chooses to use it). The decision maker can insist that his subordinates work out many different perceptual interpretations of a given issue. The private citizen is rarely exposed to such an adversary setting. Even in such an adversary environment, there are no assurances that the correct perspective will emerge. But then again, that is not the objective. The objective should be to expose the individual to different interpretations of the same event. Thus the individual can see and understand how alternative images exist and why these images might produce different kinds of behavioral responses. Even in decisional groups, however, it is often difficult to implement a devil's advocate strategy. Group dynamics often prevent an environment where both popular and unpopular views are tolerated. In crisis situations particularly, unpopular ideas tend to be excluded. While there are definite costs with a devil's advocate strategy, these appear to be outweighed, for the moment, by its benefits. Increased communication, the development of cooperative enterprises, and the use of multiple advocacy are only a few of the possible ways that our findings on images can be translated into policy and action. They do suggest, however, the general directions that we might take.

Directions for Future Analysis

We began this text with the idea that one could not understand human conflict without integrating the various social sciences into an intellectually satisfying instrument of analysis. Our objective was to build an intellectual framework within which the various elements of conflict could be identified and analyzed. Each chapter has described and analyzed some of the major dimensions of this framework. Obviously much additional theoretical and empirical research must be done. It must focus not only on the antecedents of social conflict but also on the complex interrelationships that exist among these factors and the processes of conflict.

Second, we contended that the student of human conflict must understand the basic dimensions of the problem(s). We have sought to strike a balance between the presentation of "basics" and a more challenging analysis of how the behavioral sciences have contributed to an explanation of conflict. Through this balance, we have sought to aid the reader in identifying the dimensions of human conflict. We believe that you, the reader, should now be able to embark on more rigorous types of analysis of the type we have identified. Hypothesis formulation, research designing, empirical analysis, and theory development should now be more meaningful to you. Much remains to be done in this field. The complexities and importance of our images of conflict should now be evident.

Index